RABELAIS

IN

ENGLISH LITERATURE

RABELAIS

IN

ENGLISH LITERATURE

BY

HUNTINGTON BROWN

1967
OCTAGON BOOKS, INC.
New York

Originally published 1933 by Harvard University Press

Reprinted 1967

by special arrangement with Harvard University Press

OCTAGON BOOKS, INC.
175 FIFTH AVENUE
NEW YORK, N. Y. 10010

LIBRARY OF CONGRESS CATALOG CARD NUMBER: 67-18756

Printed in U.S.A. by
NOBLE OFFSET PRINTERS, INC.
NEW YORK 3, N. Y.

TO
MY FATHER

" Wir wollen stark Getränke schlürfen. "

PREFACE

The English speaking reader of to-day who turns for the first time to Rabelais, whether in the translation of Urquhart and Motteux or in the original, is sure to be struck at the outset by its masculine strength, its gay and hairy ribaldry, and its apparent want of form. If his previous knowledge of French literature begins with Racine and Molière, he may find himself momentarily at a loss to think of Rabelais as French at all, marvelling not to find *Gargantua and Pantagruel* the work of some hard bitten countryman of his own.

The truth is that, since the Renaissance, Rabelais has been better appreciated in England, at least until very recent years, than in his own country ; in England also more than in Italy, whence he drew much of his inspiration, or in Germany, the land of his earliest non-French adaptor. No systematic commentary of his writings appeared in France before the eighteenth century, no modern French version until the nineteenth. The earliest German translation, that of Gottlob Regis, was published 1832-41, and the earliest Italian, that of Gennaro Perfetto, begun in the year of the world war, is still incomplete. His first two lexicographers—and one knows the importance of lexicography in the study of Rabelais—were Englishmen of the reigns of Elizabeth and James, and the earliest and greatest of all the translations of his work was made by a Scottish Cavalier.

The presence of his influence in English literature has never been quite a secret, for most of the faithful have acknowledged their discipleship, but such information as is available about it exists only in brief and scattered monographs and footnotes ; nowhere is it viewed fully and systematically. The present work is an attempt to supply the deficiency. The time appears to be ripe, for Rabelais's popularity among English speaking peoples is in the ascendant. Several new editions of Urquhart and Motteux have appeared in the last few years, and a new translation, that of Mr. Samuel Putnam, the third in our language, and at least three new biographies in English, have been published since 1928.

The present survey, then, is the first of its kind of any substantial length. The error most frequent in the study of literary influence is that of confusing what one individual owes to one other individual with what may be due to accidental similarities of genius or to common traditions and circumstances. I have been careful to provide the fullest documentation as the only adequate safeguard against this error. The material I have gathered should interest both the student of Rabelais, as a notable memorial of his vitality, and the student of English literature, as the makings of a tradition. I may claim to have pointed out traces of the influence in several unsuspected places, as for example, in a masque of Ben Jonson, an epistle of Sir Thomas Browne, and a paper of Addison, and to have analyzed it with some fullness in the many authors in whom it has been known or thought to be present, as for example in Swift and Sterne. *Tristram Shandy* is the latest work considered, for it is the last important example of the Rabelaisian manner that we have. English letters since the revolutionary period of the eighteenth century have been for the most part unhappily " genteel, " and hence proportionately barren of anything like true Pantagruelism. Sterne himself was tainted with the new plague, as he betrays in his devious and itching treatment of sex. Smollett, indeed, his contemporary, is to be regarded, by virtue of *The Adventures of an Atom*, as the last of the bold bad imitators.

It seemed advisable to undertake an analysis of Rabelais's style in some detail at the outset in order to provide a convenient body of facts and examples for reference in the ensuing chapters. For this analysis I am greatly indebted to the excellent and thorough work which has been done on the subject by Messrs. Huguet, de la Juillière, Lefranc, Plattard, Sainéan, Schneegans, Spitzer, and others. My contribution here is of the slightest, and the same is true of my brief accounts of Claudius Holyband's *Dictionarie*, Sir

John Harington's *Metamorphosis of Ajax*, Robert Dallington's *The View of Fraunce*, Bishop Hall's *Mundus Alter et Idem*, and the translation of Urquhart and Motteux, which are based upon the researches of Miss Lucy E. Farrer and Messrs. Rehfeld, Sainéan, and Salyer. In using borrowed material I have been at pains to make due, and I may say here, grateful, acknowledgement of my source in every instance. On the other hand I have felt no obligation to record that certain of my independent findings agree with those of one or more of my predecessors.

H. B.

Kirkland House, Cambridge, Massachusetts.
August 1st, 1933.

CONTENTS

RABELAIS IN ENGLISH LITERATURE

CHAPTER I

INTRODUCTORY

An analysis of Rabelais's work. A view of kindred literary types in England before his influence began to be felt. General aspects of the Renaissance.

Pantagruel, the earliest instalment of Rabelais's great romance, saw the light in 1532 or '33, and *L'Isle Sonnante* or Book V, the last, in 1562, nine years after the author's death. The first recorded mention of his name in England occurs between 1567 and '79, but there is no positive evidence that his authentic works were read until some time later. By the end of the nineties his influence had been powerfully felt. Rabelais prophesied in 1542 : "Angleterre, Escosse, les Estrelins, seront assez mauvais Pantagruelistes[1]." The cult, he thought, could not flourish so far north of the wine-growing zone. The history of his English following, to which the present work is devoted, would probably have surprised him, but the comparative tardiness of its incidence suggests that there was some element of more than accidental truth in the prophecy. It seems, indeed, to have been more than justified in the year 1542, and the vicissitudes of English life in the following half century, which were so to liberalize English thought as to make something like a genuine appreciation of Rabelais possible, were, many of them, so unforeseen, that one cannot but be struck by the patness

---

1. *Pantagrueline Prognostication*, 1542, Ch. vi. All quotations from Rabelais agree with the text of Moland unless otherwise indicated. This passage does not occur in the edition of 1532.

of his not more than half serious and, as to time, indefinite prognostication.

Rabelais was an intellectual pioneer, even in his own country,
which had already produced a group of men of the most advanced
and liberal culture. His books were relished at once by a sympathetic and powerful aristocracy, as well as by many of his fellows,
at the same time that Reformers and Inquisitors were clamoring
for his destruction. The most outspoken of all satirists of Church
and State, he was indulged and admired by the anointed heads of
both. The facts of his life provide most interesting material in
which to study the newly emerging democracy of learning and letters, and its relation to the Reformation, on the one hand, and the
various ranks of the Church, on the other. It will be remembered
that Rabelais was the son of a provincial attorney, and that he
spent something between ten and twenty years in monastic life, in
which he found the leisure and, among others, from Erasmus and
Guillaume Budé, the friendly encouragement, to which he owed
much of his encyclopedic learning. Having been initiated, probably at a very early age, into the Franciscan Order, he was trans-
ferred in 1525 to the Benedictine. He withdrew from this in or
before 1530, for he came as a secular priest in that year before the
faculty of Montpelier to receive his first degree in medecine. It
does not appear that he ever divested himself completely of Holy
Orders in the remaining twenty three years of his life, though
from this time forward his main pursuits were clearly medecine and
writing. It is good to reflect that he numbered a Bishop and two
Cardinals among his patrons, that the dispensation by virtue of
which he moved from the Franciscan into the Benedictine Order
was made by the Pope himself, and that two kings officially sanc-
tioned and protected the printing of his books. The sanction of
Francis I was given after he had, very probably at the instigation
of the genial Queen of Navarre, caused *Gargantua and Pantagruel*
to be read aloud to him, and it was renewed by Henry II.

His one gigantic work, which occupied him intermittently from
1532 to his death, was written for a public whose taste had been
prepared for lengthy prose narratives by the interminable and
numerous prose redactions of the romances of chivalry. It envi-

sages the two worlds of obsolescent scholasticism, superstition, and chivalry, on the one hand, and of humanism and everyday life, on the other. Ostensibly a sustained and uproarious satire, the author declares that he wrote it for the delight and health of the sick [1]. Laughter was his medicine, and medicine his chosen profession. Vice and virtue, wisdom and folly, were weighed in his scales, but only as aspects of the human comedy, never in the abstract. The old writers of allegory had spent time enough in their wearisome crusades against the seven deadly sins. Rabelais was indignant at the wastefulness of the scholastic system of education, but indignation was not his element. He was content to define a healthy attitude toward abuses, a very different thing from pretending that they could or should be eradicated. He did not, in other words, attempt the impossible. Narrow-mindedness was the one all-corrupting, curable, and therefore unnecessary disease, a heritage, as he saw it, of a dessicated past, and he filled his bowls to wash it away, and give life to its stunted victims, in the wine of Pagan antiquity.

The revival of learning and the voyages of discovery increased both the methods and the materials of literature, and stimulated the boldest experimentation. Extravagance, in the literal sense of the term, that is " wandering outside, " was an essential phase of the process. New centers of orientation in a rapidly expanding physical and intellectual world could only be perceived in relation to its external limits, and these required to be explored. Rabelais was hardier than most in the variety of experience which he undertook to express, and in the idiom he selected in which to do so. Some of his material and some of his language were in his own time, and still are in ours, abhorrent to certain tastes. Those aspects of his work answer to aspects of the continental life of his time which have scarcely been paralleled in the history of England, and they have largely conditioned our appreciation of his art from the beginning. One might illustrate the limits of ferocity to which public affairs on the continent were sometimes conducted, by reference to the history of the Waldensian war, or the same in private

---

1. *Pantagruel*, Prol.

affairs, by reference to the autobiography of Benvenuto Cellini. It is rather more significant in the present instance to notice the robustious nature of continental gaiety. A certain Gaspard de Tavannes, for example, is said to have taken a corpse from a gibbet, and to have placed it, for a practical joke, in a lady's bed. Gallantry was oddly conceived by the same individual, who offered to establish the priority of Queen Catherine's beauty by cutting off the nose of her nearest rival, Diana of Poitiers. The little court of Madame de St. Pol in the province of Cotentin laughed aloud at a battle between her pages and ladies, in which one of the latter broke a leg, another was cut in the breast, and a third seriously wounded in the head with a kitchen spit [1]. A most enlightening document in the history of continental manners and humor is a letter written by Rabelais himself to Cardinal de Guise, in which he describes a sham battle fought in the Piazza Sant'Apostoli in Rome, on Thursday, March 14th, 1549, in celebration of the birth of Charles of Orléans, second son of Henry II [2]. The description is ecstatic.

... du chasteau fut tant tiré d'artillerie, tant jetté de mattons, micraines, potz et lances à feu, que tout le voisinage en retondissoit, et ne voiyoit on autour que feu, flambe et fumée, avec tonnoirres horrifiques de telle canonnerie [3].

Engagements were fought single handed, in which lances were broken and horses killed, to the accompaniment of fifes and trumpets. These were followed by a mass engagement, marked by " hurlemens espouventables. " When this was over, and the combatants had retired, two dead men were seen to have remained upon the field, " desquelz l'un avoit le bras gauche couppé, et le visage tout en sang ; l'autre avoit un transon de picque à travers le corps souz la fante du harnois. "

Autour desquelz fut recréation nouvelle, ce pendant que la musique sonnoit. Car Frerot, à tout son accoustrement de velours incarnat feuilleté de toille d'argent, à forme d'œsles de souris chauve, et Fabritio

1. Schneegans, *Gesch. d. Grot. Sat.*, 502.
2. *La Sciomachie*, Rabelais, *Œuvres*, II, 360 ff.
3. *Ibid.*, II, 366-67.

avecques sa couronne de laurier, soy joingnirent à eux. L'un les admo-nestoit de leur salut, les confessoit et absolvoit comme gens morts pour la foy ; l'autre les tastoit aux goussetz et en la braguette pour trouver la bourse. Enfin, les descouvrans et despouillans, montrerent au peuple que ce n'estoient que gens de foin. Dont fut grande risée entre les spec-tateurs, soy esbahissans comment on les avoit ainsi là mis et jettez durant ce furieux combat [1].

During a final display of fireworks a squib balloon was thrown from a balcony.

Et couroit ledit ballon parmy la place, jettant feu de tous costez, qui estoit chose espouventable : fait par l'invention de messer Vincentio, romain, et Francisque, florentin, bombardiers du Pere Saint. Frerot, faisant le bon compagnon, courut prés ce ballon, en l'appellant gueulle d'enfer et teste de Lucifer ; mais, d'un coup qu'il frappa dessus avecques un transon de picque, il se trouva tout couvert de feu, et crioit comme un enragé, fuyant deçà et delà, et bruslant ceux qu'il touchoit [2].

Rabelais's only comment upon the accident is this : " Puis devint noir comme un Ethiopien, et si bien marqué au visage qu'il y paroistra encores d'icy à trois mois. "

As to England, one cannot assert that savagery was unknown to her civilisation, but it is not one of the phases of English life which the historians have particularly emphasized. The butche-ries of Tower Hill were quite as cruel, though not nearly as nume-rous per head of population as those inflicted by the Inquisition in Spain or in France. The jocular curdling and spilling of the blood of men would seem, in any case, to have been confined in the period of the Reformation to the lower orders of society, as in Chaucer. One even hears little of the tormenting of animals, as in bear and bull baiting, which is said to date from the reign of Henry II, and which was later relished by all classes, including royalty. The feeling of political insecurity which the divorce pro-ceedings of Henry VIII aroused, the survival of orthodox dogma and ritual in the newly reformed Church, and the traditional ear-nestness of the English as a whole in regard to religion, but parti-cularly the earnestness of the Reformers and their followers from

---

1. *Œuvres*, II, 368.
2. *Ibid*, II, 369.

Wycliffe to the Martyrs, made for an atmosphere of tension and
piety wholly inhospitable to the spirit of Rabelaisian satire, no
matter what it might have been directed against. Rabelais and
the Reformers had certainly something in common, their most
obvious affinity being a cordial abhorrence of the abuses of the
Catholic church. This is not all, for Rabelais makes Pantagruel
use terms narrowly characteristic of the language of the Evange-
lists, in vowing to spread the Holy Gospel among his subjects, and
elsewhere agrees with them in the importance he assigns to the
reading of the Scriptures by laymen [1]. Calvin, however, condemned
Rabelais in 1550 for a materialist, and Rabelais despised Calvin [2]. The mutual antipathy of the two men was not a mere matter
of doctrine, it was the fundamental opposition of the Protestant
versus the Catholic temperament. The program of the Reformers was inflexible, and, because of the odds which it challenged,
involved, after the example of Christianity in ancient Rome, a
philosophy of martyrdom. Rabelais, on the contrary, though he
always maintained his beliefs with the utmost enthusiasm, de-
clined explicitly and repeatedly to risk burning for them, because,
he says, through the mouth of Pantagruel, " Je suis de ma nature
assez alteré, sans me chauffer davantaige [3]. " So genial a confession could not but arouse the profoundest suspicion of his sincerity
among men dedicated to a cause which would certainly have been
lost had they permitted themselves the luxury of a sense of humor.
In England, therefore, it was not until a kind of new Catholicism
developed after the breach with Rome, that one can imagine her
people cultivating Rabelais. If one, or some, English Rabelaisians
did exist before the reign of Queen Elizabeth, they have remained
to posterity mute and inglorious.

Rabelais's work has been defined by a certain critic as grotesque
satire [4]. The definition, though by no means comprehensive, is

---

1. Plattard, *Vie de Rabelais*, 112 ff. See *Pantagruel*, Ch. xxix, and *Gargantua*, Ch. xxiii.
2. Plattard, *Vie de Rabelais*, 201, 217 ff. Rabelais speaks of " les Demoniacles
Calvins, imposteurs de Geneve, " in Bk. IV, Ch. xxxii.
3. Bk. II, Ch. v.
4. Schneegans, *Gesch. d. Grot. Sat.* See especially Pt. I, Ch. i and Pt. II, Ch. i.

both interesting and convenient. As burlesque differs from mere drollery in having an object, namely the ridicule of something revered or sublime, so satire differs from burlesque in the permanent and moral, as opposed to the superficial, poetic, or merely playful justice of its attack. Satire envisages " something which should not be " (a " Nichtseinsollend "). Grotesque satire is distinguished from other varieties by a monstrous exaggeration combined with a feigned adherence to fact. The last point is of especial importance as the dividing mark between the grotesque and allegory. Allegory, reduced to its essence, is merely a sustained figure or symbolization of an abstract idea or theory. Its main business is to be consistent, any other interest which it may offer being accidental. Many of Rabelais's chapters are clearly allegorical, but with him pseudo-realism, learned high-jinks, sheer nonsense, or some other motive beyond the exigencies of the allegory itself, almost invariably predominates. He set so little store by systematic philosophy that allegory, merely as such, was of little use to him. Allegory, then, is simply a conventional use of symbols, which may or may not be intrinsically interesting, whereas the grotesque is, as truly as tragedy, an imitation of life in the Aristotelian sense. Professor Santayana has observed that grotesque forms are ones " which nature has not, but might conceivably have offered [1]. " The grotesque writer must make his departures from what is normal orderly and plausible, for once the reader relaxes his hold upon reality, all things become automatically possible, and the spell is broken. If the reader then attempts to find umbrage in allegorical meanings where none have been intended, his disappointment will be complete. Forms have to be invented for which no models exist and which obey no law save that of inner and dynamic necessity. Their author must possess the widest knowledge of life and a supreme imagination.

In accordance with the principle that the background of the grotesque is realism, prose would seen to be the most convenient medium for its expression in literature, being a nearer approximation than verse to everyday speech, though there is certainly no

---

1. George Santayana, *The Sense of Beauty* (New York, 1896), p. 256.

ultimate reason why verse, in proper hands, should not be superior here, as it is for the expression of other highly imaginative motives. Rabelais's prose is peculiarly fine in the evenness of its transitions from the rhythms and diction of tap-room chatter to those of Ciceronian eloquence. As the need arises to suit the language to some peculiarly grotesque fantasy, he takes every possible liberty with prose conventions, though he does not tamper with syntax. He varies his word order to produce the most striking effects, and sometimes abandons the familiar form of the sentence upon the printed page to place huge catalogues of nouns or adjectives in parallel columns. The periods riot in repetitions, interruptions, and parentheses.

Rabelais may, then, be conveniently named a grotesque satirist and stylist. Doubtless it is in these capacities that he is chiefly distinguished among all who have shared them, and differentiated from those whose achievements in other directions he has rivalled or surpassed. He has been styled the Michelangelo of the grotesque. He was, however, much more than that, and no simple formula can adequately suggest, much less describe, his mighty genius. One can scarcely overemphasize the error of those who classify his work narrowly as satire. A certain John Dunlop, falling into that error, concludes most unthoughtfully that " no satirical writings have suffered more by lapse of time than those of Rabelais [1]. " Evidence does not support his view. The remark suggests the simple truth, of which its writer appears to have no idea, that the modern reader is *less* interested in whatever *local* and *temporary* satire there may be in Rabelais than in other elements of his work. Satire of that kind often loses interest for posterity, its vitality depending less upon the chance that its precise object will remain a matter of concern to human society than upon the extent to which it furnishes analogies, and, as in all fiction, upon the vigor of its characters and setting. Friar John, for example, doubtless caused many waggings of ecclesiastical heads in the sixteenth century, and many sly

---

1. John Dunlop, *Hist. of Fiction* (Edinburgh, 1814), III, 66, cit. Regis, *Garg. und Pant.*, III, 1428.

winks among their enemies, — nay, among the more narrow minded in both groups, he may have evoked little, if any, other response ; but at this distance the discrepancy between his unclerkliness and his calling, like that between the worldliness of Sir John Falstaff and his rank of knighthood, is clearly seen to be more significant as an element of portraiture than it is as an attack upon a human institution. The imagination which conceived the Friar was, indeed, of the same order with that which conceived the Knight.

Gargantua and Pantagruel appeared, it will be remembered, in five installments. It consists of a new treatment of material found chiefly in the romances of chivalry, in the mediaeval chronicles and farces, and in the poetry of Folengo, Pulci, and Bojardo. The immediate inspiration of Book I was a folk tale, of which the earliest surviving version in writing was published in 1532, and entitled : *Les grandes et inestimables Cronicques du grant et enorme geant Gargantua : Contenant sa genealogie, La grandeur et force de son corps. Aussi les merveilleux faictz darmes quil fist pour le Roy Artus comme verrez cy apres* [1]. Its story, as it happens, was known to the English in a form which differs widely from the version of Rabelais, before and independently of Rabelais's own, and came to be confused therewith.

The chronicle of 1532 tells how Merlin created a giant, Grandgosier, upon the top of the highest mountain in the orient from the blood of Lancelot's wounds and the bones of a male whale, and his mate, Gallemelle, from the bones of a female whale and the parings of Queen Guinevere's finger nails [2]. Their son, Gargantua, after performing sundry feats of strength in France, and after losing his huge mare, is brought into England by Merlin upon a cloud for the purpose of succoring King Arthur in his wars. He is much needed, for Arthur is in serious difficulties. Gargantua at once subdues a hostile race of giants named after Gog and Magog, and likewise the Irish and the Dutch. The Irish campaign is treated in detail. The hero puts whole armies into

---

1. See " Works and Editions Cited " under " Girault, " below, p. 242.
2. This and the next three paragraphs repeat more or less closely certain passages of my introduction to Girault, *The Tale of Gargantua and King Arthur.*

the folds of his clothing, eats shiploads of food, and drinks barrels of cider at a single gulp. He is nevertheless comparatively temperate and serious minded. The numbers of his victims, the measurements of his apparel, and the like, are stated exactly. His laugh is heard for seven leagues, he slays two hundred thousand Irish and Dutch. Having served King Arthur two hundred years, three months, and four days, he is carried to Faërie by Gain la Phee and Melusine, and is there to this day.

Gargantua had long been a familiar personage in French folk lore. He was characterized primarily by beneficence, huge size, and a huge appetite. His name seems to mean gullet, or some derivative, than which nothing could better suggest bigness and geniality. Monsieur Lefranc has emphasized the significance of his rôle as savior. This, he suggests, may be connected with the legend of St. Michael, who suppressed the revolt of Lucifer, since the cult of that saint is associated in several countries of Europe with mountains named Gargan or Gargano, and the present legend makes the hero toss the rock of Mont Saint Michel into the sea [1].

Rabelais takes over many details of the chronicle of 1532, including the stature, the appetite, the costume, and the homely good nature of the giant, as well as the names of his parents, the mare, the visit to Paris, the episode of the cathedral bells, the war club, and the inundation, but he eliminates all the Arthurian connections.

A three fold expansion of the story appeared c. 1534, entitled *Les croniques admirables du puissant Roy Gargantua*, sometimes known as the *Seconde Chronique*. It contains borrowings from Rabelais's *Pantagruel*, three chapters of which [2] it embodies in their entirety. It was written or, more properly speaking, compiled, by François Girault, the author of a poem entitled *Le moyen d'avoir de l'argent*. This was the *Gargantua*, assuming there was but one, which was translated into English in or before the reign

---

1. See Lefranc, *Œuvres de Rabelais*, I, Introd., Ch. ii, xlvi-xlix ; H. Gaidoz, " Gargantua ; essai de mythologie celtique, " in *Rev. Arch.*, nouv. sér., XVIII (1868), 172-191 ; and Paul Sébillot, *Gargantua dans les traditions populaires* (Paris, 1883), *passim*.
2. Bk. II, Ch. i, ii, and iii.

of Elizabeth. The evidence for this statement is presented in the introduction to my edition of the text, where I have shown that the tradition of the Gargantua of folk lore in England was originally quite independent of the influence of Rabelais.

One of Rabelais's earliest publications was a mock almanac of 1532, the *Pantagrueline Prognostication.* Its elaborate fooling with proverbial wisdom and its style are highly characteristic, and it was the only one of the minor works to influence English litterature.

Rabelais's Gargantua retains the size and strength of him of the chronicles [1]. These qualities are mainly emphasized in the account of his early years, and the former, like that of Dame Philosophy in Boethius, is variable. He is tall enough to lean upon the towers of Notre Dame, and yet small enough to enter into houses and to drink with men of normal build. His pedigree goes back to the creation, and includes all the well known giants of sacred and profane mythology. Born crying for drink, he inherits the kingdom of the Butterflies, and takes to wife Badebec, daughter of the King of the Unknown People in Utopia. The fruit of their union is Pantagruel, King of the Dipsodes, the central personage of the last four books. He is an exemplary prince, like his father and grandfather, the whole line being marked by a surpassing thirst and a progressively excellent scholarship.

Gargantua sucks milk from the udders of seventeen thousand nine hundred and thirteen cows, as well as floods of Septembral juice, plays at two hundred and sixteen games, and anoints his soul with thirty masses each day. The first fifty years of his education are entrusted to a pair of schoolmen who all but demoralize him completely, with the result that his father pays them off in dudgeon, and causes a new programme, now famous in

---

1. It has been deemed advisable to include here for purposes of convenient reference, and without further apology, a brief review of certain aspects of *Gargantua and Pantagruel* which are, no doubt, perfectly familiar to all readers of Rabelais.

Rabelais's works were published at the following dates : *Pantagruel* (Bk. II), 1532 or '33 ; *Pantagrueline Prognostication* , 1532 ; *Gargantua* (Bk. I), 1534 ; Bk. III, 1546 ; Bk. IV, 1553 ; Bk. V (posthumously), 1562.

the history of education, to be instituted. He retains certain
preceptors, each of whom has a Greek name signifying some
virtue or capacity for service, and they thereafter form the nucleus
of his court and of the court of his son. Their teaching is based
mainly upon the Greek and Roman classics. It takes full account
of the exigencies of practical life, and provides for the welfare of
the body as well as of the mind.

Both father and son are able generals and magnanimous
conquerors. Gargantua's war against Picrochole introduces the
most delightful character in the whole romance, the drinking,
fighting, and fornicating " claustral Monk, called Friar John, "

young, gallant, frisk, lustie, nimble, quick, active, bold, adventurous,
resolute, tall, lean, wide-mouthed, long-nosed, a fair dispatcher of morning prayers, unbridler of masses, and runner-over of vigils ; and to
conclude summarily in a word, a right Monk, if ever there was any,
since the Monking world monked a Monkerie : for the rest a Clerk
even to the teeth in matter of breviary [1].

His defense of the vineyards of his close is rewarded by the
building of the Abbé de Thélème, representing what monasticism
might be in a holiday world. Here the sexes cohabitate in liberty and opulence and in the pursuit of happiness, under no
restraint save that imposed by their own good taste.

The Second Book introduces Panurge, a foil to Friar John, a
personage of almost equal charm. He is friendly, brilliant, a
vandal and a coward, reminiscent in sqme ways of François Villon,
and Pantagruel takes him to his heart, remonstrating but mildly
at his shortcomings. In this book attention should be drawn
especially to the drollery of Panurge as linguist, litigant, and
practical joker, of his disputation by signs, and of Epistemon's
Lucianic account of the lower world, and to the satire in the
passages about the Limousin scholar, the Library of St. Victor,
and Baisecul versus Humevesne.

Book III deals with the consultation of various oracles by
Panurge in an attempt to decide whether he shall marry. It

---

1. Bk. I, Ch. xxvii.

displays the author's erudition in more concentrated form than any of the other books, and the chief characters are richly developed. Among its more important contents may be mentioned Panurge in praise of debt ; why new married husbands are exempt from military service ; why the codpiece is the most important piece of armor ; Judge Bridoye, who judges by casting dice ; and a description of the Pantagruelion herb, hemp. The oracles and methods of divination include dreams, passages selected at random out of Homer and Virgil, a necromancer (Her Trippa), a theologian, a poet (Raminagrobis), a physician (Rondibilis), a philosopher, and a lunatic. They may the taken, according to the genius one sees in Rabelais, as a satirical attack upon prophecy as a whole and prophets in particular, or merely as a pleasant representation of things which, however odd and possibly pernicious, may not be other than they are. Satire and Rabelais are rooted together in the minds of many readers, but what at first appears in him to be satire is ever bursting its clothes, most often, no doubt, at the waistband, and is ever emerging as a higher type of creative art. This is true of Panurge and the soothsayers, and especially of what has been miscalled Rabelais's satire on women.

Rabelais was friends with the lawyer Tiraqueau and an admirer of his reactionary treatise, *De legibus connubialibus*, in which women are strictly recommended to the government of their men, and also with a certain Amaury Bouchard, author of a feminist reply to the *De legibus*, entitled Τῆς γυναικείας φυτλῆς *apologia*. Throughout Book III Rabelais assumes the proposition that women are infallibly given to the cornification of their husbands, and his characters examine marriage upon this basis exhaustively. It is proven that women both must be, and cannot be, controlled. Elsewhere, in the accounts of Thélème, of la Reine Quinte, and of the Isle of Lanterns, especially the first, he appears as an ardent champion of their intelligence and taste. Their charm is never called in question. At Thélème it is they who decree what costumes shall be worn, and they have an equal voice with the men in determining the day's undertakings. So stands Rabelais in relation to the " querelle des femmes. " He takes the middle ground, or rather, no ground at all. Human character is at the center of his thought, and all things are referred to it. Systems and doctrines are fallible ; truth, to Rabelais, is as various as man.

Panurge finds all his advisors unsatisfactory. Pantagruel therefore forms a project to sail with his men to the Oracle of the Bottle, which he feels confident will resolve his friend's dilemma. A fleet of twelve ships is accordingly prepared, and they sail in the month of June. This Lucianic voyage, occupying the last two books, takes the adventurers to distant corners of the earth, where they encounter strange lands and peoples. These are imaginative idealizations of divers institutions, ideas and abuses. Some of the material is satirical, some allegorical, and some merely droll, the three kinds being, moreover, variously and subtly combined. The portrayal of character is never neglected, the chief interest remaining with Panurge and Friar John, though Pantagruel is a close third, and a whole gallery of new figures is introduced. Rabelais displays a vast knowledge of contemporary geography, and digresses, as usual, upon many topics.

The Fourth Book tells how messages are carried by homer pigeons ; how Panurge overreaches a sheep merchant ; why monks haunt kitchens ; of the strange ways of bailiffs ; how Panurge behaves in the tempest ; how Pantagruel considers the passing of heroes and the meaning of the death of Pan ; of the gluttony of Quaresmeprenant, or Lentkeeper ; how Pantagruel slew a whale ; of his war against the Andouilles, or sausages ; of the impudence of the Papefigues, or Pope-mockers ; how a devil was cheated by a farmer ; of the Papimanes, or Romish fanatics ; how their bishop praises the Decretals ; how Pantagruel hears frozen words ; how Gaster (the belly) is the mother of invention ; of the island of thieves, called Ganabin ; and the whole of the final chapter is given to a description of how Panurge, for the twentieth time, it may be, this time as the result of a vision of damned souls which came to him in a dream, beshits himself.

Book V, originally *L'Isle Sonnante*, continues the adventures. The Ringing Island is visited, which was once inhabited by Siticines (musicians who played upon the tombs of the dead), now transformed into a filthy and parasitical race of birds, whose ranks are named after those of the Church, Papegaut, Cardingaux, Clergaux, Monagaux, Abbegesses, Monagesses, etc. The fleet touch at the isle of Weapons ; the isle of Furred Law-cats ; the isle of the rapacious Apedeftes (the ignorant) ; and the kingdom of la Quinte Essence, called Entelechie (inner perfection). Life in this realm moves upon well oiled wheels. The Queen has never so much as to raise her voice, and while she is able to entertain her guests with the daintiest and most plentiful fare (her servants lead them " to Apollo, " like the hospitable Lucullus in Plutarch), herself subsists upon food which is predigested. She maintains an academy of " abstractors, " " spodizators " (alchemists), tasters, and other scientists, whose researches are prosecuted with the utmost ingenuity. Some are engaged in effecting novel cures, such as that of St. Francis' disease, which is treated by paying the patient's debts and tying a purse of gold about his neck ; some in sanitation, the pestilent air of close houses being purified by throwing the house out of the window ; some in extending the frontiers of pure science by cutting fire with a knife, breaking sausages across the knee, measuring the jumps of fleas, and the like. Other ports of call are the isle of Odes (moving highways) ; the isle of Esclots (wooden shoes), inhabited by droning and laconic Friars ; the isle of Satin or tapestries, where the author is granted a vision of the ancient gods and men by Ouy-dire, or Hearsay ; and last, the isle of Lanterns, and the Oracle of the Bottle. The Queen of the Lanterns — all the Lanterns are female — furnishes Pantagruel with guides to his long sought goal. Thirteen chapters are devoted to the account of the Oracle, its priestess Bacbuc, and the ritual of consultation. Before the temple is a fountain of water, which has the quality of wine in the estimation of all who taste it, and over the shrine is inscribed 'Εν ο''νῳ ἀλήθεια.

Panurge gibbers with fear now that his momentous question is to be answered, and Friar John, against whom eighteen devils would be powerless, holds him firmly by the arm. The priestess warns him to listen with but one ear, and when the rites are accomplished, he becomes aware of a murmuring and fizzling in

the Bottle, punctuated at last by the usual monosyllable which
bottles pronounce, " Trinc. " The unanswerable is answered.
The delighted pilgrims leap for joy, spout poetry, and drink like
Templars. At last they sail away, apprized of the knowledge that
there is treasure in the earth for those who will dig plough deep, and
that man's essential needs are but two, for God and companionship.

Nobody can begin to comprehend the wide rage of human
experience embraced by this unique and ample work who has
not read it often and thoughtfully. There is little plot, but the
characterization is masterly and the movement swift.

The movement is that of an athletic and disciplined mind on a
holiday [1]. Never doubting that there is such a thing as eternal
truth, Rabelais is fond of the lore of proverbs, and makes them
his stock in trade. For all that he is an independent thinker,
he speaks sincerely and characteristically in proverbial language,
and such language he pays the repeated homage of parody. The
account of Gargantua's adolescence is full of inverted truisms
and of figurative meanings used literally. Thus Gargantua
" tournoyt les truies au foin, battoyt le chien devant le lion,
mettoyt la charrette devant les boeufz [2]. " Rabelais even invents
expressions which sound like proverbs in order to play with them,
as when he says, " Le grand Dieu feist les planetes, et nous faisons
les platz netz [3]. " At times he uses such expressions blasphe-
mously, as when he makes a drinker say, " J'ay la parolle de Dieu
en bouche : Sitio [4]. "

He drew freely upon the classics for embellishment, illustration,
and authority. Parables abound, in the form of adaptations
and quotations, chiefly from Plato and Plutarch, Pausanias and
Atheneus, Suetonius and Strabo, Pliny and Lucian ; and from
the orators, especially Cicero. He draws to a limited extent upon

1. For a fuller treatment of Rabelais's style see Lefranc, *Œuvres de Rabelais*,
I, Introd. ; Plattard, *L'Œuvre de Rabelais*, 338 ff. ; Schneegans, *Gesch. d. Grot.
Sat.*, Pt. II, Ch. iii ; Sainéan, *La Langue de Rabelais* ; P. de la Juillière, *Les
Images dans Rabelais* ; Spitzer, *Wortbildung als Stil. Mittel, exemplif. an Rabelais* ; from which works the present observations are largely derived.
2. Bk. I, Ch. xi.
3. Bk. I, Ch. v.
4. Bk. I, Ch. v.

the poets, Homer, Virgil, Horace, Catullus, Ovid, and Martial, but neither they nor the dramatists, not even Aristophanes, interested him as much as the prose writers. Not being a philosopher, he was little concerned with philosophies in themselves or with the great movements of history, but was ever alert for " faicts et dicts memorables, " the apt anecdote and the handy phrase. Analysis shows that he cites *almost all the personages of classical fable and history* [1]. He was acquainted with most of his materials at first hand, but also made use of anthologies and imitations. The way in which he fuses his erudition into an essentially popular tale without pedantry or vulgarity is one of the wonders of literature. He is rarely obscure unless for purposes of irony. It is essential to remember the taste of his age, for his readers were insatiable of learned writing, increasingly so, to judge by the considerably greater amount thereof in Book III than in Books I and II, and were no doubt educated to be critical of the manner in which it was presented to them.

His style is frequently grotesque, but it is to misunderstand Rabelais if one remembers him primarily for his catalogues and galimatias. Most of his phrasing is economical and dramatic. He takes pains to represent gestures, tones, and the movement of the lips, and to suit the word to the person who utters it. His " formlessness " is a delusion, as was perceived by one of the most narrowly formal of all critics, Thomas Rymer. Rymer went so far as to place his dramatic propriety above that of Shakespeare [2].

The more serious portions of the work, e. g. the epistles of Grandgousier and Gargantua [3], are couched in the periods of Cicero, the style cultivated by nearly all writers of prose in the Renaissance. Rabelais handles this style with respect, never confusing the real thing with mere pompousness, though he understood its comic uses, for did not Friar John excuse his profane swearing on the ground that it was " rhetorique ciceroniane [4] ? "

---

1. Thus Jupiter is cited twenty-five times in the first four Books, Hercules twenty, Bacchus fifteen, Plato twenty-four, Homer twenty-two, Aristotle sixteen, and so forth, and so forth. See de la Juillière, 55 56.
2. See below, p. 149 ff.
3. Bk. I, Ch. xxix, and Bk. IV, Ch. iii.
4. Bk. I, Ch. xxxix.

Rabelais's colloquial manner, however, is that in which he wrote
the bulk of the work and in which he excelled. One can scarcely
turn to a page of his writing without wishing to read it aloud.
There is much introduction of the author in person—he represents himself as an old man—and the reader is continually addressed as " vous. " This " vous, " like his proverbs and some
of his archaisms, betokens the popular raconteur. The expletive
or ethical dative is frequent, and the word order arranged in such
a way as to command attention, as thus, " Qui fut bien esbahi
et perplex, ce fut Gargantua [1]. " Oaths abound, and there are
many coughs, spittings, and clearings of the throat [2]. The
rhythms are those of everyday speech [3]. The fervor of conviction is carried by repetitions of both important and unimportant
words [4]. In dealing with objections to the argument in hand, the
concessive clause is discarded in favor of an implied interruption
of the reader [5].

It has been estimated that two thirds of the work is " discours. "
If, as Monsieur Plattard says, the author wishes to emphasize
the newness of his tale [6], the quickness of Pantagruel [7], the
ingenuity of Gaster [8], or the strangeness of the death of Bringuenarilles [9], he works up an argument, he proves by comparisons,
he exalts and celebrates by apostrophes and exclamations, like
a popular orator. In heated or serious talk he is fond of grouping
his expressions in two and three ; but when he mounts his high
horse there is no use counting. Friar John calls Panurge one
hundred and seventy-two kinds of cullion in a single breath, and

---

1. Bk. II, Ch. iii.
2. For example, in the harangue of Janotus de Bragmardo, Bk. I, Ch. xix.
3. See for example Bk. I, Ch. v.
4. Thus Panurge praises man " comme animant, non plante ; comme animant (diz je), né à paix, non à guerre ; animant né à jouissance mirificque... ;
animant né à domination pacificque sur toutes bestes. " —Bk. III, Ch. viii.
5. Thus : " vous dictez que au rugissement du lion toutes bestes loing à
l'entour fremissent... Il est vray... Je vous certifie que au mandement de
messere Gaster tout le ciel tremble. " —Bk. IV, Ch. lvii.
6. Bk. II, Prol.
7. Bk. IV, Ch. xxxiv.
8. Bk. IV, Ch. lxii.
9. Bk. IV, Ch. xvii.

Panurge retorts with one hundred and sixty-eight [1]. Another
eruption of adjectives numbers two hundred and ten [2]. Yet the
sentences are by no means always long, for when the aforesaid
pair chirp over a bottle, or when strenuous action is afoot, the
periods are abrupt and pointed.

The range of Rabelais's vocabulary is staggering, and was
probably one of the chief obstacles to a widespread appreciation
of his work by the English before Urquhart. It may be measured
by the images used in his figures of speech, of which a thorough
analysis has been made [3]. These include, in the first four books
alone : fourteen varieties of food, thirty animals, six insects,
four fishes, twenty-two birds, ten fabulous or distinctly exotic
animals, twenty-one fruits and vegetables, six terms from architecture, eight from navigation, twenty-five more or less from
theology, fourteen from natural science, fourteen from the art
military, three from astronomy, three from geometry, six from
jurisprudence, seven from hunting and fishing, fifteen from music,
twenty-five more or less from general anthropology, twenty-five
names of crafts and professions, three of nationalities, ten games,
twenty-six vessels or receptacles, seven artisans' tools, five agricultural implements, four toilet articles, twenty garments, six
diseases, five cures, and forty or fifty miscellaneous objects. These
terms, be it noted, are not merely ones of which he knew the
meaning, but with which he was sufficiently familiar to use for comparison and reference. He delights in synonyms, of which he
has, for example, twenty-nine for the carnal act, twenty-five for
the male genitals, fifteen for monk, and nineteen meaning to eat [4].
They frequently occur in pairs, one of which is a neologism and
the other a familiar word which explains its meaning. A complete

---

1. Bk. III, Ch. xxvi, and xxviii.
2. Bk. III, Ch. xxxviii.
3. See de la Juillière, *Les Images dans Rabelais.* Rabelais draws on the classics for no less than two hundred and ninety-six comparisons in the first four
Books, on the Bible for seventy-eight, on mediaeval and modern history for a
dozen or more, and on geography and the lore of the sightseer for a dozen or so
each. — *Ibid.*, Ch. ii, iii.
4. De la Juillière, 113 ff.

gloss of Rabelais would amount to a dictionary of both the standard and the colloquial French of his time.

Many of his words are new formations. When he is in an eruptive mood and has exhausted the legitimate vocabulary of his own tongue and its dialects, he unbungs his Greek and Latin, and with the free use of analogy and sound conformities, delivers himself of notable creations. They range all the way from modest formations with active prefixes and suffixes to sesquipedalian monsters. Some are merely playful, as *chascunière* [1] ; others burlesque, as *torcheculatif* [2] (a parody of words like *speculatif*, which are comparatively weighty) ; and others frankly satirical, as *Sorbonagre* (from *Sorbonne* + ὄναγρος, wild ass). The Sorbonne moved him to a well known *tour de force* when he spoke of " maraulx de Sophistes, Sorbillans, Sorbonagres, Sorbonigenes, Sorbonicoles, Sorboniformes, Sorbonisecques, Niborcisans, Borsonisans, Saniborsans [3]. "

He shows a strong tendency to similarly sounding word endings and word beginnings in his synonym groups, as in " joye, soulas, et liesse [4]. " When there are three or more he usually ends with a full toned word, often metrically feminine [5]. From rhythm to rhyme is only a step, and a rhyme ending is often made to serve a purpose equivalent to that of brackets in algebra, as in " mocqueries, folatries, et menteries joyeuses [6], " where *joyeuses* modifies all three nouns. A noteworthy feature of his wit is the inclusion of an object of satire in a rhyming list with which its sense is not normally parallel. Thus he deals with teachers of predestination : " abuseurs, predestinateurs, imposteurs, et seducteurs [7]. "

His sounds take the most elaborate patterns, and these are no doubt largely owing to the complicated rhyme schemes which

---

1. " Chascun s'en va à sa chascunière. " — Bk. II, Ch. xiv.
2. Bk. I, Ch. xiii.
3. Bk. II, Ch. xviii.
4. Bk. I, Ch. x.
5. E.g. " joye, plaisir, delices et rejouissance. " — Bk. I, Ch. ix.
6. Bk. I, Prol.
7. Bk. II, Prol.

were being cultivated in the contemporary poetry [1]. When he has the choice of associating words by either sense or sound, he often favors the latter. This is illustrated by the following :

et dedans y apparoissoit la Lune, en figure et mouvement telle qu'elle est au ciel, pleine, silente, croissante, ou decroissante [2],

where the order of the phases of the moon is interrupted by *silente* for the sake of its rhyme. A rhyme ending often runs into word-play, for example,

Appelez vous cecy fiansailles ? Je les appelle fiantailles de merde [3].

In lists he frequently begins with a scheme of word formation, and then proceeds mechanically, without regard to sense, as in " pou-drebif, brandif, positif, gerondif, genitif, actif [4]. " His ebullience sometimes, though rarely, spoils the effect of a crescendo, as when he speaks of " l'enorme, indicible, incroyable, inestimable me-chanceté [5], " where *inestimable* is less strong both tonically and logically than *incroyable*.

A common type of word–play involves a contrast between the historical and a derived meaning of the stem, for example, *cardi-naliser*, to dye red, as a lobster ; and there is another, sometimes confused with it, called the *figura etymologica*, in which the stem of a word that has been used once is preserved without change of meaning and added to in some way as a more convenient mode of expression than the choice of a different word. This has been illustrated in *chascunière*. Rabelais makes rich use of both for-mations.

It is conservatively estimated by Monsieur Sainéan that of all the French latinists whose practise and authority caused the

---

1. The practise of linking associated words by various sound conformities had been characteristic of the Italian Macaronic poets. See Schneegans, pp. 129, 131, 133.
2. Bk. V, Ch. xlii.
3. Bk. IV, Ch. xv.
4. Bk. III, Ch. xxvi.
5. Bk. V, Ch. xi.

introduction of the following words into French, Rabelais's was the most decisive. I shall include only those of Monsieur Sainéan's list (of over ninety) to which there are closely analogous forms in English [1].

RABELAIS	EARLIEST USE OF ANALOGOUS ENGLISH FORM RECORDED BY OXF. DICT.
abhorrer (1534)	abhor (1449)
acclamation (1552)	acclamation (1585)
agriculture (1534)	agriculture (1603)
apparat (1534)	apparate (apparatus c. 1600)
	apparatus (1638)
articulation (1546)	articulation (1597)
aspect (1534)	aspect (1386, Chaucer)
athlète (1546)	athlete (1528)
cadavre (1534)	cadaver (1398, Trevisa)
candide (1534)	candid (1630)
correct a. (1532)	correct v. (c. 1374, Chaucer)
	correct pp. (1460)
	correct a. (1676, Dryden)
crépuscule (1532)	crepuscule (dawn, c. 1391, Chaucer)
culinaire (1546)	culinary (1638)
décadent (1546)	decadent (1837)
décimer (1546)	decimate (1600)
maritime (1534)	maritime (1598)
modal (1546)	modal (1625)
offensif (1534)	offensive (before 1548)
officieux (1546)	officious (1565)
ovation (1534)	ovation (1533)
panique n. (1534)	panic a. (1603)
	panic n. (1627)
parallèle (1552)	parallel (1549)
pénurie (1532)	penury (1432-50)
perversion (1546)	perversion (1388)
prélude (1534)	prelude (1599, Ben Jonson)
prolifique (1546)	prolific (1650)
pétrifier (1552)	petrify (1594)
rare (1532)	rare (c. 1420)
sacrosaint (1546)	sacrosanct (1601)
sceptique (1546)	sceptic a. (c. 1575)

---

1. *La Langue de Rabelais*, II, 71-72.

sidéral (1534)

spiral a. (1534)
stagnant (1546)
succès (1552)
superfétation (1534)
tergiverser (1532)

tropique (1532)
éjaculation (1552)

exclusif (1532)
excrément (1534)
exotique (1552)
explorer (1546)
fréquent (1552)
frugal (1534)
génial (1546)

génie (1532)
guttural (1532)
horrifique (1534)
hyperbolique (1546)
imperméable (1546)
importeur (1534)

imposture (1534)
inculquer (1546)
indigène (1532)
inerte (1534)
inhiber (1534)
inscription (1534)
instant a. (1534)
interpolation (1546)
intimider (1546)
linéament (1532)
turbine (1534)

tutélaire (1552)
valide (1552)
ventriloque (1552)

vermiforme (1532)

sceptic n. (1587)
sideral (1594)
sidereal (1634, Bishop Hall)
spiral a. (1551)
stagnant (1666)
success (1537)
superfetation (1603)
tergiversation (1583)
tergiversate (1654)
tropic (1391, Chaucer)
ejaculate v. (1578)
ejaculation (1610)
exclusive (1570)
excrement (1565)
exotic(k) (1599, Ben Jonson)
explore (1585, Queen Elizabeth)
frequent a. (1531)
frugal (1598, Shakespeare)
genial, (generative or nuptial, 1566 ; festive 1620),
genie (1655)
guttural (1625)
horrific (1653, Urquhart)
hyperbolic (1646)
impermeable (1697)
import v. (1508, Skelton)
importer n. (1700)
imposture (1537)
inculcate (1550)
indigenous (1646)
inert (1647)
inhibit (1460)
inscription (1538)
instant a. (1477)
interpolation (1623)
intimidate (1646)
lineament (1570)
turbinal (top-shaped, 1584)
turbinated (top-shaped, 1615)
turbine (1842)
tutelary (1611)
valid (1571)
ventriloquy (1584)
ventriloque n. (1681)
ventriloque a. (1826)
vermiform (1730)

The *Oxford Dictionary* cites Rabelais as precedent for *impermeable, inscription,* and *prelude.* The dates given show that at least ten of the words existed in English before his time, and the extent to which he may have contributed towards our adoption of the other fifty or more can scarcely be estimated exactly. One knows that the *Dictionary* is not infallible as a guide to the earliest ocurrence of a word in the language, and likewise that word invention was a feature of Renaissance culture at large. Coincidences must have been frequent. That *horrific* is not recorded before Urquhart seems to point clearly to Rabelais, and I am inclined to attribute to him also *exotic* and *prelude,* since they are first recorded in a writer well versed in his works [1]. The list is given in the present instance, however, not to argue Rabelais's influence, but rather his sure sense in making use of so many new words, whether of his own invention or not, which the passage of time was to standardize in two languages.

Rabelais is no prose-poet in the usual sense ; he does not attempt melodic sweetness nor sustained cadences ; his rhythmic patterns are intermittent, like those of Wagnerian opera. His style as a whole has been well described as the *orchestration of ideas.* One idea is passed through two or more different vocabularies as a musical theme is taken up by different instruments. Thus,

Pour ce que, selon le dict de Hesiode, d'une chascune chose le commencement est la moytié du tout, et, scelon le proverbe commun, à l'enfourner on faict les pains connuz... [2].

Rabelais, it may be said, is generally recognized as a writer of universal significance, though not yet of universal appeal. Perhaps he will never be that. Though he wrote of all things, and though he dedicated Book III to the Queen of Navarre, he addressed himself implicity to men. He shares woman's conservatism as regards underlying values ; but he is preponderantly masculine in his intellectual and sometimes revolutionary treatment of externals. Women will probably always enjoy his portrayal of

---

1. Ben Jonson is treated below, pp. 81 ff.
2. Bk. IV, Ch. iii.

character, but never to the same extent his exaggerations. Farce has never been popular with the sex, and Rabelais is generally farcical even when serious. That this is no paradox may be illustrated by the true pathos of the first chapter of *Pantagruel*, where Gargantua alternately roars like a calf in his joy at the birth of his son, and weeps like a cow in his grief at the death of the mother. It would certainly be unwise in this place to argue his universality. Faithful readers are aware, in any case, that each new reading reveals something hitherto unobserved, perhaps the admirable characterization of a spirited woman in the lady of Paris abused by Panurge in Book II, chapters XXI and XXII ; the beauty of the dying speech of Raminagrobis in Book III, chapter XXI ; or the sublimity of the passage on the death of Pan in Book IV, chapter XXVIII. " Universal " or not, his ways are unique, and it is only in terms of these that his influence can be traced, for no man can bequeathe his genius. One of his ways is a consistent leaning toward the ugly and the horrific. Monsieur de la Juillière finds in his study of Rabelais's images that the ugly is generally chosen when it offers : devils, asses, monkeys, goats, and the like [1]. Rabelais's very exaggeration of things to the point of impossibility is at first blush ugly, and so illustrates the description of his work first advanced, to wit, that it is grotesque.

The grotesque had almost no tradition in England in the century of Rabelais. Her history was comparatively chaste ; so was her literature. There are, however, distinctly Rabelaisian elements in Dunbar, Skelton, and John Heywood. Dunbar, for instance, writes with pseudo-realism in his satires on the Abbot of Tungland. The Abbot, it seems, boasted he would fly to France from Stirling Castle, but fell in the first attempt and broke his leg. The story is told as a vision in two poems. In one he is represented as a griffin copulating with a female dragon and generating the Antichrist in the clouds ; in the other he is surrounded by birds who attack him, and force him down into a bog. The style is vigorous and fluent. It gives the impression not only of speed, but of the strength behind the movement of great mass. The following

---

1. *Les Images dans Rabelais*, 51.

example, taken from his poem *The Tua Mariit Wemen and The Wedo*[1], illustrates the characteristic gusto of his earthy imagery, his feeling for words which almost define themselves, and his fertility. One notices that his preoccupation with sounds is by no means confined to alliteration.

I haue ane wallidrag [2], ane worme, ane auld wobat [3] carle,
A waistit wolroun [4], an worth bot wourdis to clatter ;
Ane bumbart [5], an dronbee, ane bag full of flewme [6],
Ane skabbit skarth [7], ane scorpioun, ane scutarde [8] behind ;
To see him scart [9] his awin skyn grit scunner [10] I think.
Quhen kissis me that carybald [11], than kyndillis all my sorow ;
As birss [12] of ane brym bair [13], his berd is als stif,
Bot soft and soupill as the silk is his sary lwme [14] :
He may weill to the syn assent, but sakles [15] his deid is.

The pertinent features of Skelton are a similar fluency, a similar earthiness, and similar mouthfuls of sound. Rabelais would have been delighted with *The Tunnyng of Elinor Rummyng*, and he might have recognized in *Philipp Sparrow* not only a similar copiousness, but also a delicacy of feeling which he himself could never have rendered. He would probably have considered *The Bowge of Court*, *Magnyfycence*, and certain other pieces, old-fashioned. Skelton, for his part, would certainly have enjoyed *Pantagruel* had he lived long enough to read it.

John Heywood, in the interlude of the *Foure PP* (c. 1530),

---

1. *Poems*, ed. Schipper, 50.
2. Poor weak creature.
3. Feeble as a worm.
4. Impotent man.
5. Lazy man.
6. Phlegm.
7. Cormorant.
8. One who scatters or pours out behind.
9. Scratch.
10. Disgust, loathing.
11. Mean fellow.
12. Bristles.
13. Fierce boar.
14. *Membrum virile.*
15. Worthless.

makes a " potycary " tell how a woman blew down a castle with
a prodigious fart [1], and again, makes a pardoner give a Chaucerian-
Lucianic-Rabelaisian account of the women in hell [2]. When these
were at last deported, he exclaims

> And how the cheymes in hell dyd rynge,
> And how all the soules therein dyd synge !

The apothecary displays a large technical vocabulary, plays upon
words, and purposely reverses the gist of proverbial expressions.
Thus, displaying his wares,

> Here is syrapus de Byzansis, —
> A lytell thynge is i-nough of this,
> For euen the weyght of one scryppull
> Shall make you stronge as a cryppull.
> Here be other : as, diosfialios,
> Diagalanga, and sticados,
> Blanka manna, diospoliticon,
> Mercury sublyme, and metridaticon,
> Pelitory, and arsefetita [3]...

The play is a contest of lies, and the second lie is said to have
been but a dream. If we discount these conventions, it must be said
that the whole is both grotesque and satirical. It makes light of
the marvellous in mediaeval lore, and aims a shaft at women's
chatter, pardoners, apothecaries, palmers, and pedlars.

It would be well if early English grotesque writing were further
investigated, yet the paucity of familiar material is significant.
Our Middle Age was not so barren, nor our early Renaissance so
lurid, as to present grotesque incongruities to the literary mirror.
A Rabelais in England would have languished for want of inspiration. Rabelais found plenty in Italy, where he was entertained
many times in the course of his life ; and one knows what the
English Protestants thought of that country. Our energy was
abundant, but we did not drink so deep nor burn so many heretics as

---

1. *The Playe Called the Foure PP.*, ll.708 ff., Repr. in Adams, *Chief Pre-
Shakespearean Dramas* (Boston, 1924), 367 ff.
2. *Ibid.*, ll.771 ff.
3. *The Foure PP.*, ll.612 ff.

our neighbors. We did not laugh so loud. The non-conformist conscience perenially exhibited by the Anglo-Saxons is largely a racial phenomenon, and manifested itself long before the Reformation. It is recorded that in the time of Rabelais an English ambassador was profoundly shocked to see the French King seated beside his mistress as he viewed the return of his queen from her coronation [1] ; and it was owing to the same kind of scruples that Chaucer, or some volunteer on his behalf, recanted for the license of his comparatively innocent " worldly vanitees [2]. " We were an earnest and decorous people, and appear to have shunned Rabelais in the beginning deliberately, for our cultivation of the French language and literature has at all times been adequate to some understanding of his work.

The proximity of the two nations and their intercourse, commercial, military and diplomatic, is primarily accountable. Conversation books in the two languages date at least from Caxton [3], and England produced the first standard grammar of French, Palsgrave's *Lesclaircissement de la Langue Française*, in 1530 [4]. It is interesting to notice that its only important forerunner, the *Champ fleury* of Geoffroy Tory, expresses the need of such a work as Palsgrave wrote, in a memorable passage, which Rabelais was to put with little change into the mouth of his Limosin scholar [5]. Palsgrave was born in France, and became a B. A. of Cambridge, M. A. of Paris, chaplain to Henry VIII, and tutor to the Princess Mary and to the King's natural son, the first Duke of Richmond [6]. He was only one of a number of native French scholars who found employment teaching French to the early Tudor aristocracy, a near rival being Giles Dewes, or Du Guez, an old tutor of the King, author of *An Introductorie for to lerne... frenche trewly* (1532) [7].

---

1. See Schneegans, *Gesch. d. Grot. Sat.*, 509.
2. *The Canterbury Tales*, T. 1084-85 (Skeat's numbering).
3. Caxton published a small volume of *Dialogues in French and in English*, c. 1483. Here is a sample : " May I here be logged ? *Ye, well and clenly...* Dame, may men goo by ship fro hens to boloyne ?... [etc.] ", pp. 46-47.
4. Repr. François Génin, Paris, 1852.
5. See *Lesclaircissement*, Intro., 7 ; and Rabelais, Bk. II, Ch. VI.
6. *Dict. Nat. Biog.*
7. Repr. with *Lesclaircissement* of Palsgrave, ed. Génin, Paris, 1852. See Intro., 14, ff., for an account of Du Guez.

Another of these scholars was Nicholas Bourbon of Vandoevre in Champagne, a neo-Latin poet praised by Erasmus, a protégé of Anne Boleyn, and tutor to Lord Hunsdon and the Dudleys [1]. His interest in the present connection is tantalizing, for he was a friend of Rabelais. Unhappily the friendship came about rather in spite than because of any admiration on his part for the latter's witings, the first of which he attacked in 1533. It is unlikely that he recommended them abroad [2].

The increasingly numerous grammars and dictionaries after Palsgrave indicate that the enthusiasm for things French continued and extended down the social scale [3]. It was inevitable that Rabelais's books should have come at last with the stream of French culture which poured into England in the eighties and nineties with the Huguenot immigrants. The population of London is said to have been augmented by some fourteen hundred of these in 1580, over fifty per cent of the total foreign population of the city in the previous decade [4]. Whatever the figure, their influence was widely reflected. The drama, for example, represented a French character for the first time in 1587 [5]. " French, " writes a grammarian of the time,

---

1. See Bastide, *Anglais et Français du XVIIe siècle*, 40 ; and Plattard, *Vie de Rabelais*, 157-58.

2. Charles Whibley writes as follows of John Leland (1506-1552), author of *The laboriouse Journey and Serche of Johan Leylande, for Englandes Antiquities* : '' Born in 1506, he studied both at Christ's College, Cambridge, and at All Souls, Oxford, and, after some years spent in Paris, where he was the friend of Budé, and may, through his mediation, have encountered Rabelais, he was appointed chaplain and librarian to Henry VIII, and rector of Pepeling in the marches of Calais. '' — *Camb. Hist of Eng. Lit.*, III, 374.

3. Some sixteen different French grammars and dictionaries, not counting reprints, appeared before 1600, and an equal number in the following half century. Holyband's *The French Littleton* went through at least seven editions, 1566 ff., *The French Schoole-Maister* eight, 1573 ff. ; G. de la Mothe de Vayer's, *The French Alphabet*, four, 1595 ff. ; and Cotgrave's celebrated *Dictionarie of the French and English Tongues* three, 1611, 1632, and 1650. A list, by no means complete, of these works is to be found in Upham's *The French Infl. in Eng. Lit.*, 9-10, n. 2.

4. See Eckhardt, *Die Dialekt-und Ausländertypen des älteren Englischen Dramas*, II, 5.

5. *Ibid.*, 94.

is a Courtly speech, spoken and vnderstood by most Princes, Noble-
men, and Gentlemen in all parts of Christendome, because still the
finest wits delight to read bookes of State, Pollicie, Marciall discipline,
Phisicke, Humanitie, Historie, Diuinitie, and a number of most rare
spirits have written thereof in French.   Some are giuen to read Poësies
& Loue-toies, the sweetest that are to be read are in French, pend by
Bartas, Marot, Ronsard, Belleau, de Portes, and diuers other wits ini-
mitable...:   some to follow armes and the conduct of warre, the French
is the onely tongue for the Marcialist: others to trafficke with the stranger, the French is the only trading tongue in Europe.   And againe, if
we marke well the scituation of Fraunce, it lyeth in the very heart of
Christianitie, and thither are sent Embassadors from al other quarters
of *Europe*, from *England, Scotland, Pole-land, Constantinople, Italie,
Barbarie, Spaine, Netherland, Germanie*... [These things] maketh
their language very famous, and in very high request and estimation [1].

The grammarian was John Eliot, one of three or four men who
acclaimed Rabelais simultaneously in 1593.   The passage quoted
prefaces his acknowledgement of that author, who, though he
does not say quite as much, was actually his chief source of inspiration.   The argument is significant in pointing to certain
French literary fashions which had, as everybody knows, already
spread to England ; though one finds that the influence of Rabelais
has been surprisingly independent of fashions from the beginning.
He is an unique figure, towering high above his time and place,
and it is not too much to say that some measure of the maturity
of England in modern times may be taken from the incidence and
nature of his effect upon her literature.

---

1. John Eliot, *Ortho-Epia Gallica*, 1593, B^r-B^v.

CHAPTER II

THE BEGINNINGS

The Gargantua of folk lore in England. The earliest traces of Rabelais. The philologists : Holyband, Cotgrave, John Eliot. Gabriel Harvey and Thomas Nashe. Sir John Harington. Robert Dallington.

a) *The Gargantua of folk lore in England.*

It is on record that a certain Fellow of Clare College, Cambridge, who died in 1546, owned a *Gargantua Gallica* [1]. From 1571 to the Restoration there occur at least thirty-six references to Gargantua in English books by twenty different authors, in which the name simply signifies the title of a popular tale or symbolizes the gigantic [2]. In addition to these there is an entry, cancelled, of " A booke entytuled *Gargantua* " in The Stationers' Registers for June 16th, 1592, and another, not cancelled, for " A booke entituled *the historie of Gargantua. & C.* " for December 4th, 1594. The references are mostly massed in the reigns of Elizabeth and James, falling off somewhat thereafter. In none of the thirty-six passages in question is there any detail by which to determine whether Rabelais's Gargantua is the object of the reference or the giant of one or another of the popular chronicles. Two passages in John Taylor, " the Water-poet, " refer quite definitely to the folk tale, which, again, is explicitly distinguished from the works

---

1. *Proc. Camb. Antiq. Soc.*, LXIII, 180 ; cit. Gaselee in a note in *Rev. du XVIᵉ siècle*, I, 261.
2. The following argument is a summary of that presented in the Introduction to my edition of Girault, where the evidence is given in detail.

of Rabelais in a play of 1603. Two passages in Gabriel Harvey, the earlier of date 1592, one in John Taylor, and one in an anonymous dramatist of 1605 contain references with certain details which not only narrow the focus to the chronicles in general, but which go back precisely to Girault's *Croniques admirables*. Since John Taylor could not read French ; since there is no unambiguous evidence of the existence of an English version of Rabelais before Urquhart ; and since Gargantua was a personage familiar to all classes of society, it seems clear that an English version of one of the chronicles must have been current at a very early date, at the latest from before 1572, while an English version of the *Croniques admirables* must have been current from 1592. It is unnecessary to assume the incidence of two or more printed English versions of an admittedly trifling bit of folk lore in order to account for the evidence. It is probably to be inferred that there was only one, and that one was a translation of the *Croniques admirables*. In view of the special difficulties which the text of Rabelais presents, even to readers familiar with the French language, the chance is remote that many, or even a fair proportion, of the early Elizabethan passages which name the giant refer to Rabelais. The chance that an early Elizabethan translation of Rabelais's *Gargantua* was made, and read, and that all it taught people was to quote Gargantua's name, is still more remote.

The direct literary influence of the chronicle was negligible. It appears to have been committed to memory by a bricklayer of Coventry in 1575 ; and it was described as " witless " by a Puritan parson in 1572, and as " hurtfull to youth " by Francis Meres in 1598. It should be observed, however, that the original Gargantua is one of the more important of the early scions of a small but distinguished family of benevolent giants who have flourished in modern literature. Rabelais's heroes derive from him and are directly related to the Morgante of Pulci and the Baldus of Folengo, and in turn furnished Swift with the model for his Brobdingnagians, and even for some of the features of Gulliver himself. Gargantua's popularity in France—Rabelais prophesied that more copies of the *Grandes cronicques* would be sold in a month than of Bibles in nine years—and in England, where he was known to persons of all ranks and degrees of education, suggest that the success of his reincarnations must be due in some degree to those features of his original character which Rabelais and Swift, in creating their giants, saw fit to preserve unaltered.

b) The earliest traces of Rabelais.

If, as is probable, the translation of the folk tale postulated for 1572 or before was the same *Croniques admirables* which was current in 1592, its readers were furnished with three chapters from the pen of Rabelais [1] with almost certainly no knowledge that their origin was different from that of the work as a whole [2]. However this may be, the earliest recorded mention of Rabelais's name which can be dated exactly occurs in 1577 in the Epistle Dedicatory to Simon Patericke's translation of Gentillet's *Discourse* against Machiavelli. Rabelais and Machiavelli were, according to Patericke, corrupting European civilisation between them, the first by joking about vice, the second by confusing it with virtue.

Hereof Fraunce is unto all ages and nations a wofull view, yet a profitable instruction at this day. For when the 'cleare light of the Gospell began first to spring and appeare, Sathan (to occupie and busie mens minds with toyish playes and trifles, that they might give no attendance unto true wisedome) devised this policie, to raise up jeasters and fooles in Courts, which creeping in, by quipping and prety conceits, first in words, and after by bookes, uttering their pleasant jeasts in the Courts and banquets of kings and princes, laboured to root up all the true principles of Religion and Policie. And some there were whom the resemblance of nature, or vanitie of wit had so deceived, that they derided the everlasting veritie of the true God, as if it were but a fable. *Rabelaysus* amongst the French, and *Agrippa* amongst the Germanes, were the standerd-bearers of that train : which with their skoffing taunts,

---

1. Girault, p. xvii.
2. Thomas Wilson wrote a mock learned letter purporting to be from a Lincolnshire gentleman, in *The Art of Rhetoric*, 1553, as a protest against affected Latinizing of the English language (Repr. Mair, 163). Saintsbury thinks it " may owe royalty either to the Limosin scholar of Rabelais [Bk. II, Ch. vi] or even to Master Francis' own original, Geoffroy Tory himself. " — *Hist. of Crit.* (4th ed., 1922), II, 150. A comparison of the texts shows that no borrowing can be proved, and that Wilson's Latinizing is much less exaggerated than that of either Frenchman.

inveighed not onely against the Gospell, but all good arts whatsoeuer. Those mockers did not as yet openly undermine the ground worke of humane society, but onely they derided it : But such Cyclopian laughters, in the end proved to be only signes and tokens of future evils. For by little and little, that which was taken in the beginning for jests, turned to earnest, & words into deeds [1].

The notion of Rabelais's wickedness has, of course, been perennially entertained among the uncritical everywhere. The part which Simon Patericke played in its dissemination was potentially substantial, for the kindred view of Machiavelli, which was even more widely held in England, seems not to have become general before his translation of the *Discourse* in question [2].

Gabriel Harvey makes a casual reference to Panurge in a marginal note, undated, in his copy of Erasmus's *Parabolœ* (which was published at Basel in 1565) [3], and in a note which he wrote between 1567 and 1579 in his *Quintilian* calls Rabelais a " spirited and magnificent " genius, like Quintilian himself, Aretino, Machiavelli, du Bartas, Luther, [Sir Thomas ?] Smith, and a jumble of others which is Shandean in the extreme [4]. Those of his writings which can be shown to owe something to the Rabelaisian influence were not written until the nineties.

---

1. The first two pages (unnumbered) of The Epistle Dedicatory to *A Discovrse vpon the Meanes of Wel Governing... Against Nicholas Machiavel... Translated into English by Simon Patericke.* (London, 1608). The Epistle is dated, " Kalends Augusti. Anno 1577. "
2. See Eduard Meyer *Machiavelli and the Elizabethan Drama,* 19 ff.
3. It occurs opposite this line on p. 145,

> Coccyx oua subdit in nidis alienis,

and reads,

> Inde fortasse nomen, Coockouldes.
> Panurge, a cuccu. —

Quoted in Harvey's *Marginalia,* ed. Moore Smith, 139.
4. " Placent lepida ; valent seria ; florent animosa et magnifica ingenia. Qualia ipsius Quintiliani, Vallae, Fortij, Lutheri, Smithi, Rami, talium perpaucorum. Huc etiam Ferdinandus Corduba, Agrippa, Morus, Paracelsus, Florauantus, Aretinus, Rabelaesius, Machiauellus, Gandinus, Cosmopolita, Bartasius. " — in Harvey's copy of Quintilian at XII, cap. x ; cit. in *Marginalia,* ed. Moore Smith, 119. It is explained on p. 110 that he bought the book in March, 1567, for 3 /6 and wrote his name twice on the title page, the second time with date 1579.

In 1585 Sir Edward Dyer speaks of " the macheronicall phanta-
sies of Merlinus Cocaius, and sleepie *Phantasmata* of Francois
Rabilois [1]. " He may perhaps, like John Taylor after him, have
been thinking of Rabelais as the author of the popular chronicle, to
which the adjective " sleepy " would better apply than to the
Rabelaisian.

Sir Philip Sidney may have had Panurge in mind when he censured the " playing wit " who " can praise, " among other things,
" the comfortableness of being in debt, " though Panurge was anticipated by a poem, *In Lode del Debito*, of Francesco Berni (d. 1536) [2].
Sidney thus expressed himself in the *Apologie for Poetrie*, probably
written in the eighties, though not printed until 1595 [3].

The anonymous author of *An Almond for a Parrat*, an anti-
Marprelate document of 1589, speaks of " That merry man Rablays,
who dedicated most of his workes to the soule of the old Queene
of Nauarre many yeares after her death for that she was a main-
tainer of mirth in her life [4]. " Rabelais dedicated Book III only to
the " spirit " (" l'esprit ") of the Queen of Navarre, the first edition being published in 1546, actually three years before her death.
The Englishman's error is easily explained either by his using a
later edition (perhaps that of 1552) or to his ignorance of the date
of her death. It has been pointed out that the verses would have
been equally appropriate had they been addressed to the departed
" soul " rather than the living " spirit. " The phrase " most of
his workes " is perhaps owing to an assumption that the dedication
of Book III applied also to the earlier books. In any case Rabelais is now known definitely in England as the author of " workes "
which include Book III.

It is possible that Shakespeare was the earliest English writer
to make use of the romance of Rabelais. The pedant in *Love's
Labour's Lost* [5] is named Holofernes. Evidence at present available

---

1. *Writings*, ed. Grosart, 114, cit. McKillop, *M. L. N.*, XXXVI, 470.
2. See Rabelais, Bk. III, Ch. III and IV, and Francesco Berni, *Opere* (Milan, 1864), I, 126-31.
3. Arber's reprint, 49.
4. Printed in *The Works of Nashe*, ed. McKerrow, III, 341.
5. The first draft of the play is usually dated 1591. It was revised for publication. and performance in 1597-98.

does not permit us to say that Shakespeare knew his Rabelais at first hand, but the application of the name Holofernes to a pedant seems to be due to Thubal Holoferne, the first preceptor of Gargantua, who taught the youthful giant his *a-b-c* so well that he could repeat it backwards [1]. " What is *a*, *b*, spelt backward...?" asks Moth of the Shakespearean Holofernes, who replies, " Ba [2]. " It is quite possible that Ben Jonson introduced Shakespeare into a nodding acquaintance with Rabelais's work, though he may never have got him to read it, for Jonson knew Rabelais well. Shakespeare's intense literary curiosity, in any case, can scarely have failed to bring him within sound of the name and something of what it stood for. A large quantity of evidence of very little value has been assembled to prove a more intimate connection than appears to have existed [3]. The name and character of the pedant alone seems to be significant. One would like to know what would have been the state of things had a translation of Rabelais been accessible to William Shakespeare.

There was published in 1591 *A Wonderfull, strange and miraculous, Astrologicall Prognostication for this yeer of our Lord God. Discouering such wonders to happen this yeere, as neuer chaunced since Noes floud. Wherein if there be found one lye, the Author will loose his credit for euer. By Adam Fouleweather, Student in Assetronomy* [4].

McKerrow points out that it " is one of a group of three published about the same time in real or pretended rivalry. The existence of the first is to be inferred from an entry in the Stationers " Register on Feb. 25, 1590-1, to W. Wright of ' A booke entituled ffrauncis fayre weather, '...The Second is the *Wonderful Prognostication* [in question].., while the third is Simon Smell-Knave's *Fearful and lamentable effects of two...Comets, which shall appear in the year... 1591, the 25 of March.* That this followed Adam Foule-

---

1. Bk. I, Ch. xiv.
2. Act V, Sc. I, ll. 49 ff.
3. See Appendix A below, pp. 210 ff. There is a reference to Gargantua in *As You Like It*, Act III, Sc. ii, l. 237, which shows that Shakespeare shared the common acquaintance with that hero.
4. Printed in *The Works of Nashe*, ed. McKerrow, III, 377 ff. On authorship see below, p. 52, n. 4.

weather's production is shown by a reference to that work with which it opens. Some joking on the days of the week, in which Monday is said to be the best of all, perhaps suggests that Anthony Munday was the author. The three pamphlets are referred to together in John Florio's dedication to Nicholas Saunder of his *Second Fruits*, 1591... [1]. " The first is a lost work, and I have not been able to examine a copy of the second.

Comic prognostications were popular in the early 16th century, and the goliardic humour of the time continued to find a various expression in satirizing astrology. Aretino wrote at least five satirical prognostications, that for the year 1534, the fifth, alone being preserved [2]. Two were produced in Latin by the German, Heinrich Bebel (1470 ?-1518), one " borrowed...from the Italian, and the other translated from an anonymous German writer by Bebel's pupil, Heinrichmann of Sindelfingen[3]." Rabelais published several almanacs besides the *Pantagrueline Prognostication* [4]. The title page of the latter first read " pour l'année 1533, " but was later changed to " pour l'an perpetuel. " The tone of the work is humorous throughout ; whereas in his *Almanack Pour L'An 1533* and another *Pour L'An 1535*, both perserved in fragments, he includes some comparatively serious remarks [5].

The *Wonderfull Prognostication* of 1591 resembles the Pantagrueline strikingly throughout. It might be thought that any two comic prognostications must be similar, but it is not so. W. F. Smith takes care to remark that while Rabelais's pamphlet " is freely adapted " from the two Latin ones of Bebel, " very little (not more than four or five sentences) " is borrowed from him [6]. I have compared it with the Latin works myself, and am convinced that

---

1. *The Works of Nashe*, ed. McKerrow, IV, 476-77.
2. See *Un Pronostico Satirico di Pietro Aretino*, ed. Aless. Luzio (Bergamo 1900).
3. *Rabelais*, Transl. Smith, II, 459, n. Both prognostications were reprinted by Regis in the notes to his *Garg. und Pant.*, II, 927-34.
4. He made almanacs for 1533, '35, '41, '46, and '50. See *Œuvres*, ed. Moland, I, LXX-LXXII. That for 1541, for example, is simply an astronomical and ecclesiastical calendar. It is reprinted in *Works*, Transl. Putnam, III, 924.
5. These fragments are included in Putnam's translation, III, 915-17.
6. *Rabelais*, Transl. Smith, II, 459.

the resemblances between the English work and that of Rabelais prove a much closer connection than exists even between Rabelais and the Latin. Both the former are longer, and richer in sheer drollery. Their humor consists in the novel expression or application of certain truisms of life at large. Even so the English is, properly speaking, a free and not a close adaptation of the French.

Each opens with an address to the reader which announces the nature of the events to be predicted. Each writer in his own way satirizes the pretensions of astrology, both solemnly guaranteeing the truth of their predictions on their title pages, though the Englishman once makes the gentle understatement that " Astrologie is not so certain but it may fayle [1]. "

The chapters of Rabelais's work are entitled : *I Du Gouvernement et Seigneur De Ceste Année, II Des Eclipses, III Des Maladies, IV Des Fruictz et Biens Croissant de Terre, V De L'Estat D'Aulcunes Gens, VI De l'Estat D'Aulcuns Pays, VII Des Quatre Saisons..., et Premierement Du Printemps, VIII De L'Esté, IX De L'Autonne, X De L'Hyver.* In Chapter II it is said that there will be eclipses of both the sun and the moon, and the English prognostication opens on this motive : *Of the Eclipses that shall happen this present yeere...* The first is that of the moon. A sub-divison is entitled, *The Eclipse of the Sunne.* The next large division is *Of the second Eclipse of the Moone.* The next is *A declaration of the generall disposition of sundrie conceited qualities incident vnto mens mindes & natures throughout these foure quarters of the yere, by the merrie influence of the Planets, together with some other tragicall events and observations...,* and is subdivided under winter, spring, summer, and autumn.

Both writers declare that Mercury will prove inconstant [2]. A few of the large number of persons dealt with by both are brokers (composeurs d'empruns), farmers (boteleurs de foing, faulcheurs, bergiers, etc.), brewers (bresseurs de biere), ale knights (buveurs) [3], sumners and pettifoggers (chicaneurs, esperucquetz) [4], monks

1. Nashe, *Works*, III, 381.
2. *Ibid.*, III, 381 ; *Pant. Prog.* Ch. ii.
3. Nashe, *Works*, III, 382 ; *Pant. Prog.*, Ch. v.
4. Nashe, *Works*, III, 383 ; *Pant. Prog.*, Ch. v.

(moines), and harlots (putains) [1]. The English says, " olde women that can liue no longer shall dye for age ; " the French, " Vieillesse sera incurable ceste année à cause des années passées [2]. " The English, " yong men that haue Vsurers to their father shal this yeer haue great cause to laugh, for the Deuill hath made a decree that, after they are once in hell, they shall neuer rise again to trouble their executors ; " Rabelais, " ...usuriers... n'auront en ceste année tout ce qu'ilz vouldroient bien [3]. " The English predicts that " The plague shall raigne mortally amongst poore men, that diuerse of them shall not be able to change a man a groate, " and also " diuerse fluxes, and especiallie in poore mens purses, for they shall be so laxatiue, that money shall runne out faster then they can get it ; " Rabelais that there shall reign (regnera) " quasi universellement une maladie bien horrible et redoutable...faulte l'argent [4]. " The English says, " poore men shall die at riche mennes doores, " Rabelais that " les riches se porteront un peu mieulx que les pauvres [5]. " The English says, " some [women] shalbe so short heeld & so quesie stomackt that they shal ly in their beds while noon, by which means they shall grow so ful of grosse humors that they shalbe troubled with strange timpanies & swellings in their bellies, vncurable for fortye weekes ; " while Rabelais aims only at nuns, " Les nonnains à peine concepvront sans operation virile [6]. " The English warns that harlots will " fetch in young Gentlemen, to the great ouerthrow of youth, if some sharpe and speedye redresse be not fetcht from the woorshipfull Colledge of the Phisitions ; " and Rabelais that all lechers of both sexes " se doibvent garder de verolle, de chancre, de pisses chauldes, poullains grenetz, " etc. [7]. The English ventures " that Hennes, Capons, Geese, and other pullin shall little haunt poore mens tables, but flye awaye with spittes in their bellies to fat Churlles houses, " and

1. Nashe, *Works*, III, 384 ; *Pant. Prog.*, Ch. v.
2. Nashe, *Works*, III, 383 ; *Pant. Prog.*, Ch. iii.
3. Nashe, *Works*, III, 383 ; *Pant. Prog.*, Ch. v.
4. Nashe, *Works*, III, 392, 394 ; *Pant. Prog.*, Ch. iii.
5. Nashe, *Works*, III, 389 ; *Pant. Prog.*, Ch. iii.
6. Nashe, *Works*, III, 384-85 ; *Pant. Prog.*, Ch. v.
7. Nashe, *Works*, III, 385 ; *Pant. Prog.*, Ch. v.

that " The Butchers shall commit wilfull murther vpon Sheepe and
Oxen ; " Rabelais that " Plusieurs moutons, beufz, pourceaulx,
oysons, pouletz et canars mourront, et ne sera sy cruelle mortalité
entre les cinges et dromadaires, " and that " bouchiers...feront...
de beaulx coups [1]. " The English touches lightly on the
Danes and the French, while Rabelais deals with numerous
nationalities [2]. The English says " I am induced to set down that
such as haue no fire shall feele most cold ; " Rabelais that " ne
seront saiges ceulx qui vendront leurs pellices et fourrures pour
achapter du boys [3]. " The English, in addition to its remarks
already quoted on diseases, says, " men shall be troubled with such
paine in the eies that they shall not know their owne wiues from
other women ; " Rabelais that " le mal des yeux sera fort con-
traire à la veuë [4]. " Both predict that drinkables will be plentiful,
the English that " bottle Ale shall be in great authoritie, " Rabelais that " on n'y veit oncques tant de vins, ny plus frians [5]. " The
English says that " sicke folke shall haue worse stomackes then
they which be whole ; " Rabelais that " les sains [se porteront]
mieulx que les malades [6]. " The English predicts the pillory and
the confessional for bakers and prostitutes, and says that " some
shal be troubled with diseases in the throate, which cannot bee
helpte without Bull the hang man plaie the skilfull Chyrurgion ; "
while Rabelais predicts beatings for a large list of evil doers subject to Mars, including cooks (coquassiers, grillotiers), and says
that " Ung des susdictz sera ceste année faict Evesque des
champs, donnant la benediction avecques les piedz aux passans [7]. "
The English ends on a somewhat disturbing note, saying that
" good fellowes this yeere for want of money shall oft times be con-
tented to part companie ; " while Rabelais's conclusion is joyous
and nonsensical, a grotesque equivalent of the lyric endings of

1. Nashe, *Works*, III, 385, 387 ; *Pant. Prog.*, Ch. III, v.
2. Nashe, *Works*, III, 386, 387 ; *Pant. Prog.*, Ch. VI.
3. Nashe, *Works*, III, 389 ; *Pant. Prog.*, Ch. X.
4. Nashe, *Works*, III, 390 ; *Pant. Prog.*, Ch. III.
5. Nashe, *Works*, III, 392 ; *Pant. Prog.*, Ch. VI.
6. Nashe, *Works*, III, 392 ; *Pant. Prog.*, Ch. III.
7. Nashe, *Works*, III, 393, 394 ; *Pant. Prog.*, Ch. v.

Shakespearean romance : " Beuvez du meilleur... et ne chiez
plus dorenavant on lict.   O o ! poullailles, faictes-vous voz nidz tant
hault [1] ? "

It is quite possible that a translation of Rabelais's prognostication is represented by the lost GARGANTUA his prophesie, entered
in the Stationers' Register for April 6th, 1592 [2], the name of
Gargantua, now familiar in England, being substituted for that
of Pantagruel.   Whether it is or not, there were entered in the
succeeding months of that year two other works of far greater importance to literary history.   Both have fortunately been preserved.   Shakespeare's Rabelais, Rabelais the " merry man, " the
corrupter, and the unacknowledged source of the Wonderfull Prognostication, were but signs and portents of the standard author
who was now to receive the homage of a lexicographer, his first in
any language, and a grammarian.   His influence had been felt ;
it was now, for the first time, to be acknowledged.

c) The Philogists.

The lexicographer was Claude de Sainliens, or Claudius Holyband, a bilingual Frenchman and Londoner by adoption [3].   Born
in Moulins, France, of a Protestant family, he joined the earliest
of the Huguenot emigrants, and was established in England from
1566 to '97, where he became the father of a family, and a protégé
of Lord Buckhurst [4].   He is known chiefly as the author of dialogues in four languages and of French grammars and dictionaries
for English readers.   The most interesting of these to the student
of Rabelais is A Dictionarie French and English, published in
1593, an augmented edition of his Treasurie of the French Tongue

---

1. Nashe, Works, III, 395 ; Pant. Prog., Ch. x. For a lost translation of
the Pant. Prog., c. 1620, and for other prognostications in the 17th century,
see below, pp. 101-02, 132, 143-44, and Appendix E, pp. 229 ff.

2. Stat. Reg., ed. Arber, II, 286.

3. I am chiefly indebted for my account of this writer to Lucy E. Farrer,
La Vie et les Œuvres de Claude de Sainliens alias Claudius Holyband (Paris,
1903).

4. Farrer, Claude de Sainliens, 7.

of 1580 [1]. Holyband had shown himself a conservative critic of French letters in a work of that year where he condemned recent authors of " un jargon de langues diverses, que l'on ne sait comment nommer [2]. " The *Treasurie* of 1580 contains no Rabelais ; but by 1593 its author had evidently changed his mind about " jargon. " The *Dictionarie* anticipates the Johnsonian method of quoting standard authors for illustrating the definitions of words, and once, at least, cites Rabelais by name [3]. It speaks also of Pantagruel [4], but even without these hints there would still be no doubt of the source of such expressions as " boire à tirelarigaud ; " " et va, Bran pour toy ; " " il est clerc jusqu'aux dents ; " " il a mangé son breviaire ; " " faire ou rendre quinaud ; " " os medulaire ; " " gueux de l'ostiere ; " " porteurs de rogatons [5]. "

Randle Cotgrave published his *Dictionarie of the French and English Tongues* in 1611 [6]. He was a scholar of St. John's College, Cambridge, in 1587, and became secretary to William Cecil, afterwards the second Earl of Exeter. It is thought that he died in 1634. Holyband's *Dictionarie* of '93 had been the most important of its kind to date, containing about a thousand more words than that of Nicot, who was regarded as the authority in 1564 [7]. Its treatment of Rabelais was intelligent and progressive, but superficial when compared with that of Cotgrave. Cotgrave undertook the interpretation of Rabelais entire, " slang, Greco-Latin neologisms, proverbs, coinages, exclamations, and oaths, even puns and typographical errors [8] ! " Monsieur Sainéan, though he admits Holyband's priority in point of time, nevertheless calls Cotgrave

---

1. It was entered in the Stationers' Register on June 21st, 1592, as *the treasure of the Frenche tonge*, — *Stat. Reg.*, ed. Arber, II, 289ᵛ. See Farrer, *Claude de Sainliens*, 22, 72.
2. This was *De pronuntiatione linguae gallicae*. The quotation is a paraphrase of the original by Farrer, — *Claude de Sainliens*, 31.
3. Farrer, *Claude de Sainliens*, 76.
4. *Ibid.*
5. *Ibid.*
6. See *Dict. Nat. Biog.* under Cotgrave, Randle.
7. Farrer, *Claude de Sainliens*, 75.
8. This is my loose rendering of a statement by Monsieur Sainéan in his admirable article, " Les Interprètes de Rabelais en Angleterre et en Allemagne " (*R. E. R.*, VII, 142), to which I am chiefly indebted for the present discussion.

Rabelais's " first and only interpreter in the domain of lexicography [1]. " Five editions of the work appeared in the 17th century [2], and it was the foundation of our standard translation [3].

A book entitled *Orthoepia gallicana. Or the parlement of pratlers*
was entered in the Stationers' Register on December 18th, 1592 [4].
The author was John Eliot, of whose life there are but scant records.
He says himself that he was born and bred in the county of War-
wick [5], and he seems to have lived some years on the continent.
He is known to have written three hack works besides the book
already mentioned, which was published in 1593, under the revised title, *Ortho-Epia Gallica, Eliot's Fruits for the French.*

It is a grammar of colloquial French for tourists, yet of a quality
which the scholar can admire. It was dedicated to Essex, who
therefore perhaps read it ; while Gabriel Harvey owned and annotated a copy which has been preserved [6]. On the final fly leaf
he wrote " Poco, y bueno. " The first part covers the details of
French grammar, and the second, much longer, is made up of
dialogues in French and English in parallel columns, entitled *The
Parlement of Pratlers* [7]. The same thing had been done in English
and Italian by John Florio, whom, it is thought, Eliot had read.
Many of the subjects are still discussed in tourists' grammars, such
as " The uprising in the morning, " " To salute men, " " The walking, " " The Exchange. " The author, however, was not content to draw only upon his everyday experience, but acknowledges
literary sources. " I have, " he says,

written the whole book in a merrie phantasticall vaine, and to confirme
and stir vp the wit and memorie of the learner I haue diuersified it
with varietie of stories, no lesse authenticall then the deuises of *Lucians*

1. *R. E. R.*, VII, 141.
2. In 1611, '32, '50, '60, and '73, and in '79 Miège published *A Dictionary of
barbarous French, or a collection of obsolete, provincial, mis-spelt, and madewords
in French, taken out of Cotgrave's Dictionary with some additions.*
3. See below, pp. 122 ff.
4. *Stat. Reg.*, ed. Arber, II, 294ᵛ.
5. *Ortho-Epia*, A2ʳ.
6. This copy is now in the Huntington Library.
7. *The Parlement of Pratlers* has been reprinted, with an Introduction, by
r. Jack Lindsay (London, 1928).

dialogues :... And if any one say I haue plowed with other mens heigh-fars, answer for me in mine absence, Countrimen, and when I am present, I will answer for my selfe :   The truth is I turned ouer some few French authors, and where I espied any pretie example that might quicken the capacitie of the learner, I presumed to make a peece of it flie this way, to set together the frame of my fantasticall Comedie, pulling here a wing from one, there an arme from another, from this a leg, from that a buttocke, and out of euery one I had some share for the better ornament of my worke.   And to the end to defraud no man of his glory, I will tell you by whome I haue best profited :   I haue taken a few pleasant conceits out of *Francis.Rabelais* that merrie Grig, an example or two out of *Lewis Viues*, a score or two of verses out of *Bartasius* :   and put all together that I haue bought, begd or bor-rowed, it will not all amount to make two sheets of printed paper, and I cannot denie but the rest is of mine owne inuention and disposition [1].

This is a generous acknowledgement, even if not strictly accurate, his borrowings from Rabelais alone making many times two prin-ted pages.   He concludes this preface in a somewhat jarring vein of literary slang, which is fortunately dropped in the dialogues themselves.

Eliot was a realist, and it is the realism of his model, rather than the extravagance, that he recognized and rendered.   Thus while he gives us its monstrous eruptiveness in his version of the Lucianic Diogenes tumbling his tub, and its learned manner in *The Painter*, it is the sputter of animated conversation, as in *The drunken mens Banket*, *The Mariner*, or *The Braggart*, in which he chiefly extends himself and is most convincing.   The book was introduced to the world with the usual prefatory compliments and apologies, and the precaution was in vain.   No contemporary notice of it except Harvey's is recorded, and no second edition was called for.

Eliot manipulates Rabelais's text and translates the result with freedom.   He alters now the phraseology and now the order of sentences, composing from separate paragraphs, chapters, and books.   Even when he is not following the Rabelaisian text he draws largely on its idioms.   Thus :   " Vous saultez du coq à l'asne [2] ; " " Creature du gran vilain diantre d'enfer [3] ; " " Quoy !

---

1. *Ortho-Epia*, B[v] ff.
2. *Ibid.*, ii, 96 (misprinted 93).
3. *Ibid.*, 98.

Debtes ! O chose rare & antiquaire ! [1] ; " " Tes males mules, pol-
tron [2] ! ; " " Tes febures quartaines ! [3] ; " " I piaffed like a bon
companion [4] ".

He rivals Urquhart himself in fertility, as may be seen in the
list of verbs in his rendering of Rabelais's passage on Diogenes and
his tub, though word-mongering is not his chief preoccupation.   He
uses seventy words in this place to Rabelais's sixty-four.   Urquhart
uses a hundred or more [5].   They come in groups, mostly of two
and three, linked by logical or acoustic similarities, as " bind it,
wind it, twind it ; " " throw it, overthrow it ; " " tugd it, lugd it. "
He might have been more generous with ἅπαξ λεγόμενα, for we find
in the Epistle the incomparable " dezinkhornifistibulated, " with
which he improves in sense upon Rabelais's mere " desincornifis-
tibulé. " " I haue, " he says, " dezinkhornifistibulated a fantasticall Rapsody of dialogisme[5]. "

His most noticeable fault is occasional gallicism.   He renders
" plus i'ay soif " by " the more thirst I haue ; " " ie n'entends pas
la Rhetorique " by " I vnderstand not the Rhetoricke ; " " En
voyla de fort bon " by " There is very good [6]. "   These lapses are
evidently due to mere carelessness, for his English is, on the whole,
idiomatic and racy.   His few mistaken renderings of the exact
sense of the French are insignificant, such as *bet* for *bette*, which is
actualy dialect for *boisson, drink* ; or *tameth* for *entamme, to cut*,
figuratively *to bite* [7].   That he did not go wrong more often is
perhaps because he was careful to avoid selecting difficult passages.
Here is a taste of his quality, from the dialogue called " The drunken mens Banket : "

Which was first, thirst or drinking ?   Drinking.   For *Priuatio presup-
ponit habitum.*   I am a clerke, I tell you, *Fœcundi calices quem non
fecêre disertum.*   Lets sing, lets drinke, lets poure it in, where is my

1. *Ortho-Epia*, II, 98.
2. *Ibid.*, II, 124.
3. *Ibid.*, II, 78.
4. *Ibid.*, A 3ʳ.
5. *Ibid.*, A 3ᵛ ; Rabelais, Bk. III, Ch. xv.
6. *Ortho-Epia*, II, 45, 46-47, 49.
7. *Ibid.*, II, 46, 157.

tonnell ?   What ?   I drinke but by a letter of Attornie.   Wet you to
drie, or drie you to wet ?   By my fay I vnderstand not the Rhetoricke.
With the pratticque I helpe my selfe a little.   Courage, I wet, I mois-
ten, I drinke, and all for feare to die.   Drinke alwayes, you shall neuer
die.   If I drinke not, I am dead.   For conclusion of mine oration I
will say vnto you, that as for me, I thinke I am descended of some
rich King or prince in old time.   For you neuer saw man, who had a
greater desire to be a King, and rich, then my selfe, to the end to make
good cheare, to take no pains at all, to care for nothing, and to enrich
my friends & all honest and learned men [1].

It is no idle conjecture that Eliot might have achieved a complete
translation worthy of his great epoch if he had put his mind to it,
and that had he done so, its effect would have been felt.   His few
shortcomings in translating as much as he did, like those of
Urquhart sixty years later, are sufficient proof of how difficult the
text of Rabelais has always been for foreigners, even when relati-
vely near to him in point of time.   English readers of the original
have all been learned ; it was a closed book to the many, even to
most of the educated.   This was not so with Cervantes.   *Don
Quixote* was imitated successfully by Beaumont and Fletcher only
seven years after the publication of Part I in Madrid in *The Knight
of the Burning Pestle* (1611), and the name became a by word by
the middle of the century, Shelton's translation appearing already
in 1619-20 [2].   It may be that the difference is due to a more spon-
taneous appeal in that work—certainly the story has an outward
unity lacking in *Gargantua and Pantagruel*—and yet, though
Rabelais is in some ways poles removed from Cervantes in spirit,
in others he duplicates him.   Picrochole's castles in Spain, the
legal enterprises of Panurge, the pathos of old Janotus de Bragmardo [3], all these things are " Quixotic ; " and if the fates did not
intend them to be popularly enjoyed in England until long after
Cervantes was to supply an adjective to call them by, we can scarcely

1. *Ortho-Epia*, II, 46-47. For the corresponding passages in Rabelais see
Appendix below, p. 217.
2. See A. H. Mayor's admirable dissertation, *Cervantes, With Especial Reference to Don Quijote in English Literature Until 1781* (1926, unpublished ; a copy
is on file in the Library of Princeton University).
3. Bk. I, Ch. xxxiii ; Bk. II, Ch. xvii ; Bk. I, Ch. xviii-xx.

suppose that, given a medium, they, not to mention Rabelais as a whole, would have quite escaped our public in the fifteen nineties. Eliot truly missed an interesting opportunity.

d) Gabriel Harvey and Thomas Nashe.

It has become a commonplace of criticism that Thomas Nashe wrote under the influence of Rabelais [1], though protesting voices have been heard [2]. It originated with Gabriel Harvey, and Harvey's opinion was seconded by that of Bishop Hall in the late nineties [3].

Harvey had some acquaintance with Rabelais's writings himself. He owned and studied a copy of Eliot's *Ortho-Epia Gallica*, which contained copious extracts from the *Five Books* [4], and his *marginalia* include two of the earliest notices of Rabelais in England [5]. The following definition of " right artificiality " occurs in the third of his *Foure Letters*, 1592.

Right artificiality (whereat I once aimed to the vttermost power of my slender capacity) is not mad-brained, or ridiculous, or absurd, or blasphemous, or monstrous : but deepe conceited, but pleasurable, but delicate, but exquisite, but gracious, but admirable : not according to the fantastical mould of Aretine or Rabelays, but according to the fine modell of Orpheus, Homer, Pindarus,... [etc., etc.] [6].

His *Pierces Supererogation*, 1593, contains *An Advertisement for Pap-Hatchet, and Martin Mar-Prelate*. In this he attacks the author of *Pappe with an Hatchet*, probably Lyly, saying,

So may he soone make-vp the autenticall Legendary of his *Hundred merrie Tales* : as true peraduenture, as Lucians true narrations ; or

---

1. See Regis, *Garg. und Pant.*, III, 1471 ; Harvey, *Works*, ed. Grosart, I, xv ; Jusserand, *The English Novel in the Time of Shakespeare*, 305 ; Whibley, " Rabelais en Angleterre, " *R. E. R.*, I, 6 ; *Camb. Hist. of Eng. Lit.*, IV, 10 ; Upham, *The French Infl. in Eng. Lit.*, 227 ff. ; Sidney Lee, *The French Renaissance in England*, 163 ; and Manus, *Eng. Lit. in Its Foreign Relations*, 92-93.
2. See Nashe, *Works*, ed. McKerrow, V, 128-31 ; and McKillop, " Some Early Traces of Rabelais in Eng. Lit., " *M. L. N.*, XXXVI, 469-74.
3. See below, p. 71.
4. See above, p. 43.
5. See above, p. 34.
6. Harvey, *Works*, ed. Grosart, I, 218.

the heroicall historyes of Rabelais :   or the braue Legendes of Errant Knights ; [etc., etc.] [1].

Harvey's forte was " railing, " and he was loud in attacking Nashe for doing the same thing.   The quarrel of these men has been called bitter, but the compliment each paid himself and the other in advertising a style of writing common to both is suspicious.   In Nashe's writing, according to Harvey,

the end is like the beginning ; the midst like both ; and euery part like the whole.   Railing, railing, railing ; bragging, bragging, bragging :   and nothing else but fowle railing vpon railing, and vayne bragging vpon bragging ; as rudely, grosely, odiously, filthily, beastly, as euer shamed Print... I wonder, his owne mouth can abide it without a phah [2].

He might have said the same of himself.   Though a devotee of Rabelais, he seriously professes to despise Nashe for being one too, like

some odd wittes forsooth, [who] will needes bee accompted Bull Beggars, and the only Killcowes of their age .... Agrippa and Rabelays but ciphers to them [3].

Nashe, he says,

interfuseth Finicallitie, sillogistrie, disputative right, hermaphrodite phrases, declamatorie stiles, censoriall moralizers, vnlineall vsurpers of iudgement, infamizers of vice, new infringement to destitute the inditement, deriding dunstically, banging abominationly, vnhandsoming of diuinityship, absurdifying of phrases, ratifying of truthable and Eligible English, a calme dilatement of forward harmefulnesse, and backward irefulnesse, and how many sundry dishes of such dainty fritters ?   rare iunkets and a delicate seruice for him that hath compiled the most delitious Commentaries *De optimitate triparum* [4].

He declares that Nashe in his youth " haunted Aretine and Rabelays, the two monstrous wittes of their languages, " and asks rhe-

---

1. Harvey, *Works*, II, 215.
2. *Pierces Supererogation*, 1593 ; Harvey, *Works*, II, 117-18.
3. *Foure Letters*, 1592, Harvey, *Works*, I, 204-05.
4. *Pierces Supererogation*, 1593, Harvey, *Works*, II, 276.   The " delitious Commentaries " are found in the Library of St. Victor, Rabelais, Bk. II, Ch. vii.

torically, " who so shaken with the furious feauers of the One ; or so attainted with the French Pockes of the other ? [1] "

Once, at least, he varies this conception, and pays Nashe an open compliment in the same coin, saying that he is " the huge Gargantua of prose, " and that he

layeth about him with... [his] quill, as if it were possessed with the sprite of *Orlando Furioso*, or would teach the clubb of Gargantua to speake English... Pore I must needes be plagued ; plagued ? na, brayed & squised to nothing, that am matched with such a Garganta-tuist, as can deuoure me quicke in a sallat... [2].

One more illustration of his galumphing invective may be given. Nashe is still the target.

Let him be the *Falanta downe-didle* of Ryme ; the *Hayhohalliday* of Prose, the *Walladay* of new writers ; the *kutthroate* of his aduersaries ; the *gallowes* of his companions ; the only *broker* of Pamflets ; or what he can for his sweltring hart : my *battring instrument* is resolute, and hath vowed to bray the braying creature to powder. We must haue at least *three Peccauies* of *Pierce Penniles* ; and *three Misereres* of the Con-futing Tospot ; or Lord haue mercy vpon thee, *three thousand times wo-full wight*. I am loth to struggle for the *Moonshine in the pudled water* : but if we must needes buckle for nifles, & grapple for naughtes ; though I cannot tell, whither I can bounse him, like a barne doore, or thumpe him, like a drumme of Flushing ; yet I may chaunce rattle him, like a baby of parchment, or kneade him like a cake of dowe, or chearne him like a dish of butter, or girke him like a hobling gig, or tatter him like a thing forspoken, or someway haue my *Penny-worthes* of his *Penniles witt*. Nay, if the *Princock* must be playing vpon them ; that can play vpon his warped sconce, as vpon a tabor, or a fiddle : let himselfe thanke himselfe, if he be kindly thummed. Sirrha, I will stampe an *vnknowne grape*, that shall put the mighty *Burdeaux grape* to bed : & may peraduenture broach a new *Tun of such nippitaty*, as with the very steame of the *nappy liquour* will lullaby thy fiue wittes, like the sences of the drunkenest sot, when his braynes are sweetliest perfumed. I fit thee with a Similitude for thy capacity : or belch a new Con-futation against the long tongues of the *Stilliarde*, and some twenty *Tauernes in London*. I could be content, a *drunken Prose* and a *mad*

---

1. *A New Letter of Notable Contents*, 1593, Harvey, *Works*, I, 272-73.
2. *Pierces Supererogation*, 1593, Harvey, *Works*, II, 272 and 224 resp. The latter alludes to Rabelais, Bk. I, Ch. xxxviii.

Ryme, were thy deadlyest sinnes.   But they are sweet youthes, that tipple their wittes with *quaffing of knauery* and *carowsing of Atheisme* [1].

Harvey was a tireless carpenter of words, and no doubt drew some knowledge of the technique from Rabelais, though it is impossible to prove that he borrowed from him.   He may have taken over " entelechy, " which he uses half a dozen times, though he could have found it in Aristotle [2], and perhaps adopted " cumane [3], " meaning huge, from Rabelais's " decumane. "   Word mongering was, as everybody knows, a feature of Renaissance culture throughout Europe, and when found in a post-Rabelais author must not be indiscriminately attributed to his influence.   Harvey forged from the Latin such jocularities as " railipotent [4], " " subboscoes [5] " (for " whiskers "), and " postpendence [6] " (for " buttocks "), but, like Rabelais, found Greek roots more to his taste.   One may mention " apistie [7], " " glossomachicall [8], " " heterocliticall [9], " " parasitupocriticall [10], " " Pantophainoudendeconticall [11], " and " parergasticall [12]. "   Some of his creations have a more popular flavor, such as " asseth [13] " (for " maketh out an ass "), " bellybiters [14] " (for " fornicators "), and " thunderblasing [15] " (for " obstreperous ").

He wrote enough of his fustian against Nashe and Martin Marprelate to fill three sizable volumes in quarto.   I have studied them with some care and agree with Mr. McKerrow that he talked

---

1. *A New Letter,* 1593, Harvey, *Works,* I, 282-83.
2. See Harvey, *Works,* I, 247 ; II, 105, 106, 107, 283, 286, 287 ; and *Oxf. Dict.* under *entelechy.*
3. Harvey, *Works,* II, 248.
4. *Ibid.* II, 17.
5. *Ibid.,* I, 116, 131.
6. *Ibid.,* III, 32.
7. *Ibid.,* II, 311.
8. *Ibid.,* III, 13.
9. *Ibid.,* II, 132-33.
10. *Ibid.,* III, 13.
11. *Ibid.,* III, 13.
12. *Ibid.,* III, 15.
13. *Ibid.,* II, 107.
14. *Ibid.,* II, 210.
15. *Ibid.,* II, 252.

more about Rabelais than he read him. It may be allowed that he responded to Rabelais the maker of noise and words, but of Rabelais the realist this archpedant had apparently not the slightest conception, and may be called without hesitation the most obtuse of all the English Pantagruelists. He was a writer of eulogy and invective, chiefly of the latter, and invective is a dull form, calling for none of the creative art of caricature. In Harvey's hands it is a mere hose of dirty water to be turned at will upon things and men. There is no place for drollery in the scope of invective writing (as there is for invective in drollery), so that Harvey's humorous attempts, whatever their quality when taken out of the context, are invariably out of place. There is plenty of both eulogy and invective in Rabelais, but they are used everywhere to hit off character, that of himself, among others, and their face value is generally corrected at once by satirical interruptions. When Bishop Homenaz, for example, has risen to ecstatic heights in praise of the Decretals, Epistemon rises to leave the company, for the " stuff, " he says, has " unbunged the orifice of his mustard barrel [1] ; " and Panurge makes a similar rejoinder to Pantagruel's eloquent denunciation of debtors and borrowers [2].

So indiscriminate a Rabelaisian was Harvey that it seems he confused the *Croniques admirables de Gargantua* with Rabelais's authentic works. This is to be inferred from three of his several allusions to *Gargantua*, two of which are demonstrably to the folk hero, and one to Rabelais, though he makes no distinction [3]. Others in very recent times have, to be sure, made the same mistake, but there is no excuse for it in anyone who has read for himself.

The question remains, was Nashe acquainted with Rabelais's work, as Harvey and Bishop Hall thought, and was his writing influenced thereby ? There is scant evidence for the affirmative either way.

---

1. Rabelais, Bk. IV, Ch. LI.
2. Rabelais, Bk. III, Ch. V.
3. See Girault, *Gargantua and King Arthur*, ed. Brown, Intro., XXVI-XXVII.

Harvey blames him equally for following Rabelais and Aretino [1], but Nashe has something to say of his own style. In his preface to Sidney's *Astrophel and Stella*, 1591, he calls it, with feigned modesty, " heauie gated, " in contrast to the " oh my loue's " and " ah my loue's" of contemporary pastoral verse, and to the pedantry of those who " retaile the cinders of Troy [2]. " The " heauie gated " manner of that very preface, however, is traceable, like that of the bulk of his prose, to more than negative scruples. Critics have called Nashe a disciple of Rabelais on the grounds of his vocabulary and his blustering, but, had he been one, he was the man to say so himself. Actually he takes a different view. After arguing at length that *any* writer of " spirit " must use a highly wrought style, he explicitly states that his master was *Aretino*. So much we read in the Epistle to the Reader of the second edition of *Christs Teares over Jerusalem*, 1594, and in the address To The Reader before *Lenten Stuffe*, 1599 [3]. " Of all stiles, " he says, " I most affect & strive to imitate *Aretines*. " Now Aretino was held in quite as bad repute by the English in the eighties and nineties as Machiavelli, which is equivalent to saying that he was altogether an influence to shun, certainly not one to acknowledge ; and had Nashe seen fit to acknowledge Rabelais, who was gaining a similar reputation among the uncritical, he could scarcely have offered stronger grounds of reproach to his enemies.

Not once in the whole course of his writings does he mention Rabelais's name, nor that of any character in the great romance except Gargantua [4]. An apparent reminiscence of Rabelais's story

---

1. See above, p. 48. Other passages comparing Nashe to Aretino are found in Harvey, *Works*, I, 201, 289, and II, 272.

2. Nashe, *Works*, III, 332.

3. *Ibid.*, II, 183-84, and III, 152, resp.

4. We have noticed the mention of Rabelais's name in *An Almond for a Parrat*, 1589 (above, p. 36), and his influence in *A Wonderfull Prognostication*, 1591. Both works have frequently been attributed to Nashe, but on quite insufficient grounds. Both were published anonymously, and the only test of their authorship is that of style. That test does not appear to be conclusive. *An Almond* is an anti-Marprelate tract, such as might have been written by Nashe, yet the author speaks of himself implicitly as an Oxford man, whose knowledge of affairs at Cambridge is that of a stranger. Nashe received his education at Cambridge and is never known to have been connected with Oxford.

of Barbarossa and the Milanese is to be found in *Have with You to Saffron Walden*[1], yet the anecdote occurs first, according to Duchat, in the *Saxonia* of Albert Kranz, lib. vi, cap. 6 (1520), and was borrowed by Rabelais from Guillaume Paradin's *De antiquo Burgundiae statu*, pp. 49-50, published by Dolet in 1542 [2]. It was undoubtedly the common property of Europe in the fifteen nineties, and is even said by Douce to have been the origin the of the current expressions *to fig*, and *to give the fig*, meaning to thrust the thumb between two closed fingers or into the mouth [3]. Nashe writes of sleeping to dream true " vnder a lawrell tree [4], " which suggests the proposal of Panurge to put laurel branches under his pillow for the same purpose [5], but Nashe's slight variation of the method, and no less than five authorities for its efficacy cited by Rabelais, are a sufficient indication that it was a common superstition. Nashe speaks of " Frenchmen who fight valiantly at the first, but quaile in the midst [6], " and so recalls

---

This argument, with others of the same import, is set forth by McKerrow in his edition of the works of Nashe, V, 59-63. The *Prognostication* of 1591 was first attributed to Nashe in the 19th century, apparently on the assumption that it was a parody of the *Astrological Discourse* of Gabriel Harvey's brother Richard, published eight years before. McKerrow points out, however, that there is " nothing remarkable in the idea of a comic prognostication...; and surely a parody of an ephemeral production which had appeared eight years earlier would be but a pointless jest ; " and furthermore that, since the pamphlet is one of a group of three, " any argument in favour of Nashe's authorship must take into account the whole group. " — Nashe, *Works*, V, 138-39. Both works are therefore to be excluded from the Nashe canon pending proof that they belong there. If Rabelais exerted the influence upon Nashe that he is supposed to have done, it should be demonstrable from the bulk of his authentic works, against which these pamphlets are but trifles in length.

1. " He... will, like a true Millanoys, sucke figges out of an asses fundament, or doo anie thing. " — Nashe, *Works*, III, 42.

2. See *Rabelais*, Transl. Smith, II, 189, n. 4.

3. See Douce's note in J. O. Halliwell's Shakespeare on *Hen. IV*, Pt. II, Act V, Sc. iii, ll. 124-25, and Pistol's lines,

> When Pistol lies, do this ; and fig me, like
> The bragging Spaniard.

4. *Have with You*, Nashe, *Works*, III, 61.

5. Rabelais, Bk. III, Ch. xiii. The resemblance is noticed by McKillop, *M. L. N.*, XXXVI, 473.

6. *Christs Teares*, Nashe, *Works*, II, 128.

Gymnaste in Rabelais [1] ; but the same criticism of the same race was heard at the beginning of the last war, and appears to be a common and vulgar error potentially ancient. Nashe spells the name of the father of Orion " Hireus [2]. " McKerrow points out that " Hyrieus " is correct [3], while Rabelais's spelling is that of Nashe [4]. In view of the freedom of Elizabethan spelling among all classes who wrote, the point is insignificant.

There is one detail in Nashe which looks like a borrowing. Nashe speaks of the Turks " that hang all men by the throates on Iron hookes, euen as our Toers hang all there Herrings by the throates on wodden spits [5]. " Panurge in Rabelais, having leapt from the fire with which the Turks were about to consume him, runs one them through with a spit, and placing it upon two iron hooks, roasts him " comme on faict les harans soretz à la cheminée [6]. " Yet the comparison may well have been proverbial.

A certain number of comparatively unfamiliar words in Nashe's vocabulary are found also in Rabelais, and might appear to have been taken from him [7]. They are : *aconitum* [Rabelais : *aconite*], *amphibology, anatomie, anatomize, antipodes, aurum potabile, bepisse* [Rabelais : *compisser*], *Brachmanicall* [Rabelais : *Brachmanes*], *Cantharides* [Rabelais : *cantharidisé*], *carcanets* [Rabelais : *carcan*], *cockatrice* [Rabelais : *coquatris*], *cormorant, coruscant. Diogenicall* [Rabelais : *diogenique*], *Electrum* [Rabelais : *electre*], *Ephemerides* [Rabelais : *ephemere*], *Ergonist* [Rabelais : *ergoté*, adj.], *hurly-burly* [Rabelais : *Saint Hurluburlu*], *phlebotomize* [Rabelais : *phlebotomie*], *Sorbonists.* Every one of these words, however, is recorded in English by the Oxford Dictionary before Nashe, except three, *Brachmanicall, Ergonist,* and *phlebotomize,*

---

1. Rabelais, Bk. I, Ch. xlviii. The resemblance is noticed by McKillop, *M. L. N.*, XXXVI, 473.
2. *Summers Last Will*, Nashe, *Works*, III, 253.
3. Nashe, *Works*, IV, 428.
4. Rabelais, Bk. III, Ch. xvii.
5. *The Prayse of The Red Herring* in *Lenten Stuffe*, Nashe, *Works*, III, 192-93.
6. Rabelais, Bk. II, ch. xiv. The resemblance noticed by McKerrow, — Nashe, *Works*, V, 381.
7. This list is taken from McKerrow's glossary, Nashe, *Works*, V, 209 ff., where full references to the text are supplied.

but in these cases there are English precedents quite as close as the Rabelaisian. Thus *bragman* is found in Caxton ; *ergo* had been current as adverb since 1400, and was used as noun and verb in 1589 ; and *phlebotomy* occurs from 1400 [1].

Here is a sample of Nashe's style, quite Rabelaisian in its breathlessness, and it is representative of a large proportion of his work. His touch is lighter than Harvey's, of whom he says,

he was cald nothing but *Gabriell Ergo* vp and downe the Colledge. But a scoffe which longer dwelt with him than the rest, though it argued his extreame pregnancie of capacitie and argute transpersing dexteritie of Paradoxisme, was that he would needs defend a Rat to be *Animal rationale,* that is, to haue as reasonable a soule as anie Academick, because she eate and gnawd his bookes, and, except she carried a braine with her, she could neuer digest or be so capable of learning. And the more to confirme it, because euerie one laught at him for a common Mounte-banke Rat-catcher about it, the next rat he seazd on hee made an Anatomie of, and read a lecture of 3. dayes long vpon euerie artire or musckle in her, and after hangd her ouer his head in his studie, in stead of an Apothecaries Crocodile, or dride *Alligatur.* I haue not yet mentiond his Poetrie, wherein he surmounteth and dismounteth the most heroycallest *Countes Mountes* of that Craft ; hauing writ verses in all kindes, as in forme of a paire of gloues, a dozen of points, a paire of spectacles, a two-hand sword, a poynado, a Colossus, a Pyramide, a Painters eazill, a market-crosse, a trumpet, an anchor, a paire of pot-hookes... [etc., etc.] [2].

Nashe, then, for all that can be proven to the contrary, may once have " haunted " Rabelais as well as Aretino, and no doubt the latter remained a favorite with him. His preference is easy to understand. He threw himself into the give and take of contemporary life with a ferocious zeal. His views were coloured by his personal contacts, and he fought his causes in writing for the purpose of defeating enemies rather than as a pretext for literary expression. One can see in Aretino, even in a casual perusal of his works those qualities to which Nashe seems to have responded : the grimness of his satire, the fearlessness of his personal attacks, his eruptive style, and his bold word coinages.

---

1. *Oxf. Dict.*
2. *Have with You*, Nashe, *Works*, III, 67.

If Nashe required a hint to give rein to his essentially similar genius, it could have come from " the scourge of princes. "

He may have read Rabelais, but I do not believe that he did. As in the case of Shakespeare we are dependent upon a single detail to prove the connection (that of the Turks and herrings), and it is even less striking than the one cited under that author[1]. Mr. A. D. McKillop wisely points out that since the parallels fail to accumulate, the presumption follows that they are coincidences and not borrowings at all [2]. Gabriel Harvey, with the name of Rabelais forever on his tongue, understood him but superficially, if he may be said to have understood him at all, and it is doubtful whether Nashe, who never mentions his name even once, was any better qualified to do so. It is likely that Nashe would have borrowed largely if he had known him at all. McKerrow has observed that in the realm of ideas we are forced to recognize that he was a preacher, a denouncer, and a reactionary, " not once... doubting that what was generally accepted in the circles in which he moved, was, and must be, the eternal truth : not once, in however trifling a matter, does he seem to have thought for himself [3] ." His invectives are mostly as downright as Harvey's, showing no sympathetic understanding of the nature of what he attacks. The thought of Rabelais, sympathetic, critical, and constructive, is on a different plane, more incisive and at the same time more humane, more learned and at the same time more simple. His wisdom is apparent even when he is warmest on the scent of the quarry — be it pedant, woman, monk, or astrologer — he is " the slayer and the slain. " Nashe attacks pedants and women with so little subtlely that he outdoes both in the qualities which he supposes distinguish them, and inveighs against gluttony and drunkenness like his worst enemies the Puritans. How should he comprehend *Pantagruel*, Greek for " all athirst, " the gracious ladies of Thelême, or the genial and babbling old Sorbonnist, Janotus ?

It has been ventured that his protests against the mis-

---

1. Above, p. 36.
2. *M. L. N.*, XXXVI, 473.
3. Nashe, *Works*, V, 130.

constructions placed upon his previous writings in *Lenten Stuffe* are imitated from the Epistle Dedicatory to *Pantagruel*, Book III ; that the account of Harvey's birth and education in *Have with You* are modelled upon those of Gargantua ; and that *The Praise of the Red Herring*, and the sainting of the herring by the Pope " would have been dear to Rabelais's heart [1]. " The resemblances, though interesting, are not close. There can be no question of influence without more tangible evidence.

Therefore let the ghost of this " English Rabelais " be laid. If it be a real ghost it has not assumed an altogether pleasing shape, and it does not appear to be real.

e) Sir John Harington.

Sir John Harington, epigrammatist and author of the Rabelaisian *Metamorphosis of Aiax*, is to be distinguished from several near contemporaries of the same name [2]. His father was a civil servant under Henry VIII, and his mother a natural daughter of the king himself. Queen Elizabeth stood godmother at his christening in 1561. " Boy Jack " she called him, for she loved him well [3], and a boy the remained all his life, though he grew into a public servant and an author, and became intimate with some of the most important men of the day.

Educated at Eton and Christ's College, Cambridge, he studied at Lincoln's Inn, and when still a young man became High Sheriff of Somerset. In this capacity he entertained the Queen at Kelston in 1592. He accompanied Essex into Ireland, and Essex knighted him there without her authority. When the expedition failed, therefore, and the Knight was sent to appease her anger, he was given short shrift. " What ! " she said, " did the fool bring you too ? Go back to your business ! [4] " and she told Lord

---

1. By A. H. Upham, in *The French Infl. in Eng. Lit.*, 236.
2. The most accurate life of Harington is that by N. E. McLure, prefixed to his edition of *The Epigrams* (Philadelphia, 1926). See also Mr. Jack Lindsay's enthusiastic introduction to his edition of *The Metamorphosis* (London, 1927).
3. Chamberlin, *The Sayings of Queen Elizabeth*, 38.
4. *Ibid*, 298.

Buckhurst to " Go tell that witty fellow, my godson, to get home. It is no season to fool it here ! [1] "

His relations with Essex smack of opportunism, though they were perhaps not downright disloyal. One suspects that the turn of affairs at the last might have seriously embarrassed or ruined a stronger or less nimble individual. He appears to have been unscrupulous in his conduct toward his brother-in-law, whom he attempted, for no good reason, to disinherit ; and he showed the most bland impertinence to James I when he petitioned that king to make him Lord Chancellor and Archbishop of Ireland. He died in 1612.

He was in truth an opportunist, like many an illustrious contemporary. But ambition was less strong in his make-up than gaiety and good sense. His well known Rabelaisian work, *The Metamorphosis of Aiax*, was published in 1596. License was refused, owing to a suspected reference to the deceased Leicester, and on its appearance the Queen banished the author to his estate at Kelston. Let not the simple-minded infer that the royal stomach was turned by this treatise on privies, for such it is, nor that she would punish any man for the venial offense of a steaming jest. It was her pride which was upset, and she acted true to one of her guiding policies, in defense of a favorite.

Harington took the rebuke in good part, and was irrepressible. So much we read in letters exchanged at this time with his cousin, Thomas Markham, and Lady Dowager Russel, and in an epigram begging the Queen's forgiveness. A second epigram acknowledges that " The Poet of the Prince obtain'd his sute [2]. "

The Metamorphosis of Aiax means, freely translated, the improvement of the " jakes " or latrine [3]. It is a prose treatise of some hundred and twenty pages in octavo, and was immediately followed by the much shorter *Anatomy* of that mighty hero whose strength, " being an inseparable accident to him, doth now only remain in his breath. "

---

1. Chamberlin, 52.
2. These documents are reprinted by Lindsay, *Metam. of Aiax*, XIX-XXII.
3. I am much indebted for the analysis which follows to G. Rehfeld's *Sir John Harington, ein Nachahmer Rabelais'* (Halle, 1914). My references to the text of Harington are to the edition by Lindsay.

The author justifies his subject in a letter signed Μ:σχχμος,
arguing, in the way of Renaissance humorists, that others have
done worse, and ending a list of these with

a seuenth (whome I would gesse by his writing to bee groome of the
stoole to some Prince of the bloud of Fraunce) [who] writes a beastly
treatise onely to examine what is the fittest thing to wipe withall, alled-
ging that white paper is too smooth, browne paper too rough, wollen
cloth too stiffe, linnen cloth too hollow, satten too slipperie, taffeta too
thin, veluet too thicke, or perhaps too costly : but hee concludes that
a goose neck to bee drawne between the legs against the fethers, is the
most delicate and cleanly thinge that may bee [1].

The Prologue describes " Great Captaine Aiax, " his quarrel
with Ulysses, his slaughter of the cattle and sheep, and his sui-
cide. It tells how his blood was turned into a hyacinth, " which
is a very notable kind of grasse or flower. " According to grazers,
" and some of them may be trusted for 100000 pounds, " the grass
retains " such pride of this noble bloud " that cattle will burst
who eat it too greedily, and sheep will rot. At this point the author
conceives a *liber fictitius* of Rabelais, and proceeds as follows :

Further I reade that nowe of late yeeres a French Gentleman sonne
to one *Monsieur Gargasier*, & a young Gentleman of an excellent spirit & towardnes, as the reuerent Rabbles (*quem honoris causa nomino*,
that is, whom I should not name without saue-reuerence) writes in his
first booke 13. Chap. but the story you shall finde more at large in
the xiiii booke of his tenth Decad. This yong Gentleman hauing taken
some three or foure score pillst o purge melancholie, euerie one as big as
a Pome Cyttern, commanded his man to mowe an halfe acre of grasse,
to vse at the priuy, & notwithstanding that the owners (to saue their hay
perhaps) sware to him it was of that ancient house of AIAX, and therefore reserued of purpose onely for horses of the race of Bucephalus,
or Rabycano, yet he would not be perswaded : but in further contempt
of his name, vsed a phrase that he had lerned at his being in the lowe
Countries, and bad *Skite vpon* AIAX. But suddenly (whether it were
the curse of the people, or the nature of the gras I knowe not) he was

---

1. *Metam. of Aiax*, 8. Harington's own marginal note reads : " This matter
is discoursed by Rabbles in his 13. Chapter of his first [misprinted " fift "]
booke. Vn moyen de me torcher le cul le plus Seigneurial, le plus excellent,
ₗe plus expedient que iamais fut veu. "

stricken in his Posteriorums with S. Anthonies fier; & dispairing of other
help, he went on pilgrimage in hope of remedie hereof to Iapana, neare
Chyna : wher he met a french Surgeon, in the vniuersitie of Miaco y^t
cured him both of that and the Verol, y^t he had before in his priorums,
with the Momio, of a Grecian wench, that Vlysses buried in his trauell
vpon the coast of the further Ethiopia : and so hee came back again
by *Restinga des ladrones*, through *S. Lazaro*, and crossing both the Tro-
picks, *Cancer* and *Capricorne*, he came by *Magellanes*, swearing he
found no straights there, but came from thence straight home. And
so in 24. houres saile, and twoo or three od yeares beside, he accomplished
his voyage, not forgetting to take freshe wine and water at *Capon de
bona speranza*. Yet ere hee could recouer his health fully, he was faine
to make diuerse vowes (for nowe hee was growen very religious with
his long trauel). Amonge which one was, that in remembrance of
China, of all meates, he woulde honour the Chine a beef moste ; an
other was, that of al offices of the house, he should doe honour to that
house of office, where he had committed that scorne to AIAX : and
that there, hee shoulde neuer vse any more such fine grasse, but rather,
teare a leaf out of Holinsheds Cronicles, or some of the bookes that lye
in the hall, then to commit such a sinne against AIAX. Wherefore
immediatly on his comming home, he built a sumptuous priuy, and
in the most conspicuous place thereof, namely iust ouer the doore, hee
erected a statue of AIAX, with so grim a countenance, that the aspect
of it being full of terrour, was halfe as good as a suppositor : & further, to honor him he chaunged the name of the house, & called it
after the name of this noble Captaine of the greasie ones (the Grecians
I should say) AIAX : though since by ill pronunciation, & by a figure
called *Cacophonia*, the accent is changed & it is called a Iakes [1].

Ajax is the great-grandson of Jupiter, and Jupiter is the son of
Saturn, alias Stercutius, the god of dung. His genealogy was
discovered " in an old Church booke in the Austen Friers at
Genoua [2], "

Which when it was made knowen vnto the whole fraternitie of the
brethren, ther was nothing but reioicing and singing, vnto their god
Sarco:heos [3], a deuout *Shaame* in honour of this *Stercutius*... Which
sonet hath a maruellous grace in their countrie, by means they do
greatly affect... *similiter desinentia*, euery Frier singing a verse & a

---

1. *Metam. of Aiax*, 12-14.
2. Compare the description of the document containing the genealogy of
Gargantua (Rabelais, Bk. I, Ch. ı) and the genealogy itself (Bk. II, Ch. ı).
3. " *Flesh-god* (Greek), " Lindsay's note, *Metam. of Aiax*, 128.

brother answering him in the tune following amounting iust to foure and twentie, which is the misticall number of their order [1].

This is the song.

1. O tu qui dans oracula
2. Scindis cotem nouacula
3. Da nostra vt tabernacula

O thou who utt'ring mystic notes,
The whetstone cut'st with razor,
In mother-tongue permit our
[throats,

4. Lingua canant vernacula
5. Opima post gentacula
6. Huiusmodi miracula
7. Fit semper plœnum poculum
8. Habentes plœnum loculum
9. Tu serva nos ut specula
10. Per longa & læta sœcula
11. Vt clerus & plebecula

Henceforth to sing and say, Sir !
To rich, material breakfasts, join
These miracles more funny —
Fill all our cups with lasting wine,
Our bags with lasting money !
To us a guardian tow'r remain,
Through ages long and jolly ;
Nor give our house a moment's
[pain

12. Nec nocte nec diecula
13. Curent de vlla recula
14. Sed intuentes specula
15. Dura vitemus spicula

From thought's intrusive folly !
Ne'er let our eyes for losses mourn,
Nor pore in aught but glasses ;
And soothe the cares that still
[return,

16. Iacentes cum amicula
17. Quœ garrit vt cornicula
18. Seu tristis ceu ridicula
19. Tum porigamus oscula

By couching with our lasses ;
Who loud as tatling magpies prate,
Alternate laugh and lour ;
Then kiss we round each wanton
[mate,

20. Tum coligamus floscula
21. Ornemus ut cœnaculum

And crop each vernal flow'r,
To deck our rooms, and chiefly
[that

22. Et totum habitaculum
23. Tum culy post spiraculum

Where supper's charms invite ;
Then close in chimney-corner
[squat,

24. Spectemus hoc spectaculum. [2].

To see so blest a sight [3] !

Then comes another etymology, " age breedes aches, " which abbreviated and corrupted by " ill orthographers " becomes " age akes " or " Aiax. "

---

1. *Metam. of Aiax*, 14-15.
2. *Metam. of Aiax*, 17.
3. Translation by Sir John Hawkins, *History of Music*, 1776, V, 438, cit. Lindsay, *Metam. of Aiax*, 128.

The purpose of the book is to provide an infallible means of combating the hero, and so ends the Prologue.

In form the Metamorphosis is a lecture, made up of a series of citations from ancient and modern literature, even from the Bible, anecdotes and sayings, puns and jokes.

There are satirical thrusts on all possible occasions at contemporary persons and events, many of which are obscure at the present day, but the satire is basically general, and so of abiding interest.

Part I is a defense of the work, and in particular of plain speaking. Here is a specimen of the argument, embodying a truth of which, if the world were cognizant, censorship might stop confusing the cloacinian with the erotic :

The chiefest of al our sensuall pleasures, I meane that which some call the sweet sin of letchery, though God knows, it hath much sowre sawce to it, for which notwithstanding, many hazard both their fame, their fortune, theyr friends ; yea their soules, which makes them so oft breake the sixt commaundement, that when they heare it read at Churche, they leaue the wordes of the Communion booke, and say, *Lord haue mercy upon vs, it grieues our hearts to keepe this law.* And when the commination is read on Ashwednesday, wherein is read, *Cursed be he that lieth wyth his Neighhors wife*, and let all the people say *Amen* : these people either say nothing, or as a neighbour of mine said, *he hem* : this surpassing pleasure, that is so much in request, and counted such a principal sollace, I have heard confessed before a most honorable person, by a man of middle age, stronge constitution, and well practised in this occupation, to haue bred no more delectation to him (after the first heate of his youth was past) then to goe to a good easie close stoole, when he hath had a lust thereto (for that was his verie phrase.) Which being confessed by him, and confirmed by many, makes me take this aduantage thereof in the beginning of this discourse, to prefer this house I mind to speake of, before those which they so much frequent : neither let any disdaine the comparison. For I remember, how not long since, a graue and godlie Lady, and Gran-mother to all my wiues children, did in their hearings, & for their better instruction, tell them a storie, which though I will not sweare it was true, yet I did wishe the auditorie would beleeue it, namely, how an Hermit being carried in an euening, by the conduct of an angel, through a great citie, to contemplate the greate wickednes daily and hourely wrought therein, met in the street a dongfarmer with his cart full laden, no man enuying his full measure. The poore Hermit, as other men did, stopt his nostrils, and betooke him to the other side of the streete, hastening from the sower cariage all he could, but the Angell kept on his way, seeming no whit offended with the sauour. At which while the Hermit maruelled, there came not long after by them, a woman gorgeously attired, well perfumed, wel attended, with coaches & torches, to conuey her perhaps to some noble mans chamber. The good Hermit somewhat reuiued with the faire sight, and sweet savour, began to stand at the gaze. On the other side, the good Angell nowe stopped his nose, and both hastened himselfe away, and beckened his companion from the place. At which the Hermit more maruelling then before, he was told by the Angell, that this fine courtesan laden with sinne, was a more stinking sauour afore God and his holy Angels, then that beastly cart, laden with excrements [1].

The Anglo-Saxon is unmistakable in this passage. For all his gaiety, he seriously arbitrates the morality of two things which Rabelais would never dream of putting in such a light. Even had Rabelais done so, the Protestant archdeacons of the world would no doubt still have to do their reading of him *sub rosa*, like Dr. Grantly in Trollope [2].

Part II is a history of the latrine and the sewer from ancient times. The first man to attend to these matters was Titus Tatius, a contemporary of the founder of Rome, who erected a statue to the goddess Cloacina " in a great priuy. " The writer considers the refinements effected by the Emperors, giving interesting testimonials of their characters and deeds. He shows that the Bible was concerned with sanitation, citing 23d Deuteronomy, 12-14. He continually digresses, discussing chimneys that smoke, eaves that drip, and the taming of a shrew, and yet continually returns. He ends the history with " certaine autenticall rules, out of a general Councell of Phisitions... sent by common consent to a great King of England, " which recommend " Doctor Diet, Doctor Quiet, & Doctor Meryman. " One wonders if by the last they meant Doctor Rabelais. The golden rule is this,

Nec mictum retine, nec comprime fortiter anum,

for

Quatuor ex vento veniunt in ventre retento,
Spasmus, hydrops, colica, vertigo, quatuor ista.

---

1. *Metam. of Aiax*, 25-26.
2. *The Warden*, Ch. VIII.

As regards the jakes,

> Aer sit mundus, habitabilis ac luminosus,
> Infectus neque sit, nec olens, fœtere cloacæ [1].

Part III sets forth the advantages of the author's privy, and praises his associates who have lent coöperation and encouragement toward its perfection. " Neither was the place inferior to the persons, beeing a castle, that I call, the wonder of the West, so seated without, as England in few places affoords more pleasures : so furnished within as China nor the West Indies scant allowes more plentie [2]. " He has made " *Stercutius* a nowne adiectiue, " for a " nown substantiue [is] that that may bee seene, felt, heard, or understood, " and Stercutius has now lost these characteristics [3]. He concludes with a disclaimer of scurrility, saying that the work has salt but not bitterness, therefore beshrew any who take it in anger.

The Metamorphosis was followed by *An Anatomie of The Metamorphosed Aiax*, published later in the same year (1596). Here the new device is technically described, ostensibly by the inventor's servant, Thomas [4]. Thomas compares himself to his master as inventor and wit in an " Apology, 1. or rather a Retractation ; 2. or rather a Recantation... [etc]. " There appears to him in a dream " a nimble dapper fellow..., one that hath [a] pretty pettifogging skill in the law, and hath been an under sheriff (but not thrice), " and is now a kind of attorney. This person tells of a company with whom he discussed several recent books : Lipsius the great politician's *de Cruce*, M. Raynold's work against Bellarmine, the new and old *Faerie Queene*, their opinion being that " some wanted rhyme, some wanted reason, and some both. " But *The Metamorphosis of Aiax* was praised, and " when they found Rabbles named, then they were at home ; they looked for

---

1. *Metam. of Aiax*, 80-81.
2. *Ibid.*, 97.
3. *Ibid.*, 101.
4. I have not seen the edition used by Rehfeld (it contains much omitted from the one reprinted by Lindsay) and have taken the following remarks entirely from his account of it. See : *Sir John Harington, ein Nachahmer Rabelais*, 79-84.

pure stuff where he was cited for an author. " When it is explained
to them that Misacmos (Harington's pseudonym) means " a hater
of filth " they are incensed, for they profess that they are " filthy
fellows among the grave grey-beards. " Misacmos is therefore
to be denounced " at a privy sessions. "

Accordingly an indictment is lodged for eleven offenses. The
jurors chosen, each gives some information about himself of very
local interest. The prosecution accuses him not only of the
offensiveness of *The Metamorphosis*, but of aiming disrespectful
comments at the whole female sex in his *Ariosto* [1], and of daring
" to compare, or rather to counfound, bawdy houses and Jakes
houses, courtezans and carters, with angels and hermits. " Misacmos is ready to retract. He is accused of vilifying the name of
a great soldier, of naming, that is, a heroic Greek in the " Latrina
lingua, " and saying that " his picture was set in so homely a
place that it might...seem to have been called after his name in
English. " In defense Misacmos cites " old Scoggin's jests, "
which all his hearers must have read, where " our kings picture "
is similarly degraded ; but the court is not satisfied until he resolves
to call the hero not Captain, nor Monsieur, but " Don Aiax. "
Lastly he is charged with Roman Catholicism, but declares that
he is not Catholic nor Protestant nor Puritan, but a " Protesting
Catholic Puritan, " and aims " to have good faith, good works,
and good words. " His writings " must be as they be taken. "
He is discharged, but his confidence is shaken, and he will never
more write such " idle toys. "

Harington stands beside John Eliot as one of the first two
Englishmen who knew how to value and to imitate Rabelais.
Both men, to the honour of their age, perceived and rendered
something of his essential spirit. Eliot caught especially the
realism of his character portrayal and dialogue, Harington the
charm of his miscellaneous learning, his mock-gravity, and his
healthy coarseness. Neither was attempting an all around imitation, yet that which each gave us is so successful that one could
wish they had written more.

---

1. Harington's translation of *Orlando Furioso* was published in 1591.

The earliest whole hearted acceptance of Rabelais's art in
English criticism has been quoted : it is " pure stuff. " No
higher praise could be bestowed, and Harington was qualified to
know the full meaning of his words.

Like Rabelais he thinks for himself in religion, though he is
no extremist. He is a " Protesting Catholic Puritan. " Disclai-
ming that his satire has any evil intent, he commits himself to
the acumen of the reader : his words " must be as they be
taken. " Rabelais says as much of *Gargantua* [1]. The mock trial
is occasioned by his pseudonym, and he is evidently proud, in
spite of its etymology, to be numbered among the " filthy fellows [2]. "
He was perfectly versed in the philosophy of the Rabelaisian
dunghill, and that he should take pains to explain his attitude
toward it (Rabelais is more subtle) is but natural in an imitator
and an Englishman.

Like Rabelais, he affects to delight in the bodily pleasures of
eating, drinking, and fornication. Like him, too, he connects
them with monks, in the " sonnet " of the Austin Friars, and
elsewhere [3]. His satire of the church includes also humorous
interpolations on circumcision and on the doctrine *ex inferno
nulla redemptio* [4]. He introduces the familiar story of the humble
suitor to the Pope, who, seeing his master kiss the pontifical toe,
fled lest " they would haue made...[him]...haue kist him in
some homelyer place [5]. " Like Rabelais, he makes merry over
casuistic lawyers, and prescribes gaiety as medecine. He praises
the Emperor Claudius for permitting inferiors to break wind in
the presence [6].

He knew the popular literature of his country well, and uses

---

1. Prologue, Bk. I.

2. It is a foolish error of Harrington's that those who indict Misacmos should
praise *The Metamorphosis*, and the prosecution condemn it.

3. " For the same sweet sinne of lechery, I would say as the Frier said, a yong
man & a young woman in a greene arber in a may morning ; if God doe not
forgiue it, I woulde. " — *Metam. of Aiax*, 65.

4. *Ibid.*, 28, 66.

5. *Ibid.*, 111. Compare Rabelais, Bk. IV, Ch. xlviii. The Papimanes
express their willingness to kiss the Pope in any part of his anatomy.

6. *Metam. of Aiax*, 55.

the classics as Rabelais had done, for their popular interest. His attitude is ever that of the raconteur : his work is one long address to the reader. He adopts the language of speech, and dilutes his erudition for general consumption. Here is a passage exactly in the manner of Rabelais's prologues :

Ho sirra bring hither the Dictionarie. Which of them, Cooper ? No no, *Thomas Coperus omisit plurima verba*. Which then, that with the French afore the latine, or *Thomas Thomas* ? Yea, bring mee them two. What hast thou brought the two dictionaries ? I meant but the two *Thomases*. Come old friend *Tom, Tom, Qui fueras quondam claræ præpositor aulæ* [1], you haue made rods to ierke mee withall ere now, I thinke I shall give you a ierke, if you do not helpe mee to some English for this worde. Looke it sirra there in the Dictionarie. *Con, con*. Tush what doost thou looke in the French ? thou wilt make a sweet peece of looking, to looke for *con fornicar* in the French : looke in the Latine for *fornicor*. *F, fa, fe, fi, fo, for, foramen, forfex, forica, forma, fornicator*, (now I thinke I am neer it), *fornix, fornicor, aris, are*. Ther, what is y [t] ? A vault, to vault or arch any thing with a compasse. Well said, carry away the books againe, now I haue it : then thus it is, he alloweth the vaulting or arching ouer the iakes [2].

The work shows a thorough acquaintance with Martial, as might be expected in an epigrammatist ; and the cue for the whole was, of course, taken from Ovid ; neither of which writers was much prized by Rabelais. But by far the greater part of the humanistic material is found in the historians, especially Livy and Suetonius. In this Harington is Rabelais's child. More than Rabelais he draws upon the church fathers, and upon political writers like Polybius and Thucydides. He differs further in passing by Herodotus, Caesar, Strabo, Pausanias, and others, and in his slight interest in the philosophers. He rarely refers to the neo-Latins of the Renaissance. More than Rabelais he inclines to digress into criticisms of history itself.

Owing perhaps to the expository rather than narrative character

---

1. " A great officer among the boies at Eaton, M. of the rods. " — Harington's note, *Metam. of Aiax*, 64.

2. *Ibid.*, 64-65. Opposite " F, fa, fe, etc. " Harington writes : " Eliots dictionarie and Coopers placed these 2. woords too neere together. "

of his work he makes proportionately *more* learned references than Rabelais. He occasionally names chapter and verse in marginal notes, sometimes inaccurately, but does not allow them to run riot as Rabelais does, and is generally content merely to name his author. Rabelais surpasses him in sharpening the contrast between the depth of his learning and the ridiculous uses to which it is put. Rehfeld's analysis of the matter leads him to the conclusion that Rabelais, affecting precision, is less accurate than Harington. He believes that Rabelais quotes from memory, Harington with the document before him.

Rabelais uses citations for two purposes, to corroborate arguments, and as the point of departure for scenes. Harington, properly speaking, has no scenes, and is therefore largely limited to the former practise. The latter is found, however, in one instance, namely in the account of the metamorphosis of Ajax after Ovid, which happens to be an adaptation more fundamental to the whole work than any corresponding one in Rabelais.

Harington is a master of low comedy, in both words and situations. We have seen some of his etymologies, and they illustrate a pervading love of word play. He is ever attentive to the single word, quick to take up its contrasting meanings and possibilities of contortion. We may recall " privy sessions, " " Latrina lingua, " " he hem " for " Amen, " and the like. Like the mediaeval writers and John Lyly himself, he exploits sound similarities ; but like them, too, he is sometimes content with patterns which are too simple. Rabelais frequently sacrifices sense to sound, but the sounds are variously composed, and owing to the " unaccented " quality of the French language, never give that painfully thumping impression which one often suffers in reading *Euphues*. Repetition and alliteration can be as unrelenting as " eeny-meeny-miney-mo " from a chorus of children, and are frequently a jarring element in Elizabethan prose. Thus Harington writes,

But from thence, you shall passe downe a streame that seemes to be no streame, by corne fieldes that seeme no fields, down a streete no streete, in at a gate no gate, ouer a bridge no bridge, into a court no court, where if I be not at home, you shall finde perhaps a foole no foole[1].

The rhetorical aspects of his style are humanistic, never quite grotesque. I believe, for example, that his longest catalogue is that of fifteen activities of the Pagans over which fifteen deities presided [2], a modest effort compared with the lists of Rabelais. He tells his anecdotes mainly for the idea they embody, not, like his model, equally for the idea and for the display of stylistic virtuosity.

The little flurry occasioned by his comparatively innocent satire is amusing when one thinks of the thunders which broke over Rabelais for his truly horrific performances. With a resignation that is suspicious he vowed to eschew such writing for the future, in almost the words used by Rabelais in the Epistle to Odet, prefixed to Book IV [3]. His work became notorious, and gave its author the soubriquet, Sir Ajax : he is so called by Ben Jonson in *The Silent Woman*, and once also in an official document. The pun was taken up by Marston in *The Scourge of Villainye*, by John Taylor repeatedly, and by Shakespeare in the Quarto of *Love's Labour's Lost*[4]. The new privy, the prototype of the modern water-closet, seems to have been duplicated for Elizabeth's ladies in waiting, though the day of its generalization was, happily, remote [5].

Sir John, the ornament of a court, soldier and schemer, inventor and wit, in whose veins flowed royal blood, is almost a puny figure beside the gigantic lawyer's son of La Devinière, and it would be ludicrous to press the comparison. That which makes him worthy of it at all is, as Mr. Jack Lindsay suggests, the dignity of the civilization he embodies. " The book may be trifling, " says Mr. Lindsay, " but it holds an impress of character which is not trifling, " and again, in conclusion, " Harington is no great

---

1. *Metam. of Aiax*, 5-6.
2. *Ibid.*, 30.
3. See above, p. 65.
4. See *Metam. of Aiax*, Intro., xxiv-xxv.
5. *Ibid.*, xxv.

poet ; but I defy any great poet to write a better book on privies [1]. "

f) Robert Dallington.

Three allusions to Rabelais have been found by Monsieur Sainéan in *The view of Fraunce*, 1598, by Robert Dallington, secretary
to the English ambassador at the Court of France. It speaks
much for the enlightenment of the age in literary values that this
writer, who was, in Monsieur Sainéan's words, a " veritable gallo-
phobe, " did not, as one might expect, or fear, attribute those
aspects of French civilization which he disliked to the influence
of the Curé de Meudon. Instead one gathers that he accepted
Rabelais as a standard author. He recalls Rabelais's proverb
that a fool can teach a wise man, and twice quotes Friar John :
first, his criticism of gorgeous palaces with poor kitchens, cold
hearths, and empty cellars, and second, his well known excla-
mation about old drunkards and old physicians [2].

---

1. *Metam. of Aiax*, ix, xv. For a discussion of *Ulysses Upon Ajax*, a spu
rious sequel to *The Metamorphosis* and *The Anatomy*, sometimes attributed to
Harington, see Appendix C below, pp. 221-22.
2. Sainéan, *L'Influence et la Réputation de Rabelais*, 242-43.

CHAPTER III

FROM BISHOP HALL TO URQUHART

The poets : Hall, Guilpin, Witaker, Dones (*i.e.* Donne ?), Coryat, Taylor, Donne, Jonson, Drayton, Hayman. The drama : Jonson, *Lingua, Albumazar,* Barnes, Webster, Shirley, Ford, Mayne. Prose : Lodge, Burton, Bacon, " Democritus Pseudomantis, " certain anonymous prognostications, Hall, Browne, Howell.

a) *The Poets.*

The influence of Rabelais can be traced continuously in English prose from John Eliot, and from 1597 it appears also in the drama and in poetry. It became general before Elizabeth died, and the circles widened against the rising tide of Cavalier formalism. The poets, to be sure, found little in him to imitate, but they could not ignore such a powerful force as he had become in the intellectual world.

Joseph Hall, poet and Bishop, author of the Rabelaisian *Mundus Alter et Idem* [1], alludes three times to Rabelais in his verse Satires, which were published in 1597. In the first satire of Book II he chides Thomas Nashe as follows :

> For shame or better write, or *Labeo* write none.
> But who coniur'd this bawdie *Poggies* ghost,
> From out the stewes of his leude home-bred coast :
> Or wicked *Rablais* dronken reuellings,
> To grace the mis-rule of our Tauernings [2] ?

---

1. See below, pp. 103 ff.
2. *Die Satiren Halls*, ed. Schulze, 35. Schulze shows that Labeo is Nashe (265). That Hall attributes the kind of writing that Nashe was known for,

Drinkers are the subject of Book III, Satire vi, and he writes of them in truly Rabelaisian imagery. Thus,

> When Gullion di'd (who knows not *Gullion* ?)
> And his dry soul ariu'd at *Acheron*,
> He faire besought the Feryman of hell,
> That he might drinke to dead *Pantagruel*.

Charon consents to let him do so, with the result that he drinks the Acheron dry, and the boat sticks fast in the mud, detaining its impatient passengers,

> Till *Gullion* his bladder would vnlode.
> They stand, and wait, and pray for that good houre :
> Which when it came, they sailed to the shore [1].

The affectation by fops of the French, Italian, and Spanish languages is ridiculed in Book VI, Satire i :

> But now can euery Nouice speake with ease,
> The far-fetch'd *language of th'Antipodes* [2],

the name given by Pantagruel to the lingo of Panurge in Rabelais, Book II, Chapter ix.

There is no reason to suppose that Hall really thought Rabelais " wicked, " he is simply invoking a popular notion.

No doubt Edward Guilpin is doing the samet hing when he says of the authors of *Lydian Airs* in *Skialetheia*, 1598 :

> Let Rabelais with his durtie mouth discourse,
> No longer blush, for they'll write ten times worse [3].

Thomas Coryat, the traveller, became the object of a great

---

and with which he was contributing to " the misrule of our tauernings, " to the influence of the proverbially obscene Poggio and Rabelais, is comparable to Harvey's accusations that he was influenced by Rabelais and Aretino. The lines do not mean that " Labeo " is necessarily a *translator*, as W. F. Smith seemed to think (see his translation of Rabelais, I, Intro., xiii-xiv).

1. *Die Satiren Halls*, ed. Schulze, 52-53.

2. *Ibid.*, 106.

3. Cit. from *Rabelais*, Transl. Urquhart and Motteux, ed. Whibley (1900), I, lxxvii-lxxviii.

outburst of ironical eulogy in verse for his *Crudities*, which he published in 1611. He had made a journey through Europe on foot three years before, and embodied his experiences in this lengthy narrative, which he passed around among his friends for their perusal before committing it to the press. Born in the seventies, the son of a Somerset clergyman, he was college bred and became a member of Prince Henry's household [1]. Here he gained a reputation for clownish wit, and his still more clownish rival, John Taylor, tavern-keeper, boatman, and " Water-Poet " to his Majesty, gave him no peace. Both men were adept in self advertisement, and Taylor knew how to make a great asset of his menial rank in society. Ben Jonson, "apparently at the desire of Prince Henry, " gave the tip to the literary world that the hunt was up, and they rallied to his standard [2]. The men he enlisted include some of the best brains of that brilliant epoch, John Donne, Inigo Jones, and Sir John Harington, to mention no more. Each addressed a poem to the delighted Coryat, and he published the lot as a preface to the *Crudities* under the title of *The Odcombian Banquet*. This formidable corpus runs to a hundred octavo pages, and is striking evidence of the felicity of ordinary Elizabethans when they turned their minds to verse, as well as of the democratic spirit of the great ones who joined in the game.

The Rabelaisian aspects of the *Crudities* are obvious and superficial. The book is a valuable and amusing source of information about the externals of the contemporary continental scene, but is quite lacking in that integration which alone can give value to a travelogue. Coryat enjoys hard drinking and practical jokes, occasionally turns a mouth filling period, and is profuse of learned reference, puns, and word coinages. He " excarnificates " his horse with his spurs [3] ; a scholar proficient in Hebrew is an " Hebrician [4], " races are " Ethnickes [5], " cannibals are

---

1. *Dict. Nat. Biog.*
2. See Esther Cloudman Dunn, *Ben Jonson's Art*, 5.
3. Coryat, *Crudities*, Repr. (Glasgow, 1905), I, 185.
4. *Ibid.*, I, 272.
5. *Ibid.*, I, 314.

" Cyclopicall Anthropophagi[1] ; " " Hunnish " becomes " Hunni-call, [2] " and " cuckolded, " " capricornified. [3] " A single illus-tration may be given of his more ambitious attempts in style :

I was imbarked at Dover, about tenne of the clocke in the morning, the fourteenth of may, being Saturday and Withsun-eve, Anno 1608, and arrived in Calais (which Caesar calleth Ictius portus, a maritime towne of that part of Picardy, which is commonly called le pais recon-quis ; that is, the recovered Province, inhabited in former times by the ancient Morini.) about five of the clocke in the afternoone, after I had varnished the exterior parts of the ship with the excrementall ebullitions of my tumultuous stomach, as desiring to satiate the gor-mandizing paunches of the hungry Haddocks (according as I have hieroglyphically expressed it in the front of my booke) with that wherewith I had superfluously stuffed my selfe at land, having made my rumbling belly their capacious aumbrie [4] .

This is the opening sentence of the work, but promises more than is realized by what follows. Such a flight may owe some-thing to Rabelais, with whom Coryat was sufficiently familiar to refer to his remarks on the cod-piece [5], and to recognize the allusions made by his critics [6] ; in any case, the latter, with whom we are chiefly concerned, struck by his vocabulary [7], the hetero-geneousness of his material [8], and his tendency to exag-

1. *Crudities*, II, 309.
2. *Ibid.*, I, 311.
3. *Ibid.*, I, 403.
4. *Ibid.*, I, 152.
5. " Which Codpiece because it is by that merrie French writer Rabelais stiled the first and principal piece of Armour, the Switzers do weare it as a significant Symbole of the assured service they are to doe to the French King in his Warres. " — *Ibid.* I, 191.   See Rabelais, Bk. III, Ch. viii, " Comment la braguette est première pièce de harnois entre gens de guerre. "
6. See below, p. 76, n. 1, 2.
7. Ben Jonson says, " He is a great and bold Carpenter of words, or (to ex-presse him in one like his owne) a Logodaedale, " and again, " It is thought he lives more by letting out of ayre [Coryat in a footnote signifies at 'the fore parts, not the hinder'], then drawing in ; and feared, his belly wil exhibite a Bill in Chauncery against his Mouth for talking away his meales.   He is alwaies the Tongue-Major of the company, and if ever the perpetual motion be to be hoped for, it is from thence. "   — *Crudities*, I, 18.
8. One William Austin writes,

> The famous booke of Mandevill
> Tell[s] not of things so strange and evill,

gerate [1], compared him freely with Pantagruel and with Rabelais.
The contribution of Lawrence Whitaker [2] is dedicated

> To the most peerelesse Poetical Prose-writer, the most Transcendent, Tramontane Traveller, and the most single-soled, single-souled, and single-shirted Observer, the Odcombian Gallo-Belgicus.

It includes the following

> *Sonnet composé en rime à la Marotte, accomode au style de l'Autheur du liure ; faict en louange de cet Heroïque Geant Odcombien, nomme non Pantagruel, mais Pantagrue, c'est à dire, ny Oye, ny Oison, ains tout Grue, accoustré icy en Hochepot, Hachis, ou Cabirotade, pour tenir son rang en la Librairie de l'Abbaye St. Victor à Paris, entre le liure de Marmoretus de baboinis & cingis, & celuy de Tirepetanus de optimitate triparum [3] ; & pour porter le nom de la Cabirotade de Coryat, ou, de l'Apodemistichopezologie de l'Odcombeuili Somerseti* (Soti), en, etc.

> Si de ce pais le pourpris spatieux,
> (D'ou est sorti ce Badin [4] precieux)
> Ou bien la Suisse, ou mesme l'Alemagne
> Pouroit fournir quelque douce compagne
> D'esprit pareil, & de condition
> Semblable à luy, le vieil Deucalion
> Et Pyrrhe en eux seroient resuscitez :
> Car ne nasquit de leurs cailloux iettez,
> Que tas de gens, et un monde nouueau :
> Ainsi des pierres, ou nostre Blaireau [5]

> Of jests, mistakings, and misprisions,
> Of Pagans, Jewes, and circumcisions,
> Of Tombs, Sepulchers, dead mens bones,
> Of Epitaphes, of stockes and stones.

— *Crudities*, I, 85.

1. John Donne writes him a " Macaronicon, " ending :

> ....I leave
> L'honra, de personne nestre creduto, tibi.

— *Crudities*, I, 39.

2. *Ibid.*, I, 41-43.
3. Rabelais, Bk. II, Ch. vii. The Rabelaisian titles envisaged are *Marmotretus, de babouynis et cingis...* ; *Beda, de Optimitate triparum* ; and *Le Tirepet des apothecaires.*
4. " Cest-à-dire, Voyageur, du mot Grec, βαδίζειν. " — Coryat.
5. " Un certain animal, qui a la veue fort percante. " — Coryat.

> A ietté l'œil (fut-ce aux Ponts ou Potences,
> Clochers, Statues, qui tiennent balances)
> Est né soudain un grand hideux volume
> De beau discours, qui s'est rendu l'enclume
> De nos esprits, un monde de fadeze,
> Dont le goutteux se resiouir soit aise.
> Tay toy Rablais, rabbaissé soit l'orgueil
> De tes Endouilles, qui d'un bel accueil
> Receurent ton Geant [1] en la Farouche [2],
> A ce Geant d'Odcombe pierre et souche
> Parla, fournit des comptes, l'entretint
> Le muguetta, voire & son sens maintint
> En ce travail : Mais scais-tu bien pour quoy ?
> Son Chef Cresté luy donna ceste loy,
> > Que des hommes du lieu ne scachant le language,
> > Parmy troncs et cailloux il passeroit sa rage.

A certain John Dones, who may or may not be John Donne, wrote as follows :

> What had he done had he ere hug'd th'Ocean
> With swimming Drake or famous Magelan ?
> And kiss'd that unturn'd cheek of our old mother.
> Since so our Europes world he can discover ?
> It's not that French which made his Gyant see
> Those uncouth Ilands where words frozen bee,
> Till by the thaw next yeare they'r voic't againe [3] ;
> Whose Papagauts [4], Andoûilets [5], and that traine
> Should be such matter for a Pope to curse
> As he would make ; make ! makes ten times worse,
> And yet so pleasing as shall laughter move [6].

The knowledge of Rabelais possessed by Dones and Whitaker could scarcely have been more intimate. Rabelais comes so readily to the pens of those who have studied him that one can hardly overemphasize the doubts already raised as to any real acquaintance with his work on the part of Nashe.

---

1. " Pantagruel. " — Coryat.
2. " Une isle ainsi appellee par Rablais ." — Coryat. See Rabelais, Bk. IV Chs. xxxv-xlii.
3. Rabelais, Bk. IV, Chs. lv-lvi.
4. *Ibid.*, Bk. V, Ch. iii.
5. *Ibid.*, Bk. IV, Chs. xxxv-xlii.
6. *Crudities*, I, 71.

Taylor must have been disappointed in the effect of this avalanche of verse. The tone of the whole *Banquet* is friendly and Coryat was clearly impervious to its ridicule, otherwise he would not have published it. The " Water-Poet " therefore hastened to satirize him on his own account, with *Odcombs Complaint* : *or, Coriats Fvnerall Epicedivm : or Death-Song, Vpon His late-reported drowning. With his Epitaph in the Barmuda, and Vtopian tongues : And translated into English by Iohn Taylor* [1]. In this he calls the traveller " Odcombian, Graecian, Latin, Great Thom Asse [2]. " The epitaph, in Bermudian, " which must be pronounced with the accent of the grunting of a hogge, " begins :

> Hough gruntough wough Thomough
> Coriatough, Odcough robunquogh [3].

The *Complaint* was followed by *Certaine Sonnets, in Praise of M*r *Thomas the Deceased* [4], and that, in turn, by *Laugh, and be Fat: or, A Commentary vpon the Odcombyan Banket* [5]. The last is Taylor's free paraphrase of all the poems of the *Banket* which he could read, those in foreign languages, of which there are a number, being too much for him. His attempt was foolhardy, and the result dismal. One would scarcely expect a man of his parts to be able to improve upon Ben Jonson or John Donne. Nothing daunted he persevered, though he must have long since begun to weary his readers. His parting shot was *Master Thomas Coriats Commendations to his friends in England. From Agra,* [6] which contains *The Copie of an Oration that I* [Coryat] *made in the Persian Tongue, to the Great Mogoll, before diuers of his Nobles.* This is another *galimatias*, intended to ridicule Coryat's pretensions as polyglot, and comes most impertinently from the unilingual Taylor. Coryat, having by now had enough, succeeded in restraining Taylor by an appeal to superior powers [7].

---

1. Taylor, *Works*, ed. Spenser Soc., Folio, 218 ff.
2. *Ibid.*, 219.
3. *Ibid.*, 221.
4. *Ibid.*, 222 ff.
5. *Ibid.*, 229 ff.
6. *Ibid.*, 243 ff.
7. *Dict. Nat. Biog.*, under Coryat.

One critic has argued at length that the influence of Rabelais is traceable in Taylors's works [1], but his evidence is unsatisfactory. Taylor was ignorant of foreign languages [2]. He omitted, moreover, all the allusions to Rabelais from his paraphrase of the *Odcombian Banquet*. There being no grounds for assuming the existence of a translation of *Gargantua and Pantagruel* at this time, it is difficult to see how Taylor might have familiarized himself with its contents. I have not found a single unambiguous allusion in all his bulky writings to anything therein, his only mention of Rabelais referring definitely to Girault's *Cronicques admirables* [3]. He could have made such extensive use of Rabelais's galimatias and popular word formations alone that one can with difficulty believe he would have passed them by.

In *Taylors Motto* is a long list of all the authors who have contributed to his writing, including Du Bartas, Montaigne, Guevara, and numerous other foreign writers, but none whose works had not been translated into English [4]. A similar list of over two hundred lines, devoted exclusively to the literature of fancy, nonsense, and superstition, is found in the *Preamble* to his *Praise of Hemp-Seed* [5]. The name of Rabelais is conspicuously absent from both. Though he frequently mentions Gargantua, not once does he name Pantagruel, nor any other of Rabelais's characters. *Taylor's Goose* [6] is a mock serious poem in praise of the usefulness of geese, extending to seven folio pages of double columns, and yet nowhere does he allude to Rabelais, Book I, Chapter XIII, as any disciple worthy the name must have done in the circumstances. No more does he mention Judge Bridlegoose.

In the face of such evidence one is not justified in appealing to Rabelais to account for the fact that Taylor wrote in praise of hemp and so recalls the herb Pantagruelion ; that some of the titles in one of his lists of popular reading are as meaningless as

---

1. Upham, *The French Infl. in Eng. Lit.*, 256 ff.
2. Girault, *Gargantua and King Arthur*, ed. Brown, Intro., XXIX.
3. *Ibid.*, XXVIII.
4. Taylor, *Works*, Repr. Spenser Soc., Folio, 217.
5. *Ibid.*, 544 ff.
6. *Ibid.*, 114 ff.

some of those in the Library of St. Victor (none is borrowed from it) ; that he wrote gibberish to satirize pedants ; or that he satirizes Lent and personifies Shrove Tueşday in a way which suggests the passages on Quaresmeprenant in *Pantagruel,* Book IV. Still less is one justified in arguing the influence from the similar taste of both men for eating and drinking and from a few similar traits of style [1]. The most conspicuous of these is the burlesque cataloguing, which is indeed monstrous in both authors, yet in both it is formally identical with that used by the mediaeval romancers. The art of gibberish is one of which every child is potentially master, and what Taylor needed to learn about coining words he could have found in Thomas Nashe, whom he is never tired of praising [2]. He professes, sincerely for all that we know, to abhor plagiarism [3] ; but whatever his work may owe to literary antecedents, Rabelais is not to be counted among them.

John Donne's fourth satire, probably written before 1600, is aimed at the vanity of the courtier. The courtier, affecting the gift of tongues, makes the following irreverent comment :

> Nay, your Apostles were
> Good pretty linguists, and so Panurge was ;
> Yet a poore gentleman, all these may passe
> By travaile [4].

The courtier, indeed,

> such wonders told
> That I was faine to say, If you had liv'd, Sir,
> Time enough to have beene Interpreter
> To Babells bricklayers, sure the Tower had stood [5].

---

1. Mr. Upham does all these things.
2. See *Works,* Folio, 168, 282, 546 ; Quarto I, *Differing Worships,* title page, etc., and *Aqua-Musae,* 3.
3. Thus in *Works,* Folio, 217 :

> And many more good Bookes I haue with care
> Lookt on their goods, and neuer stolc their ware.

4. Donne, *Poems,* ed. Grierson, I, 160-61, ll. 58-61.
5. *Ibid.,* ll. 62-65.

The poet is nauseated :

> I belch, spue, spit,
> Looke pale, and sickly, like a Patient ; Yet
> He thrusts on more [1].

The last passage is reminiscent of the " unbunging " of Epistemon's " mustard barrel " in Rabelais, Book IV, chapter II.

Rabelais is mentioned by Michael Drayton, a poet quite innocent of his influence, in 1627.

> Olde Chavcer doth of Topas tell,
> Mad Rablais of Pantagruell,
> A latter third of Dowsabell,
> With such poor trifles playing [2].

Robert Hayman (d. 1631 ?) was an epigrammatist and governor
of Newfoundland[3]. His epigrams, which are quite undistinguished,
were published in London in 1628, under the title of *Quodlibets, Lately Come Over from New Britaniola, Old Newfovnd-land...
With two Epistles of that excellently wittie Doctor, Francis Rablais* :
Translated out of his French at large. The first of the latter is
" A rayling Epistle... Wherein, " says the author, " though I
follow him [Rabelais] not verbatim, yet whoso can compare them,
shall find I haue done him no wrong [4]. " The second is " Another
Epistle...translated as the former [5]. " Both are extreme examples
of the kind of liberties that have been taken with the name of
Rabelais by educated dolts. What Hayman understood by the
term " translation " is difficult to say. Neither of these *Epistles*
bears the remotest resemblance to any portion of Rabelais's extant
works ; and the chance that they resemble, much less duplicate,
some lost writings of that author is remote. One would have to
imagine Rabelais expressing indignation at the turpitude of bawdry

---

1. Donne, *Poems*, I, 163, ll. 109-11.
2. The opening lines of *Nimphidia*, 1627. — *Nimphidia & The Moses Elizium*,
ed. John Gray (1896), III.
3. See *Dict. Nat. Biog.*
4. *Quodlibets* (London, 1628), 5th page from end of book (the pagination is
irregular).
5. *Ibid.*, 3d page from end of book.

for eighty lines, and a non-conformist's admiration of matronly chastity for sixty-eight more. One would have further to imagine him writing these sentiments in heroic couplets, or some equivalent.

b) The Drama.

It has been suggested that the tenuous connection of Rabelais with Shakespeare may have been owing to the mediation of Ben Jonson [1]. Ben himself has often been mentioned beside Rabelais by the critics, and the theory of the Rabelaisian influence on his work expressed [2], though with little primary evidence. I have latterly been able to supply what was wanting in this regard [3].

The connection dates from his earliest play, *The Case is Altered*, which is generally assigned to 1597-98 [4], and on at least two occasions he appears to have had the text before him as he composed. The first is in Act V, Scene II, of *The Devil Is An Ass* (1616). Pug, " the less devil, " succeeding poorly with his mischief on earth, invokes his master, saying,

> O Call me home again, dear chief, and put me
> To *yoking foxes, milking of he-goats,*
> *Pounding of water in a mortar,* laving
> The sea dry with a nut-shell, gathering all
> The leaves are fallen this autumn, *drawing farts*
> *Out of dead bodies,* making ropes of sand,
> Catching the winds together in a net,
> Mustering of ants, and numbering atoms ; all

---

1. Above, p. 36.
2. Thus, for example, Herford and Simpson write of *The New Inn* : " Joyous reminiscences of Rabelais and Cockayne linger, faded and subdued, about this hostelry of the Light Heart, this Host who so pleasantly enforces the ' great charter ' of his Thelema which will tolerate everything sooner than the sullen guest. " — *Ben Jonson*, ed. Herford and Simpson, II, 195. See also G. Gregory Smith, *Ben Jonson*, 168 ; A. H. Upham, *The French Influence in English Literature*, 241 ff.
3. In an article, " Ben Jonson and Rabelais, " *M. L. N.*, XLIV, 6-13.
4. In Act IV, Sc. IV, Juniper refers to Jacques, the miser, as " the old Panurgo, " meaning " the old villain. " For the date of the play, see Herford and Simpson, I, 305-06.
My quotations from Jonson conform to the text of *The Works*, ed. Gifford-Cunningham, 9 vols. (1875).

> That hell and you thought exquisite torments, rather
> Than stay me here a thought more : *I would sooner*
> *Keep fleas within a circle, and be accomptant*
> *A thousand year, which of them, and how far,*
> *Out-leap'd the other*, than endure a minute
> Such as I have within...

All the expressions in italics are taken from Rabelais's account of the academicians of La Reine Quinte in Book V, Chapter xxii. The author saw some of them bleaching negroes in a basket by rubbing their bellies, while

> Autres à trois couples de renards sous un joug aroient le rivage areneux, et ne perdoient leur semence.
>
> . . . .
>
> Autres tiroient eau des Pumices, que vous appelez Pierre-ponce, la pillant long temps en un mortier de marbre, et luy changeoient sa substance.
>
> . . . .
>
> Autres tiroient laict des boucs, et dedans un crible le recevoient, à grand profit de mesnage.
>
> . . . .
>
> Je vis un jeune Spodizateur, lequel artificiellement tiroit des pets d'un Asne mort, et en vendoit l'aune cinq sols.
>
> . . . .
>
> Autres dedans un long parterre songneusement mesuroient les sauts des pusses : et cestuy acte m'affermoient estre plus que necessaire au gouvernement des Royaumes, conduictes des guerres, administrations des Republiques, alleguant que Socrates, lequel premier avoit des cieux en terre tiré la Philosophie, et d'oisive et curieuse, l'avoit rendue utile et profitable, employoit la moitié de son estude à mesurer le saut des pusses, comme atteste Aristophanes le Quintessential.

For the rest, " laving the sea dry with a nutshell " and " catching the winds together in a net " are proverbial expressions, but in the present instance were doubtless suggested to the writer by near equivalents in the Rabelais passage, namely,

> Autres chassoient au vent avec des rets, et y prenoient Escrevisses Decumanes.
>
> . . . .
>
> Autres.. puisoient l'eau avec un rets.

Jonson returned to the second figure when he made Lovel say, in *The New Inn* (Act IV, Scene III), " I will go catch the wind first in a sieve. " " Drawing farts out of dead bodies " is an accomplishment of " the brotherhood of the Rosie Cross " in *The Staple of News* (1625, Act III, Scene I).

The Comus of the masque *Pleasure Reconciled to Virtue* (1619) is closely modelled upon Rabelais's Messere Gaster. One should consult the full account of the visit of Pantagruel and his men to Gaster's island (Bk. IV, Chs. LVII-LXII).

The masque opens with a " Hymn, " a merry drinking song, by the " full chorus. " It calls the Belly (i.e. Comus) " Prime master of arts, " " the founder of taste, " and the inventor of various foods, and of certain agricultural implements for harvesting and milling grain and of kitchen equipment for baking bread and meats. All this is taken from Rabelais, who calls Gaster " le noble maître es ars " (Bk. IV, Ch. LXI).

Des le commencement il inventa l'art fabrile, et agriculture pour cultiver la terre, tendant à fin qu'elle luy produisist Grain... Il inventa les moulins à eau, à vent, à bras, à aultres mille engins, pour Grain mouldre et reduire en farine ; le levain pour fermenter la paste ; le sel pour luy donner saveur...le feu pour le cuire, les horologes et quadrans pour entendre le temps de la cuycte de pain, créature de Grain.

Gaster's foods, detailed in the preceding two chapters, form one of Rabelais's most imposing catalogues.

After the " Hymn " the Bowl-bearer in a long speech describes the " belly-god : "

Do you hear, my friends ? to whom did you sing all this now ? Pardon me only that I ask you, for I do not look for an answer ; I'll answer myself : I know it is now such a time as the Saturnals for all the world, that every man stands under the eves of his own hat, and sings what pleases him ; that's the right and the liberty of it. Now you sing of god Comus here, the belly-god ; I say it is well, and I say it is not well ; it is well as it is a ballad, and the belly worthy of it, I must needs say, an 'twere forty yards of ballad more, as much ballad as tripe. But when the belly is not edified by it, it is not well ; for where did you ever read or hear that the Belly had any ears ? Come, never pump for an answer, for you are defeated : our fellow Hunger

there, that was as ancient a retainer to the Belly as any of us, was turn'd
away for being unseasonable ; not unreasonable, but unseasonable ;
and now is he, poor thin-gut, fain to get his living with teaching of
starlings, magpies, parrots and jack-daws, those things he would have
taught the Belly. Beware of dealing with the Belly, the Belly will
not be talk'd to, especially when he is full ; then there is no venturing
upon Venter, he will blow you all up, he will thunder indeed la ! Some
in derision call him the father of farts ; but I say he was the first inventor of great ordnance, and taught us to discharge them on festival
days, would we had a fit feast for him, i' faith, to show his activity ;
I would have something now fetched in to please his five senses, the
throat ; or the two senses, the eyes : pardon me for my two senses ;
for I that carry Hercules's bowl in the service, may see double by my
place ; for I have drunk like a frog today :   I would have a tun now
brought in to dance, and so many bottles about him.   Ha ! you
look as if you would make a problem of this ; do you see, do you see ?
a problem :   Why bottles, and why a tun ?   and why a tun and why
bottles, to dance ?   I say, that men that drink hard, and serve the
Belly in any place of quality, (as the jovial tinkers, or the lusty kindred,)
are living measures of drink, and can transform themselves, and do
every day, to bottles or tuns, when they please :   and when they have
done all they can, they are as I say again (for I think I said somewhat
like it afore) but moving measures of drink, and there is a piece in the
cellar can hold more than all they.   This will I make good, if it please
our new god but to give a nod, for the Belly does all by signs ; and I
am all for the belly, the truest clock in the world to go by.

The borrowing is detailed.   Comus has no ears ; Gaster " sans
aureilles feut créé " (Rabelais, Bk. IV, Ch. LVII)[1].   Hunger, a
cashiered retainer, now earns his living teaching certain birds what
he would have taught the belly ; Gaster teaches the same birds
" ars desniées de Nature : "   " Les Corbeaulx, les Gays, les Pape-
gays, les Estourneaulx, il rend poëtes :   les Pies il fait poëtrides,
et leur aprent languaige humain proferer, parler, chanter.   Et tout
pour la trippe, " hunger being, of course, the motive, though it is
not separately personified (Bk. IV, Ch. LVII).   Comus is dangerous ;
" Beware of dealing with the Belly,...he will blow you all up, he
will thunder indeed... "   Similarly in Rabelais :   " au mandement

1. The classical Comus, so far as we know, was never represented thus.   See
W. H. Roscher's *Ausführliches Lexikon der Griechischen und Römischen Mythologie* (Leipzig, 1890 ff), under *Komos*, and the references there given.

de messere Gaster tout le ciel tremble, toute la terre bransle...   A loy aulcune n'est subjecte, de toutes est exempte.   Chacun la refuit en tous endroictz, plus toust s'exposans es naufrages de mer, plus toust eslisans par feu, par mons, par goulphres passer, que d'icelle estre apprehendez " (Bk. IV, Ch. LVII).   Comus " was the first inventor of great ordnance ; " Gaster " avoit inventé recentement Canons, Serpentines, Coulevrines, Bombardes, Basilics, jectans boullets de fer, de plomb, de bronze... "   (Bk. IV, Ch. LXI).   The dance of the tun and bottles, which is the next episode of the masque, is clearly a reminiscence of " le grand flasque (nostre Lanterne l'appelloit Phlosque) gouverneur de la dive Bouteille, accompagné de la garde du temple, et estoient tous Bouteillons François " (Bk. V, Ch. xxxv).   Comus " does all by signs ; " Gaster " ne parle que par signes " (Bk. IV, Ch. LVII).   The Belly is " the truest clock in the world to go by, "—an idea expressed by Pantagruel in a chapter following closely upon the Gaster episode, " il n'est horologe plus juste que le ventre " (Bk. IV, Ch. LXIV [1]).

Two other passages in Jonson deserve mention.

Lickfinger, the master cook in *The Staple* of *News* (1625, Act III, Scene I), asks, " What news of Gondomar ? " and the barber, Thomas, replies,

> A second fistula,
> Or an excoriation, at the least,
> For putting the poor English play, was writ of him,
> To such a sordid use, as, it is said, he did,
> Of cleansing his posteriors.

And Lickfinger cries, " Justice !   Justice ! "   Friar John, in Rabelais, tells of suffering in a similar manner for putting the Fifth Collection of Decretals to the same use, and Homenaz, Bishop of the Papimanes, declares, " ce feut evidente punition de Dieu " (Bk. IV, Ch. LII).

---

1. Jonson borrows from Rabelais as he does from the classics, selecting and piecing together in a fashion which used to be called plagiaristic.   He never mentions him by name, as indeed he might well have done in the present instance, for it was his frequent practise to indicate the sources of his masques in accompanying commentaries.

Doctor Rut, in *The Magnetic Lady* (1632, Act II, Scene i) prescribes for Placentia as follows :

> Give her a vent,
> If she do swell. A gimblet must be had ;
> It is a tympanites she is troubled with.
> There are three kinds : the first is anasarca,
> Under the flesh a tumour ; that's not her's.
> The second is ascites, or aquosus,
> A watery humour ; that is not hers neither.
> But tympanites, which we call the drum,
> A wind-bombs in her belly, must be unbraced,
> And with a faucet or a peg, let out,
> And she'll do well : get her a husband.

Rabelais tells of a similar cure achived by a doctor of the Quintessence (Bk. V, Ch. xxi).

> Un autre je vy hydropiques parfaitement guarir, timpanistes, ascites, et hyposargues, leur frappant par neuf fois sur le ventre d'une besaguë Tenedie sans solution de continuité.

Gimlet, *faucet*, and *peg* are all names of the phallus used by Gargantua's nurses, that is, *teriere*, *dille*, and *bondon*, *bouchon* (Bk. I, Ch. xi).

One may add that there is a close resemblance between the argument of Carlo Buffone in praise of debt in Act I, Scene i, of *Every Man Out of His Humour* [1] and that of Panurge in Rabelais, Book III, chapter iii. " Debt ! " says Carlo, " why that's the more for your credit, Sir, " and continues :

> O ! look where you are indebted any great sum, your creditor observes you with no less regard, than if he were bound to you for

---

1. The Farmer, Sordido, in this play, who holds his grain against a dearth, and attempts to hang himself when the harvest proves plentiful (in Act II, Scene iii), might be thought to have been suggested by Rabelais, Bk. III, Ch. iii, where he speaks of " les usuriers de Landerousse, qui n'a gueres se pendirent, voyans les bleds et vins ravaller en pris, et bon temps retourner. " The idea of hanging in such circumstances may have been proverbial. It is mentioned in *Macbeth*, Act II, Sc. iii, l. 5 : " Here's a farmer that hang'd himself on the expectation of plenty. " This, considering the dates, was perhaps an allusion to Jonson's play. Jonson's treatment of the theme delighted John Taylor, the " Water-Poet. " See his *Part of This Summers Travels*, 1639, *Works*, ed. Spenser Soc., Qu. I, 16-18.

some huge benefit, and will quake to give you the least cause of offense, lest he lose his money.   I assure you, in these times, no man has his servant more obsequious and pliant, than gentlemen their creditors : to whom, if at any time you pay but a moiety, or a fourth part, it comes more acceptably than if you gave them a new-year's gift.

Panurge says to Pantagruel :

Crediteurs sont (je le maintiens jusques au feu exclusivement) créatures belles et bonnes.   Qui rien ne preste est créature laide et mauvaise, créature du grand villain diantre d'enfer.   Et faict, quoy ? Debtes. O chose rare et antiquaire ! Debtes, diz je, excedentes le nombre des syllabes resultantes au couplement de toutes les consonantes avecques les vocales, jadis projecté et compté par le noble Xenocrates. A la numerosité des crediteurs si vous estimez la perfection des debteurs, nous ne errerez en Arithmeticque praticque. Cuidez vous que je suis aise, quand, tous les matins, autour de moy, je voy ces crediteurs tant humbles, serviables et copieux en reverences ? Et quand je note que, moy faisant a l'un visage plus ouvert et chere meilleure que es autres, le paillard pense avoir sa depesche le premier, pense estre le premier en date, et de mon ris cuyde que soit argent comptant. Il m'est advis que je joue encores le Dieu de la Passion de Saulmur, accompaigné de ses Anges et Cherubins. Ce sont mes candidatz, mes parasites, mes salüeurs, mes diseurs de bons jours, mes orateurs perpetuelz.

Panurge, Pantagruel, and the Oracle of the Bottle are all mentioned [1] ; so is Gargantua [2].   The last, considering the omnivorous-

---

1. On Panurge see note 54 above.   In *The New Inn*, 1629, Act I, Sc. i, Lovel explains that the studies of his master, Lord Beaufort, have been in classical, not in romantic, literature :

> He had no Arthurs, nor no Rosicleers,
> No knights o' the Sun, nor Amadis de Gauls,
> Primalions, Pantagruels, public nothings.

In *The Staple of News*, 1625, Act IV, Sc. i, Lickfinger says to Madrigal,

> Heretic, I see
> Thou art for the vain Oracle of the Bottle.
> The hogshead, Trismegistus, is thy Pegasus.

Rabelais calls the Oracle " la Bouteille trimegiste " in Book V, Ch. xlvi.   In *The New Inn*, again, Act IV, Sc iii, the Host says to the Nurse, who has let her ward escape,

> ....Where is your charge ?...
> Go ask the oracle
> Of the bottle, at your girdle, there you lost it.

2. *Every Man in His Humour*, Act II, Sc. i.

ness of Jonson, may have been associated in his mind either with Rabelais or with folk-lore. Other scattered ideas and phrases which could have come conveniently to his use from Rabelais, though they were not the latter's exclusive property, are : the figure of teeth chattering like virginal jacks (i. e. piano keys) [1] ; licking figs out of the posteriors [2] ; and making a meal of a savoury odor [3]. He employs *Holofernes*, the name of the preceptor of Gargantua, as a general term of abuse, and names an allegorical character Philautia, possibly after the common noun *philautie* found in Rabelais, Book III, chapter xxix. He may have taken over also the words *exotic* [4], *paranomasie* [5], and *prelude* [6], the earliest use of which in English is credited to him by the *Oxford Dictionary*. One might mention also the following, though they are all recorded earlier :   *Brachman* [7], *Massoreth* [8], *metoposcopy* [9], *myrobalanes* [10], *quintessence* [11], *truchman* [12].   Like Rabelais he uses *tripe* in various figurative senses [13], and at least once the characteristic (but not exclusively) Rabelaisian phrase " 'bove e-la " [14].   Like Rabelais he is fond of drawing upon the Greek. We have mentioned *Philautia* in *Cynthias's Revels*, and the same play contains also, in the Induction and in two interpolated masques, the allegorical names, *Aglaia*, *Anteros*, *Apheleia*, *Eucolos, Eucosmos, Eupathes, Euphantaste, Gelaia*,

---

1. In *Volpone*, 1605, Act II, Sc. i ; Rabelais, Prol., Bk. II.
2. In *The Alchemist*, 1610, Act I, Sc. i ; Rabelais, Bk. IV, Ch. xlv ; cf. under Nashe, above, p. 53.
3. In *The Alchemist*, Act. I, Sc. i ; Rabelais, Bk. III, Ch. xxxvii.
4. The word occurs in *Every Man Out of His Humour*, Act IV, Sc. iv.
5. In the *Poetaster*, Act III, Sc. i, and in *Timber*, § CXXIX, *Consuetudo*. A certain E. K. is recorded by *Oxf. Dict.* as using *Paranomasia* in 1579.
6. In *Cynthia's Revels*, Act V, Sc. ii.
7. In *The Fortunate Isles*, a masque.
8. In *The Magnetic Lady*, Act I, Sc. i.
9. In *The Alchemist*, Act I, Sc. i.
10. In *Volpone*, Act III, Sc. ii, and in *The Alchemist*, Act IV, Sc. i.
11. In *Volpone*, Act II, Sc. i.
12. In *Cynthia's Revels*, Act V, Sc. ii.
13. For *whore* in *Bartholomew Fair*, Act I, Sc. i ; for *a large quantity* in *Pleasure Reconciled to Virtue* (see above, p. 83) ; for *guts* in *The Staple of News*, Act. IV, Sc. i.
14. " You had some strain Bove e-la " = " you fornicated, " in *The Devil Is An Ass*, Act V, Sc. iii.   In Rabelais " nous sommes au-dessus de Ela " means " we are in the soup, " in Bk. IV, Ch. xix.

Hedon, and *Storgé*, which, though they are not duplicated in Rabelais, remind us of those of the retainers of Gargantua and Pantagruel. Others are found in *Part of King James's Entertainment in passing to his Coronation*. The *Fortunate Isles* (1626) contains a character, Father Outis, who recalls some of Rabelais's Utopian names in Book IV, Chapter II, and elsewhere, *Medamothi, Udem, Achorie*, etc. He makes a facetious use of learned words such as *agnomination* [1], *amphibolies* [2], *cosmogrified* [3], *fricatrice* [4], *gigantomachized* [5], and *mangonizing* [6]. He is fond of such popular compounds as *un-in-one-breath-utterable* [7], *un-to-be-melted* [8], *un-to-be-pardoned* [9], *turdy-facy-nasty-paty-lousy-fartical* [10], and of popular etymologies like *Maecen-asses* [11], *Aristarchus or stark ass* [12], and *Breeches quasi bear-riches* [13].

He revels in sounds, and yet is not carried away by the monotonous jingles of Euphuism. A few illustrations will suffice to justify comparison with Rabelais. Bobadil, in *Every Man in His Humour*, says of Downright, who " has not so much as a good phrase in his belly, " that " he was born for the manger, pannier, or pack-saddle [14]. " The motive recurs in *A Tale of a Tub*,

> I could get up upon a pannier, a pannel,
> Or, to say truth, a very pack-saddle [15].

Is not this an echo of a line which was later to catch the ear of Laurence Sterne ?

---

1. In *The Poetaster*, Act III, Sc. I.
2. In *The Magnetic Lady*, Act II, Sc. I.
3. In *The Case Is Altered*, Act IV, Sc. IV.
4. For *whore* in *Volpone*, Act IV, Sc. I.
5. In *Every Man Out of His Humour*, Act V, Sc. IV.
6. In *The Poetaster*, Act III, Sc. I.
7. In *Every Man In His Humour*, Act I, Sc. III.
8. In *The Devil Is An Ass*, Act III, Sc. I.
9. In *The New Inn*, Act V, Sc. I.
10. In *Volpone*, Act II, Sc. I.
11. In *The Case Is Altered*, Act I, Sc. I.
12. In *Every Man Out of His Humour*, Induction.
13. In *Cynthia's Revels*, Act IV, Sc. I.
14. *Every Man In His Humour*, Act I, Sc. IV.
15. *A Tale of a Tub*, Act IV, Sc. III.

Que nuist sçavoir tousjours et tousjours apprendre, feust ce d'un sot, d'un pot, d'une guedoufle, d'une moufle, d'un pantoufle [1] ?

Ben calls the Jews " goggle-eyed grumbledories [2] ; " scribblers are " poets, poetaccios, poetasters, poetitos [3] " ; and a certain Miles would change his name

To Guiles, Wiles, Piles, Biles, or the foulest name
You can devise [4].

The affinity of the two writers may be further illustrated in the realm of ideas in passages in which one would not be justified in attempting to prove imitation.   Captain Bobadil on one occasion boasts how he and nineteen gentlemen might fight all the Queen's wars by capturing and killing the enemy twenty at a time [5], in precisely the tone of Rabelais's Duc de Menuail, who plans a conquest of the world for King Picrochole [6]. The famous purge of Crispinus (Marston) in *The Poetaster*, which makes him puke up his monstrous vocabulary, is closely imitated from the *Lexiphanes* of Lucian [7], and yet the realism of certain of the details suggests with almost equal force Rabelais's episode of the Limousin scholar.

Crispinus. O — !... O, I am sick — !
Horace. A bason ; a bason, quickly : our physic works. Faint not man.
Crispanius. O — retrograde — recriprocal — incubus.

" Tu escorches le latin, " says Pantagruel to the Limousin, " par sainct Jan, je te feray escorcher le renard, car je te escorcheray tout vif, " and his threat brings on a torrent of the man's incom-

---

1. Rabelais, Bk. III, Ch. xvi.   On Sterne see below.
2. In *Every Man Out of His Humour*, Act V, Sc. iv.
3. In *The Magnetic Lady*, Induction. Compare Rabelais's " Sophistes, Sorbillans, Sorbonagres, etc., " cit. above, p. 20.
4. In *A Tale of a Tub*, Act IV, Sc. i.
5. *Every Man In His Humour*, Act IV, Sc. v.
6. Rabelais, Bk. I, Ch. xxxiii.
7. *The Poetaster*, Act V, Sc. i. See *Works*, ed. Gifford-Cunningham, II, 497, note.

prehensible dialect [1]. Volpone as mountebank [2] suggests divers of Rabelais's characters, Her Trippa, for example, in volubility [3], Panurge in deceit [4]. The pseudo-quixotic projects of Sir Politic Would-Be [5] are comparable in their fatuous and nice triviality to the law suits of Panurge [6]. *Epicœne or the Silent Woman* has been traced in outline and in many details to one of the *Orations* of Libanius [7], yet we find the tone of it suggesting Rabelais throughout in its satire on female shortcomings, its praise of Pythagorean silence, and in its farcical sound and bustle. Truewit describes the whole play when he says, in Act IV, Scene I, of the Epicœne-Morose menage,

> The spitting, the coughing, the laughter, the neezing, the farting, dancing, noise of the music, and her masculine and loud commanding, and urging the whole family, makes him think he has married a fury.

It is pertinent to recall that Rabelais once acted in a farce whose plot was probably taken from the same source [8]. The Rabelaisian " Patelinage " of *The Silent Woman*, and the cheerful villainy of Panurge reappear stronger than ever in *The Alchemist*, together with necromantic lore which, again, suggests Rabelais's Her Trippa [9]. Jonson is an adept in Rabelaisian abuse, which is to say that he understands how to make abuse convincing, and even friendly, as well as colorful, far surpassing the gaudy attempts of Harvey and Nashe. *Volpone, The Silent Woman*, and *The Alchemist* illustrate this *crescendo*, and it rises to new heights in the mouth of Ursula, the pig-woman, in *Bartholomew Fair*. " Though

---

1. Rabelais, Bk. II, Ch. vi.
2. *Volpone*, Act II, Sc. I and II.
3. Rabelais, Bk. III, Ch. xxv.
4. Rabelais, Bk. II, Ch. xvii.
5. *Volpone*, Act IV, Sc. I.
6. Rabelais, Bk. II, Ch. xvii.
7. See *The Silent Woman*, ed. Henry, Intro., xxviii-xxxii, and *Volpone*, ed. Rea, Intro., xxii-xxiii.
8. " La morale comedie de celluy qui avoit espousé une femme mute. " Rabelais outlines its plot in Bk. III, Ch. xxxiv, and says, " Je ne riz oncques tant que je feis à ce Patelinage. "
9. See note 3 above.

you be captain of the roarers, " she says to Knockem, " and fight
well at the case of piss-pots, you shall not fright me with your
lion-chap, sir, nor your tusks ; you angry ! you are hungry.
Come, a pig's head will stop your mouth, and stay your stomach
at all times. " She is, in the words of Justice Overdo, " the very
womb and bed of enormity [1]. " We are further reminded of the
lawsuits of Panurge [2] in this play by Quarlous's speech to Winwife
chaffing him for his zeal in pursuing old whores [3]. Panurge
the polyglot [4] very possibly inspired a passage in *The Devil Is An
Ass*, in which Fitzdotterel jabbers four languages in a pretended
fit [5]. In the masque *News From The New World Discovered in The
Moon* Ben draws upon Lucian's *True History* for the conception of
a race of bird men, like Rabelais in the opening chapters of *Pantagruel*, Book V. We have noticed Lickfinger's mention of the
Oracle of the Bottle in *The Staple of News* [6], and the speech in
which it occurs is an eulogy of the culinary art worthy of the author
thus invoked. We have also noticed a borrowing in *The Devil Is
An Ass* from the Quintessence chapters of Rabelais's Book V [7].
The motive of the quintessential researches is used with a new set
of illustrations in *The New Inn*, where such practises as

> ...poring through a multiplying-glass
> Upon a captivated crab-louse, or a cheese-mite

are attributed to the abstemious Lovel by mine Host [8]. *The Fortunate Isles*, a masque, contains a Lucianic account of the shades
in the lower world. *The True History* and *The Dialogues of the
Dead* have inspired many imitations, both direct and indirect, and
although Jonson was no doubt well versed in both, he seems here
to have been equally inspired by the experience of Epistemon in

---

1. Act II, Sc. i.
2. Rabelais, Bk. II, Ch. xvii.
3. Act I, Sc. i.
4. Rabelais, Bk. II, Ch. ix.
5. Act. V, Sc. v.
6. See p. 87, n. 1, above.
7. See above, p. 81.
8. Act I, Sc. i.

Pantagruel, Chapter xxx. This is to be inferred from the presence of a couple of Rabelaisian words (*Outis* and *Brachman*), and from the use of certain anachronisms. Zoroastres, for example, " is confuting a French almanack. "

Jonson was a hearty animal, honest, convivial, and frank to the point of bearishness, and his excess of spirits frequently found vent in the grotesque vein that distinguishes so much of Rabelais's work. This vein was checked only by the proprieties of the stage, which, indeed, were comparatively free in his day. He wrote a mock-heroic poem (Epigram CXXXIII) upon the subject of a nocturnal crossing of the Thames, which is bolder and more odorous than any passage in his dramatic work. At Bridewell, for example,

> several ghosts did flit
> About the shore, of farts but late departed,
> White, black, blue, green, and in more forms outstarted,
> Than all those *atomi* ridiculous
> Whereof old Democrite, and Hill Nicholas,
> One said, the other swore, the world consists.

His scholarship was as vast as that of Rabelais, and surpassed it in the poetic field. One remembers that he is the author of " Drink to me only with thine eyes, " and that of all the lyrists of his time, none was more attentive than he to form. The stylistic traditions of the masque were especially rigid, and it is perhaps no wonder that he was unable to bend them successfully to the expression of a Rabelaisian theme in *Pleasure Reconciled to Virtue*. This attempt was a failure in two performances [1] and has been well described by Mr. Gregory Smith as " Pantagruel without the spice [2]. "

The legitimate drama was not so stubborn, and contains Ben's happiest efforts in the expansive manner. His realism at its best is Rabelaisian, at its worst commonplace. The former appears by fits and starts, with the result that a character may be a mere auto-

---

1. See Reyher, *Les Masques Anglais*, 56, and Jonson, *Works*, ed. Herford nd Simpson, II, 305, 309.
2. G. Greg. Smith, *Ben Jonson*, 168.

maton in one scene and a whirlwind of life in the next. His theory of the " humours " has been held accountable generally for the unevenness of his art, and with much justice. More Jonson and less theory, more Rabelais and less " humours, " would have been good medecine.

Ben came under Rabelais's influence only because the two men shared important traits of mind and temperament. Both were intellectually as tough and independent as any two men who have ever lived. Had there never been a Rabelais, it cannot be supposed that Ben would have been in any important respect different from the man that we know. The influence may or may not have been more profound than appears on the surface. The Rabelaisian parallels to those phases of Jonson's thought and style which have been considered in the foregoing pages may have been to a great, or to a very slight, extent a shaping factor. Thus, though Jonson was much less narrowly preoccupied with Rabelais than Sir Thomas Urquhart or Swift or Sterne, he is a more striking illustration of the essential affinity between Rabelais and the English mind, and has therefore an unique claim to be considered the most important of Rabelais's English disciples.

The next playwright to be noticed is the author of *Lingua* : *or the Combat of the Tongue and the Five Senses for Superiority* (produced before 1603, published 1607). He is of modest importance compared with Jonson, with whom one scholar has nevertheless suggested an identification [1]. It is more likely that he is a certain Thomas Tomkis, of whom we know little more than that he was a Fellow of Trinity College, Cambridge in 1604, and the author of another comedy, *Albumazar*, in 1613 [2].

The character Mendacio in *Lingua* speaks as follows in Act II, Scene I [3] :

---

1. See Jonson's *The Staple of News*, ed. De Winter, 167.
2. See *Dict. Nat. Biog.*, under Tomkis, Thomas ; Schelling, *Elizabethan Drama, 1558-1642* (Boston, 1908), II, 70. Winstanley argues that the play is by Anton Brewer ; see *Dodsley's Old Plays* (1825), V, 101. That the play was produced before 1603 seems likely from a reference in Act IV, Sc. VII, to " our queen. "
3. Apparently the first to observe the following parallels with Rabelais was Regis in his *Garg. und Pant.*, II, 250, 304, 739.

I help'd Herodotus to pen some part of his Muses, lent Pliny ink to write his history, rounded Rabelais in the ear when he historified Pantagruel ; as for Lucian, I was his genius [1]...

In Act III, Scene v, occurs this echo of the Lucianic accou nt of the lower world in *Pantagruel*, Chapter xxx.

For in hell they say Alexander is no better than a cobler [2].

In Act IV, Scene i [3], we encounter Rabelais's messere Gaster, the account of the latter's " art et moyen de non estre blessé ne touché par coups de canon [4] " being here skilfully split up into dialogue.   Like the *Parlement of Pratlers* this passage is the best possible evidence of the essentially colloquial quality of Rabelais's writing.   Heuresio thus addresses Anamnestes on his device " to withstánd the stroke of the most violent culverin : "

Lingua	Rabelais
Mendacio. I must needs confess this device to pass all that ever I heard or saw ; and thus it was, first he takes a faulcon, and charges it without all deceits, with dry powder well camphired ; then did he put in a single bullet, and a great quantity of drop shot both round and lachrymal. This done, he sets me a boy sixty paces off, just point blank over-against the mouth of the piece. Now in the very midst of the direct line he fastens a post, upon which he hangs me in a cord, a siderite of Herculean stone.	Dedans un faulconneau de bronze il mettoit sus la pouldre de canon curieusement composée, degressée de son soulfre, et pro-portionnée avecques Camphre fin, en quantité competente, une bal-lotte de fer bien qualibrée, et vingt et quatre grains de dragée de fer, uns ronds et sphericques, aultres en forme lachrymale. Puys ayant prins sa mire contre un sien jeune paige, comme s'il le voulust ferir parmy l'estomach, en distance de soixante pas, au mylieu du chemin entre le paige et le faul-conneau en ligne droyte suspen-doit sus une potence de bois à

---

1. Text according to *Dodsley's Old Plays* (1825), V, 129.

2. *Ibid.*, V, 156. Rabelais, Bk. II, Ch. xxx : " Car je veis Alexandre le Grand qui repetassoit de vieilles chausses, et ainsi gaignoit sa pauvre vie. "

3. *Dodsley's Old Plays*, V, 171-72.

4. Rabelais, Bk. IV, Ch. lxii.

Anamnestes. Well, well, I know it well, it was found out in Ida, in the year of the world—by one Magnes, whose name it retains, though vulgarly they call it the Adamant.

Mendacio. When he had hang'd this Adamant in a cord, he comes back, and gives fire to the touch-hole : now the powder consumed to a void vacuum—

Heuresis. Which is intolerable in nature ; for first shall the whole machine of the world, heaven, earth, sea, and air, return to the mishapen house of Chaos, than the least vacuum to be found in the universe.

Mendacio. The bullet and drop shot flew most impetuously from the fiery throat, of the culverin ; but, O strange, no sooner came they near the adamant in the cord, but they were all arrested by the serjeant of nature, and hovered in the air round about it, till they had lost the force of their motion, clasping themselves close to the stone in most lovely manner, and not any one flew to endanger the mark ; so much did they remember their duty to nature, that they forgot the errand they were sent of.

Heuresis. ......and I have an addition to this, which is to make the bullet shot from the enemy to return immediately upon the gunner :...

une chorde en l'air une bien grosse pierre Siderite, c'est-à-dire Ferriere, aultrement appellée, Herculiane, jadis trouvée en Ide on pays de Phrygie par un nommé Magnes, comme atteste Nicander. Nous vulgairement l'appelons Aymant.

Puys mettoit le feu au Faulconneau par la bouche du pulverin. La pouldre consommée, advenoit que pour eviter vacuité (laquelle n'est tolerée en Nature ; plus toust seroit la machine de l'Univers, Ciel, Air, Terre, Mer reduicte à l'antique Chaos, qu'il advinst vacuité en lieu du monde) la ballotte et dragées estoient impetueusement hors jectées par la gueule du Faulconneau, affin que l'air penetrast en la chambre d'icelluy, laquelle aultrement restoit en vacuité, estant la pouldre par le feu tant soubdain consommée. Les ballotte et dragées ainsi violentement lancées sembloient bien debvoir ferir le paige ; mais sus le poinct qu'elles approchoient de la susdicte pierre, se perdoit leur impetuosité et toutes restoient en l'air flottantes et tournoyantes autour de la pierre, et n'en passoit oultre une, tant violente feust elle, jusques au paige.

Mais il inventoit l'art et maniere de faire les boulletz arriere retourner contre les ennemis, en pareille furie et dangier qu'ilz seroient tirez et en propre parallele.

In the other play, *Albumazar*, the rogue of that name advises his apprentices that " The world's a theatre of theft [1], " and his argument appears to be taken from Panurge on debt and debtors [2] :

Alb. The world's a theatre of theft. Great rivers
Rob smaller brooks, and them the ocean.
And in this world of ours, this microcosm,
Guts from the stomach steal, and what they spare,
The meseraicks filch, and lay't i' the liver :
Where, lest it should be found, turn'd to red nectar,
'Tis by a thousand thievish veins convey'd,
And hid in flesh, nerves, bones, muscles, and sinews,
In tendons, skin, and hair ; so that the property
Thus alter'd, the theft can never be discover'd.
Now all these pilf'ries, couch'd and compos'd in order,
Frame thee and me. Man's a quick mass of thievery.

Pantagruel is mentioned in Barnabe Barnes' *The Devil's Charter* (1606-07) [3], and a bit of Epistemon's vision of the shades is quoted by Webster in *Vittoria Corombona* (1612). [4]   Shirley speaks of "A chimera out of Rabelais " in *The Triumph of Peace*, a masque

---

1. Act I, Sc. i, *Dodsley's Old Plays* (1825), VII, 110-11.
2. Rabelais, Bk. III, Ch. iv.   Panurge says : " ...figurez nostre microcosme (*id est*, petit monde, c'est l'homme), en tous ses membres, prestans, empruntans, doibvons, c'est-à-dire en soin naturel. Car nature n'a créé l'home que pour prester et emprunter... L'appetit, en l'orifice de l'estomach, moyenant un peu de melancholie aigrette, que luy est transmis de la ratelle, admoneste de enfourner viande. La langue en faict l'essay, les dens la maschent, l'estomach la recoit, digere et chylifie. Les veines mesaraïcques en sugcent,...puys la portent au foye ; il la transmue de rechef, et en fait sang. "
3. Act III, Sc. v, l. 1498, ed. McKerrow, 43 ; noticed by Koeppel, *Ben Jonson's Wirkung*, 203.
4. Act V, Sc. vi, *Works*, ed. Lucas, I, 187 ; noticed by Regis, *Garg. und Pant.*, II, 304.   Flamineo says : " Whither shall I go now ? O *Lucian*, thy ridiculous Purgatory ! To find *Alexander* the Great cobling shooes, *Pompey* tagging points, and *Julius Caesar* making haire buttons, *Haniball* selling blacking, and *Augustus* crying garlike, *Charlemaigne* selling lists by the dozen, and King *Pippin* crying Apples in a cart drawn with one horse !" In Rabelais, Bk. II, Ch. xxx, Alexander mends shoes, but Pompey and Julius Caesar are caulkers of ships, Hannibal is a cook, and Augustus, Charlemagne, and Pepin are not mentioned at all. Mr. A. F. Bourgeois believes that Webster was also familiar with the drawings once attributed to Rabelais, called " Les Songes drôlatiques de Pantagruel. " — " Rabelais en Angleterre. " *R. E. R.*, III, 83.

(1633) [1] ; and Ford has a certain Futelli in *The Lady's Trial* say of an upstart gallant,

> ...we have resolv'd him,
> He is descended from Pantagruel
> Of famous memory, by the father's side [2].

Jasper Mayne, finally, makes Rabelais a minor accessory to the plot of *The City Match* (1639). Penelope is addressed as follows by Plotwell on her tricked up betrothal to Plotwell's uncle :

> I have transform'd an English poet into
> A fine French teacher, who shall join your hands
> With a most learned legend out of Rablais [3].

The poet is named Salewit, and he performs the ceremony :

> I've read a fiction out of Rablais to 'em,
> In a religious tone, which he believes
> For good French liturgy. When I had done,
> There came a christening.
>
> *Plotwell.* And didst thou baptize
> Out of Rab'lais too [4] ?

The uncle is at last disabused.

> *Plotwell.* Wonder not, sir : you
> Were married but in jest. 'Twas no church-form
> But a fine legend out of Rablais [5].

Nobody has as yet made a complete drama from Rabelais's narrative. What might not Ben Jonson have done with it ? or Chapman, or Middleton ? The opportunity remains for the experimental theatre of to-day, and may yet be realized.

---

1. In a speech of the character Opinion, *Dramatic Works and Poems*, ed. Gifford-Dyce, VI, 270 ; noticed by Koeppel, *Ben Jonson's Wirkung*, 230.
2. Act I, Sc. II ; text according to the *Dramatic Works of Massinger and Ford*, 2d part, 150 ; noticed by Koeppel, *op. cit.*, 229.
3. Act IV, Sc. II ; *Dodsley's Old Plays* (1825) IX, 292.
4. Act V, Sc. I ; *ed. cit.*, 309.
5. Act V, Sc. IX ; *ed. cit.*, 325.

c) *Prose.*

The idea was widely current that Rabelais was " wicked. " We have found it expressed by several Elizabethans, some of whom doubtless knew better. Thomas Lodge, for example, writes : " Hire him [Blasphemy] to write a comedie, he is as arrant an Atheist as Rabelais in his Pantagruel [1]. " Certain passages in Burton's *Anatomy of Melancholy* (1621) illustrate the same view. How far Burton himself agreed with it, is not quite clear. " Ask one of...[our Philosophers], " he says, " of what Religion he is, he scoffingly replies, a Philosopher, a *Galenist,* an *Averroist,* and with *Rabelais* a Physician, a Peripatetick, an Epicure [2]. " As scurrilous as Petronius, Aretino, or Boccalini [3], Rabelais is a drunkard to boot. The intemperate, says Burton, " triumph in villainy, and justify their wickedness ; with *Rabelais,* that French *Lucian,* [they say] drunkenness is better for the body than physick, because there be more old drunkards than old physicians [4]. "

Francis Bacon, on the other hand, was fair to " the great jester, " and it needs no apology for setting down his scattered tributes to him.

The Twoo Bookes of Francis Bacon of the Proficience and Advancement of Learning Divine and Humane were published in 1605, and in both occur unmistakable reminiscences of the Prologue to *Gargantua.* In the first, observing how the vulgar misconstrue the levities of learned men, he refers them

to that which Plato said of his master Socrates, whom he compared to the gallypots of apothecaries, which on the outside had apes and owls and antiques, but contained within sovereign and precious liquors and confections ; acknowledging that to an external report he was not without superficial levities and deformities, but was inwardly replenished with excellent virtues and powers [5].

---

1. In *Wits Miserie and the World's Madnesse,* 1596, *Works,* IV, 65-66 ; noticed by McKillop, *M. L. N.,* XXXVI, 471.
2. Pt. III, Sect. IV, Mem. II, Subs. I, *Anat. of Mel.* (London, 1926), III, 440.
3. Pt. I, Sect. II, Mem. IV, Subs. IV, *ed. cit.,* I, 391.
4. Pt. I, Sect. II, Mem. II, Subs. II, *ed. cit.,* I, 262.
5. *Works,* ed. Ellis and Heath, III, 280. The Latin version of the *Advance-*

In the second occurs the following :

Surely of those poets which are now extant, even Homer himself, (notwithstanding he was made a kind of Scripture by the later schools of the Grecians), yet I should without any difficulty pronounce that his fables had no such inwardness in his own meaning ; but what they might have upon a more original tradition, is not easy to affirm ; for he was not the inventor of many of them [1].

In Book VI of the same work, published first in 1623, Rabelais is explicitly and joyfully acknowledged. Bacon writes in the dedicatory chapter :

It is permitted to every man (excellent King) to make merry with himself and his own matters. Who knows then but this work of mine is copied from a certain old book found in the most famous library of St. Victor, of which Master Francis Rabelais made a catalogue ? For there is a book there entitled " The Ant-hill of Arts. " And certainly I have raised up here a little heap of dust, and stored under it a great

---

ment, published in 1623, is found in I, 423 ff. Notes by Ellis and Spedding in I, 448, point out that the reference goes back ultimately to Plato, *Symposium*, 215A, where Alcibiades says that Socrates " is exactly like the busts of Silenus, which are set up in the statuaries' shops, holding pipes and flutes in their mouths ; and they are made to open in the middle, and have images of gods inside them " (Jowett's Translation, Oxford, 3d ed., 1892, I, 586) ; but that Bacon's changes and elaborations of the Platonic simile are clearly imitated from Rabelais. Rabelais cites Alcibiades' comparison of his master to " Silenes, " with the following explanation :   " Silenes estoient jadis petites boites, telles que voyons de present es bouticques des apothecaires, pinctes au dessus de figures joyeuses et frivoles, comme de harpies, satyres, oysons bridez, lievres cornuz, canes bastées, boucqs volans, cerfz limonniers et aultres telles pinctures contrefaictes à plaisir pour exciter le monde à rire (quel fut Silene, maistre du bon Bacchus) ; mais au dedans l'on reservoit les fines drogues comme baulme, ambre gris, amomon, musc, zivette, pierreries et aultres choses precieuses. Tel disoit estre Socrates, parce que, le voyans au dehors et l'estimans par l'exteriore apparence, n'en eussiez donné un coupeau d'oignon, tant laid il estoit de corps, et ridicule en son maintien, le nez pointu, le reguard d'un taureau, le visaige d'un fol,...mais, ouvrans ceste boite, eussiez au dedans trouvé une celeste et impreciable drogue, entendement plus que humain, vertu merveilleuse, couraige invincible, sobresse non pareille, contentement certain, asseurance parfaicte, " etc., etc. — Rabelais, Prol., Bk. I.

1. *Works*, III, 345. Rabelais writes as follows : " Croiez vous en vostre foy qu'oncques Homere, escrivant l'*Iliade* et *Odysée*, pensast es allegories lesquelles de luy ont calfreté Plutarche, Heraclides Ponticq, Eustatie, Phornute, et ce que d'iceulx Politian a desrobé ? Si le croiez, vous n'approchez ne de pieds ne de mains à mon opinion. " — Rabelais, Prol., Bk. I.

many grains of sciences and arts ; into which the ants may creep and rest for a while, and then prepare themselves for fresh labours [1].

The Library of St. Victor is again cited in Essay III, *Of Unity in Religion*, first published in 1625.

There is a master of scoffing, that in his catalogue of a feigned library sets down this title of a book, *The morris-dance of Heretics*. For indeed every sect of them hath a diverse posture or cringe by themselves, which cannot but move derision in worldlings and depraved politics, who are apt to contemn holy things [2].

Apophthegm 46 (included in the first collection, 1625) refers to one of several remarks that have been attributed to Rabelais in his last hours.

When Rabelais lay on his death-bed, and they gave him the extreme unction, a familiar friend of his came to him afterwards, and asked him ; *How he did ?* Rabelais answered ; *Even going my journey, they have greased my boots already* [3].

Apophthegm 44 (contained in the second edition of the *Resuscitatio*, 1661, not in the original collection) is as follows :

Rabelais tells a tale of one that was very fortunate in compounding differences. His son undertook the same course, but could never compound any. Where-upon he came to his father, and asked him, *what art he had to reconcile differences ?* He answered, *he had no other but this : to watch when the two parties were much wearied, and their hearts were too great to seek reconcilement at one another's hands ; then to be a means betwixt them, and upon no other terms.* After which the son went home, and prospered in the same undertakings [4].

It is said by W. J. Harris that there was published in 1620 *Pantagruel's Prognostication, Certain, True and Infallible. Tr. by Democritus Pseudomantis* [5]. This book appears to be a lost work.

---

1. *Works*, IV, 438. The " old book " is entitled *Formicarium artium* (Rabelais, Bk. II, Ch. vii).
2. *Works*, VI, 381-82.
3. *Ibid.*, VII, 131.
4. *Ibid.*, VII, 170.
5. W. J. Harris, *The First Printed Translations*, 119.

Its loss is not of great consequence, but one would like to know more of the history of the mock prognostication in the 17th century. It would seem that a vogue was inaugurated by the three works of 1590-91 mentioned in the last chapter (of which one was found to be imitative of Rabelais, and which were followed in 1592 by the lost work with the puzzling title *Gargantua his prophesie*). In 1603, for example, was published *The whole prophecie of Scotland, England and some part of France and Denmark, prophesied bee mervellous Merling, Beid, Bertlington, Thomas Rymour, Waldhave, Eltraine, Banester, and Sibbilla, all according to one* [1]. In the next year we find *A Piece of Friar Bacon's Brazen-heads Prophecie. By William Terilo.* Two years later comes *Newes from Rome of two mightie armies...also certaine prophecies of a Jew called Cabel, Shilock...Translated out of Italian by W. W.* In 1609 appeared *The Ravens Almanacke* ; *foretelling of a Plague, Famine, and Civill Warre, that shall happen this present year 1609*, which has been ascribed to Thomas Dekker. Two other such works were *Cobbes Prophecies, his signes and tokens, his Madrigalls, Questions, and Answeres, with his spirituall lesson. 1614*, and *The Owles Almanacke* ; *prognosticating many strange accidents that shall happen. 1618...by Jocundary Merrie-braines.*

I have been unable to come at any of these works except the one ascribed to Dekker. That is an amusing pamphlet, gossipy and satirical, and perhaps typical of the lot. One would like to know. It cannot be shown to owe anything directly to Rabelais. The vogue apparently ceased with the translation of Rabelais's *Prognostication* by " Democritus Pseudomantis. "

Considering the slight possibility that the early Latin prognostications of Bebel might have been disseminated in England, the still more slight chance that Aretino's manuscript *Pronostici* ever passed outside of Italy, and the connection which exists between the *Wonderfull Prognostication* of 1591 and the *Pantagrueline*, it is possible that we are in the presence of a phenomenon which begins and ends under Rabelais's influence, or, at least, ends tem-

---

1. See bibliography of " Prognostications, Serious and Burlesque " in *Camb. Hist. of Eng. Lit*, IV, 604-05.

porarily, for prophecy of a satirical cast was popular with Grub Street in the Restoration.

Joseph Hall, bishop of Exeter and Norwich, already noticed for his verse satires, published his *Mundus alter et idem* in Latin prose in the same year that saw the first two books of the *magnum opus* of Bacon (1605). It is such an important illustration of the Rabelaisian influence that it must be briefly considered, although its language places it outside the strict category of English literature.

It has been ably analyzed by Mr. S. M. Salyer [1] and I cannot do better than set down some of the results of his study. The *Mundus*, like Books IV and V of *Pantagruel*, represents a fictional voyage, both following Lucian's *True History* and anticipating Cyrano de Bergerac and *Gulliver*. Like all these it is a satire on the vices of humanity at large, of nations, and of religious sects. Like *Pantagruel* " it is a burlesque on the monstrous travel yarns of the Middle Ages, and even on the serious but unreliable accounts of voyages of the author's own day. A thread of allegory runs through most of it, and the place-names have clever double meanings that defy translation but are inordinately amusing. "

" Hall depicts the discovery of a new world at the South Pole, where all the old-world vices are applauded as virtues, and where the prevailing modes of conduct are quite the opposite of those in the lands left behind. The new continent is people by four distincts nations, the gluttons of Crapulia, the viragoes of Viraginia, the fools of Moronia, and the brigands and mountebanks of Lavernia. Crapulia has two main divisions, Pamphagonia, whose inhabitants are gourmands, and Yvronia, where none but drunkards reside. "

There are numerous influences present, but the strongest are those of More, Erasmus, and Rabelais. Mr. Salyer calls Hall " a pigmy Rabelais, " a satirist who is " neither so buoyant" as the Master, " nor so saturnine as Swift, " but who partakes " in a measure of each of these qualities. " The description is apt, though one

---

1. " Renaissance Influences in Hall's *Mundus Alter et Idem*, " *Philol. Quart.*, VI, 321-34.

would not agree that Hall is " almost the sole representative of this [Rabelais's] manner from Rabelais himself to Swift. "

" The most striking Rabelaisian influence in the whole of the *Mundus* is seen in the Journey to the Sacred Bottle which occupies all of Chapter VII, in Book I, Part II. Clearly the main idea in this was suggested by Pantagruel's expedition,... although the narrative details are dissimilar. "

Rabelais's satire on the geographers includes remarks about " the Troglogytes, the Hymantopodes, or crump-footed nation, the Blemiae, people that wear their heads in the middle of their breasts ; the Pigmies, the cannibals, the Hyperboriae and their mountains [1] " ; and Mr. Salyer finds that " Hall [also] pokes fun at all these myths. "

In Lavernia, or Thief Land, " a terrible forest on a mountain, infested with banditti, is described, and one county of the kingdom is given over to the plagiarists " (Bk. IV, Ch. II and VII). The conception is apparently taken from Rabelais's isle of Ganabin, " terre des voleurs et larrons " which Pantagruel bombards " pour saluer les Muses de cestuy mons Antiparnasse [2]. "

The name of the free city, Ucalegon, in Pamphagonia (in Bk. I, Ch. VIII) is taken from a nick-name of Panurge (in Rabelais, Bk. IV, Ch. XXII). It is placed on a rocky height, difficult of access, like the country of Gaster in Rabelais (Bk. IV, Ch. LVII), and the name of the latter evidently suggested that of Cagastrius, the emperor of Crapulia. The tactics of the Pamphagonians, who go to war with spits and forks as weapons, recalls Friar John's attack on the Andouilles (Rabelais, Bk. IV, Ch. XLI). The luxurious indolence of the citizens of Ucalegon may be partly owing to the example of the courtiers of Rabelais's la Reine Quinte (in Bk. V, Ch. XX and XXIII).

In Book IV, Chapter V, of the *Mundus* it is said that the worst disease in Lavernia is the " argentangina, " or silver quinsey. Pantagruel on one occasion says to Panurge, " Je vous vendroys plus tost silence et plus cherement, ainsi que quelques foys la vendit Demosthenes moyennant son argentangine " (Bk. IV,

---

1. Rabelais, Bk. V, Ch. XXXI.
2. Bk. IV, Ch. LXVI.

Ch. LVI). " In describing a bigot a whose devotion so essentially consists in kissing a cross that he must always have one at hand, Rabelais represents him as crossing his thumbs... [Bk. IV, Ch. LIII]. Hall has similar bigots in Moronia who can walk only with a cross gait " (Bk. III, Ch. VII, § 1).

The drinking in Yvronia was no doubt coloured by Rabelais, and at least one detail seems to be borrowed. Rabelais calls a distillery " une chapelle d'eau rose, " and Hall places a Burning Chapel in Pyraenia, or Whiskey-town (Bk I, Pt. II, Ch VII).

" Frequent word plays such as Rabelais indulges in are characteristic of Hall...[who]...feels bound to append a full glossary at the conclusion of his work... In his list of Paracelsan words (Bk. III, Ch. III, § 3) there is an imitation of many Rabelaisian catalogues of a like sort. Wherever Mercurius Britannicus travels he finds, as do Pantagruel and Panurge, old coins, epitaphs, and inscriptions over gates, all with their own clever fitness to the subject in hand, and all kindred in spirit. "

While Hall did well in looking backward for the best of the matter and manner of the *Mundus*, it is unfortunate that he also looked backward in choosing his language. Had the principal works of Erasmus and More been written in some modern tongue or tongues, they would probably be better known to-day than they are, so thorny is Latin for the many, and the same is true of the *Mundus*.

Sir Thomas Browne was as ardent a disciple of Rabelais as Bacon. A great scholar has stated that " it is but natural that he [Browne], for whom Lucian was the Rhetorick of Satan, should depreciate Rabelais [1] " ; actually Sir Thomas did nothing of the kind. On the contrary he saw fit to advise the student of French, a favorite language with him [2], to persevere even until he should master its Languedocian peculiarities, *solely a means to the exact understanding of that author* [3]. He alludes familiarly to two well

---

1. Rabelais, Transl. Urquhart and Motteux, ed. Whibley, I, LXXVIII.
2. See his letters written in the sixties to his son who was in France in *Works*, I, 3, 6, 7, 8, 14, 119, in which he is forever reminding him to work at his French.
3. *Miscellany Tracts*, No. VIII, *Works*, IV, 209-10 : " ...but although you are so well accomplished in the French, you will not surely conceive that you are

known passages in Books I and II, how Gargantua eat six
pilgrims in a salad [1], and the catalogue of the famous Library
twice cited by Bacon [2]. If evidence of his minute study of Rabelais were wanting, it is amply supplied by the following letter,
which has an interest of its own. It was reprinted by Wilkin
from *MS Sloan* 1827, as a footnote to *Miscellany Tract* No. VIII,
" Of Languages. " Whether it was ever sent to a correspondent is
uncertain.

Now having wearied you with old languages or little understood,
I shall put an end unto your trouble in modern French, by a short
letter composed by me for your sake, though not concerning yourself ;
wherein, though the words be plain and genuine, yet the sense may
afford some trouble.

Monsieur,—Ne vous laisses plus manger la laine sur le dors. Regardes
bien ce gros magot [3], lequel vous voyez de si bon œil. Assurement il
fait le mitou [4]. Monsieur, vous chausses les lunettes de travers, ne

---

master of all the languages in France, for to omit the Briton, Britonant, or old
British, yet retained in some part of Britany, I shall only propose this unto your
construction.

Chavalisco d'asquestes Boemes chems an freitado, lou cap...

This is part of that language which Scaliger nameth Idiotismus Tectofagicus
or Langue d'oc, counterdistinguishing it unto the Idiotismus Francicus or
Langue d'ouy.....

Without some knowledge herein you cannot exactly understand the works
of Rabelais... "

1. *Pseudodoxia Epidemica*, first published 1646, Bk. VII, Ch. xviii, § 5,
Works, III, 365. Speaking of Milo, he says, " And if that be true which Athe-
næus reporteth, he was little beholding to custom for his ability ; for in the
Olympic games, for the space of a furlong, he carried an ox of four years upon
his shoulders, and the same day he carried it in his belly ; for as it is there delivered, he eat it up himself. Surely he had been a proper guest at Grandgousier's
feast, and might have matched his throat that eat six pilgrims for a salad. "
The references are to Rabelais, Bk. I, Ch. iv, v, and xxxviii. Cf. Harvey,
above.

2. *Religio Medici*, written c. 1635, pub. 1642, *Works*, II, 31. " There are a
bundle of curiosities, not only in philosophy, but in divinity, proposed and
discussed by men of most supposed abilities, which indeed are not worthy our
vacant hours, much less our serious studies. Pieces only fit to be placed in
Pantagruel's library, or bound up with Tartaretus, *De Modo Cacandi*. "

3. Rabelais uses this word repeatedly in both singular and plural, referring
no doubt to the " Gotz et Magotz " of the *Grandes Croniques*, meaning *lout* or
calf, always as a term of abuse. Thus in Bk. I, Ch. liv, and Bk. IV, Ch. xix
and lvi.

4. " He is playing the hypocrite. " Cf. *mitouard*, meaning *hypocrite*, in
Rabelais.

voyant point comme il pratique vos dependants. Il s'est desïa gueri [1]
de mal Saint François [2], et bride sa mule a vostre depens. Croyez-moi,
il ne s'amusera pas à la moutarde [3] ; mais, vous ayant miné et massacré
vos affaires, au dernier coup il vous rendra Monsieur sans queue.
Mais pour l'autre goulafie et beuueur a tire la rigau [4], qui vous a si
rognement fait la barbe, l'envoyes vous a Pampelune [5]. Mais aupara-
vant, a mon advis, il auroit a miserere jusques a vitulos [6], et je le ferois
un moutton de Berry [7]. En le traittant bellement et de bon conseil,
vous assuyes de rompre un anguille sur les genoux [8]. Ne lui fies poynt:
il ne rabbaissera le menton, et mourra dans sa peau. Il scait bien que les
belles paroles n'escorchent pas la guele, les quelles il payera a sepmaine
de deux Jeudies [9]. Chasses le de chez vous a bonne heure, car il a esté
a Naples sans passer les monts [10] ; et ancore que parle en maistre, est
patient de St. Cosme [11].
Soucies vous aussi de la garcïonaire, chez vous, qu'elle n'ayst le
mal de neuf mois. Assurement elle a le nez tourné à la friandise, et les
talons bien courts [12]. Elle jouera voluntiers a l'Home ; et si le hault ne
defend le bas, avant la venue des cicoignes [1], lui s'enlevera la juppe.

1. Wilkin, *queri.*
2. A disease cured by a doctor of the Quintessence, namely poverty, in Bk. V,
Ch. xxi.
3. Rabelais often uses this phrase in its culinary sense, and at least once
figuratively, in Bk. II, Ch. xxi : " ...feut faicte une Chanson, dont les petitz
enfans alloyent à la moustarde. "
4. Rabelais, " boyre à tyre larigot, " Bk. I, Ch. vii, Bk. II, Ch. xxviii ; " Leur
boitte fut en tirelarigotz, " Bk. V, Ch. xxxiii *bis.* For etymology see *R. E. R.,*
VII, 353 ff. Wilkin, *benueur* for *beuueur.*
5. The name of a dance, according to the author of the probably apocryphal
chapter xxxiii *bis* in Rabelais, Bk. V.
6. *Miserere* and *vitulos* are the first and last words of the seven Penitential
Psalms. See Rabelais, Bk. III, Ch. xxiii.
7. " C'est vn mouton de Berry, il est marqué sur le nez. *He hath gotten a rap
ouer the nose (whereon the Shepheards of* Berry *marke their Sheepe*). "—Cotgrave,
Dictionary, 1632, under " mouton. "
8. " You are attempting the impossible. " The expression is evidently taken
from the title of Chapter xli of Rabelais, Bk. IV, " Comment Pantagruel Rompit
Les Andouilles aux Genoulx. "
9. That is, " never. "
10. " He has got something for nothing. " Wilkin, *estè* for *esté.*
11. Another expression meaning, " he has deceived you. " It seems to refer
to one of Gargantua's games, " Saint Cosme, je te viens adorer " (Bk. I, Ch. xxii).
This game, as played in the 16th century, was used as a means of playing a practical joke upon the uninitiated. The victim was made to play the saint, and
was seated on a chair, blindfolded. The others, pretending to " adore " him,
blackened his face. See note 154 in Lefranc edition, Vol. I, p. 205.
12. Meaning, " she is given to falling on her back. " One of the doctors of the
Quintessence, in Rabelais, Bk. V, Ch. xxi, rejuvinates old women, by recasting

Mais, pour le petit Gymnosophiste chez vous, caresses le vous aux bras ouverts. Voyez vous pas comme a toutes les menaces de Fortune il branle comme la Bastille ? Vrayment, il est Stoic a vingt-quatre carrats [2], et de mesme calibre avec les vieux Ascetiques. Alloran [3] lui vault autant que l'Isle de France, et la tour de Cordan [4] lui vault le mesme avec la Louvre.

Serviteur très-humble,
Thomas Broune [5].

For all the study of Rabelais that this document represents, Sir Thomas seems to have been surprisingly obdurate to his influence. As a coiner of words he may have been to some extent inspired by him, but in this capacity he needed no other motive than the bent of his own mind and the supreme command of classical literature which he possessed. Should some academician of the Quintessence, of Lagado, or of Erewhon, pause from his more exacting labours to undertake an analysis of Browne's vocabulary, he would probably find it as vast as Rabelais's own and as a whole quite independent of it. It is certainly lacking in the popular element. Rabelais's virtuosity with words is pervaded by the jocularity of a drinker and scholar addressing drinkers and the pockified ; but Browne, as Walter Pater remarks, addresses no public at all, only the " friendly reader [6]." To him the grave scientist unfolds his sonorous pedantry with no fear

---

every part of them " excepté seulement les talons, lesquels leur restoient trop plus courts que n'estoient en leur premiere jeunesse. Cela estoit la cause pourquoy elles, d'orenavant, à toutes rencontres d'hommes, seront moult subjettes et faciles à tomber à la renverse. " Short heels are one of the qualities of the " garses " of the Frere Fredon in Bk. V, Ch. xxviii.

1. Understatement intended to mean " sooner or later, " a modification of Rabelais's expression " a la venue des coquecigrues, " which, since there are no such birds, means " never. " See Book I, Ch. xlix.

2. The idiom occurs in Rabelais, Bk. III, Ch. xxxviii. Triboullet is " Fol à XXIIII caratz. "

3. " Alloran, Allusama, or Insula Erroris ; a small desolate barren island, whereon nothing liveth but coneys, in the Mediterranean sea, between Carthagena and Calo-de-tres-furcus, in Barbary. "—Author's note.

4. " A small island or rock, in the mouth of the river Garonne, with one tower in it, where a man liveth, to take care of lights for such as go to, or come from, Bordeaux. "—Author's note.

5. *Works*, IV, 210-11, n. 8.

6. " Essay on Sir Thomas Browne, " *Works* (1901), V, 127.

that it will be misunderstood or treated as a public utterance, which is perhaps the same thing. Lacking " humor " in the general sense, he followed a " humour " in the Jonsonian, and however much he may seem to impose upon the patience of his confidant, the critic has no right to protest.

A single strand of influence may be perceived in his *Musæum Clausum, or Bibliotheca Abscondita : Containing Some Remarkable Books, Antiquities, Pictures, and Rarities of Several Kinds, Scarce or Never Seen by Any Man Now Living* [1].

This tract is droll, and yet gravely droll, if not drolly grave. The obvious parallels in Rabelais are the Library of St. Victor, which is equally fantastic, but different in having both a satirical and a farcical color, and the pictures bought by Panurge and Epistemon (Bk. IV, Ch. ii).   Here are some of the more pleasing treasures : " An exact account of the Life and Death of Avicenna, confirming the account of his death by taking nine clysters together in a fit of the colic, and not as Marino, the Italian poet, delivereth, by being broken on the wheel :   left with other pieces by Benjamin Tudelensis, as he travelled from Saragossa to Jerusalem, in the hands of Abraham Jarchi, a famous Rabbi of Lunet, near Montpellier, and found in a vault when the walls of that city were demolished by Lewis the Thirteenth " ; " Epicurus *De Pietate* " ; " a Tragedy of Thyestes, and another of Medea, writ by Diogenes the Cynick " ; " Seneca's Epistles to St-Paul. " Most of the titles are " curious " rather than humorous.   Thus among the pictures there is :   " An elephant dancing upon the ropes, with a negro dwarf upon his back ; [and] Another describing the mighty stone falling from the clouds into Aegospotamos or the goats' river in Greece, which antiquity could believe that Anaxagoras was able to foretel half a year before. "   Other rarities include: " A large ostrich's egg, whereon is neatly and fully wrought that famous battle of Alcazar, in which three kings lost their lives " ; " *Batrachomyomachia,* or the Homerican battle between frogs and mice, neatly described upon the chisel bone of a large pike's jaw. "   " He who knows where all this treasure

---

1. *Miscellany Tracts*, No. XIII, *Works*, IV, 239-50.

is, " says Sir Thomas, " is a great Apollo.   I'm sure I am not he. "

The last matter to be mentioned in this place us a mock will of James Howell, historian, poet, and editor of Cotgrave. This is found in a letter dated March 26th, 1643, in which he bequeaths his knowledge of French " to my most honour'd Lady, the Lady *Core*, and it may help her something to understand *Rabelais* [1]. "

---

1. In *Familiar Letters*, ed. Jacobs (1892), II, 422 ; noticed by Upham, *The French Infl. in Eng. Lit.*, 261.

CHAPTER IV

THE AGE OF DRYDEN

The translators: Urquhart, Motteux, Ozell. Imitators and critics: John Hall, *Bibliotheca Fanatica*, *A Catalogue of Books*, John Phillips, Samuel Butler, N. D., M. Y., John Eachard, John Oldham, Tom Brown, Sir William Temple, Thomas Rymer, Peter Motteux, and others.

a) The Translators.

The work of Rabelais was like a mold into which the supple, nay the fluid, Sir Thomas Urquhart poured himself. Not only his translation of *Gargantua and Pantagruel*, but his independent works and much of his inner life itself were shaped by it. So long as the mold remained in place, the cast was perfect : the translation was, in spite of its departures from the letter, which the critics have faithfully noted, an ideal one. In it Rabelais lives again, for it represents the wedding of the genius of the Master to a technique no whit inferior to his own. The mold removed, the cast, while still retaining much of the outward impression, breaks under its own weight : in the works outside the translation the constructive art, the symmetries, the strength, of the Master are wanting.

Sir Thomas Urquhart was born in 1611 [1]. He was the eldest son (he had five brothers and two sisters) of another Sir Thomas, whose ancestry is traceable from about 1300. The senior had inherited the estate of Cromarty unburdened in any way, but

---

1. The best lives of Urquhart are that by Thomas Seccombe in the *Dict. Nat. Biog.*, and one entitled *Sir Thomas Urquhart of Cromartie Knight*, by John Willcock (Edinburgh and London, 1899).

he proved a notable spender, and his son's life from his thirty-first year, when he came into possession, was harried by debt. The father had been the first of his tribe to abandon Catholicism, and he remained a loyal Episcopalian all his life, refusing to subscribe to the Covenant of 1638. The family life seems to have been generally affectionate and happy.

There can be no doubt of the thoroughness of Urquhart's education, and it was apparently gained under difficulties. His eccentric and recondite learning seems to have been largely owing to the inspiration of a great uncle, John Urquhart. Thomas matriculated at King's College, Aberdeen, and on leaving the University made the grand tour of France, Italy, and Spain. He took the pride of a true polyglot in being able to conceal his nationality, and yet was equally proud to defend it when occasion required. He tells of entering the lists thrice against men of three different nations in order to vindicate his own. He disarmed his opponents, spared their lives when they had " acknowledged their error, " and made friends with them all [1].

He returned about the beginning of 1639 to a career of the most strenuous activity as soldier, author, and squire. He fought against the Covenanters at the Trott of Turreff, and soon after joined forces of Charles I, by whom he was knighted in '41. He published his three books of Epigrams in London in that year.

His father's creditors seem to have been as unscrupulous as his management of the estate was incompetent. Neither the son nor his trustees were able to satisfy them, and it was no thanks to their importunities that he was able to settle to prolific writing in 1645, after another sojourn of three years on the continent. In that year he published the *Trissotetras* in London, an incomprehensible essay on trigonometry, and the extent of his ensuing labors may be gauged by the report of their frustration at the Battle of Worcester in '51. On this occasion he lost most of " an hundred manuscripts ", which amounted to 642 " quinternions " of five sheets each and filled three trunks [2]. He was imprisoned

---

1. *Logopan.*, *Works*, 311.
2. 'Εκσκυβ., *Works*, 189-90.

first in the Tower, and then in Windsor Castle, but his good conduct won his release on parole, and he resumed publication. Among those who exerted themselves on his behalf at this time he takes pains to thank especially " that reverend preacher, Mr Roger Williams of Providence in New England [1]. " His Παντοχρονοχάνον and 'Εκσκυβάλαυρον appeared in 1652, and the *Logopandecteision* and translation of Books I and II of Rabelais in 1653 [2].

No traces of his subsequent life have been found. It is thought that he remained in London for a few years at work on Book III of Rabelais (it was published posthumously in 1693), and that he died abroad.

Such was the external life, and it illustrates the inner man but meagrely. His subjective life was another story, one which has very little to do with ordinary reality. He lived in the past the future, projecting in detail the most Utopian political and educational reforms. So far from appearing to seek an escape

---

1. *Logopan.*, Epilogue, *Works*, 409.

2. The catalogue of the Bodleian Library of 1674 contains, under the name of Rabelais, this entry : " First Booke of his Workes into English. *Lond.* 1653. 8°. " The first edition of Urquhart's translation (in two volumes) contains both of the first two books, entitled, according to the *Dict. Nat. Biog.* (under Urquhart), " 'The First [and ' The Second Book '] Book of the Works of Mr. Francis Rabelais, Doctor in Physick... now faithfully translated into English by S. T. U. C.,' London, for Richard Baddeley, 1653 (2 vols. 8 vo). " Whether the entry in the catalogue refers to Urquhart's work or to that of some other translator is an open question. The commendatory verses accompanying Motteux's translation of the last two books in 1694 contain two disparaging references to earlier translators (verses by H. Denne and William Pittis ; see Rabelais, Transl. Urquhart and Motteux, ed. Whibley, III, 29 ff., ll. 28-33, and Regis, *Garg. und Pant.*, II, 1397, ll. 5-12). These references might be thought to point to some predecessor or predecessors of Urquhart, or to Urquhart himself. It seems unlikely, however, that Motteux's admirers should seriously belittle Urquhart. Both Nicéron and Regis believe in the possibility that Urquhart was anticipated (Nicéron, *Mémoires pour servir à l'Histoire des Hommes Illustres dans la République des Lettres*, XXXII, 390-391 ; Regis, *Garg. und Pant.*, II, CLXXI-CLXXII). Both quote the Bodleian catalogue entry, but neither quotes the title page of Urquhart's first edition. I venture the view that the verses of Dennis and Pittis refer to the lost English version of Girault's *Croniques admirables* (see above, Ch. II, a). That work used to be ascribed to Rabelais, not only by ignorant men like John Taylor (see my edition of Girault, Intro., XXVIII), but even by certain critics of the 19th century (see, e.g., the Introduction by Paul Lacroix to *La Seconde Chronique de Gargantua et de Pantagruel*, Paris, 1872).

from his environment, he grappled with it tirelessly in the hope of subduing it to his quixotic ideals.

Many Urquhartians are familiar with the following anecdote in *Logopandecteision* which illustrates his highly individual notions of right living. One day a guest at Cromarty went shooting birds, the weather being raw and wintry, and returned with a full pouch to receive the congratulations of the neighbors. Urquhart, being blamed for not giving himself to the same kind of exercise, answered :

though the gentleman deserved praise for the evident proof he had given that day of his inclination to thrift and laboriousness, that nevertheless I was not to blame, seeing whilst he was busied about that sport, I was imployed in a diversion of another nature, such as optical secrets, mysteries of natural philosophie, reasons for the varietie of colours, the finding out of the longitude, the squaring of a circle, and wayes to accomplish all trigonometrical calculations by sines, without tangents, with the same compendiousness of computation, which, in the estimation of learned men, would be accounted worth six hundred thousand partridges, and as many moor-fowles.

Urquhart turned from his researches next day to break a wild horse, while his rival was unable to rise out of bed, " by reason of the Gout and Sciatick [1]. " The moral of the tale, in view of the risks attendant upon breaking horses, is not very clear. A more telling illustration of the devious workings of the Urquhartian logic is the book in which he supposed that he was simplifying the science of trigonometry, namely the *Trissotetras*. Its title page alone suffices to betray the paradox of its author's claim, even to the non-mathematically minded.

He suppressed the authentic genealogy of his family, and, with the same zeal which went into *The Trissotetras*, invented another. He published it under the title of the Παντοχρονοχάνον.

God the Father, Son and Holy Ghost, who were from all eternity, did in time of nothing create red earth ; of red earth framed Adam, and of a rib out of the side of Adam fashioned Eve. After which creation, plasmation, and formation, succeed the generations [2].

---

1. *Logopan.*, § 51, *Works* (Edinburgh, 1834), 331-32.
2. Παντοχρον., *Works*, 155.   The genealogy fills some twenty pages in 4⁰, and contains accounts of the more memorable scions.   It was reprinted minus the biographical matter in the Ἐκσκυβάλαυρον.

Sir Thomas was one hundred and fifty third in descent from the
" red earth, " the male line being as follows :

1. Adam	42. Hypotyphos	83. Astioremon
2. Seth	43. Melobolon	84. Phronematias
3. Enos	44. Propetes	85. Lutork
4. Cainan	45. Euplocamos	86. Machemos
5. Mahalaleel	46. Philophon	87. Stichopaeo
6. Jared	47. Syngenes	88. Epalomenos
7. Enoch	48. Polyphrades	89. Tycheros
8. Methusalah	49. Cainotomos	90. Apechon
9. Lamech	50. Rodrigo	91. Enacmes
10. Noah	51. Dicarches	92. Javan
11. Japhet	52. Exagastos	93. Lematias
12. Javan	53. Denapon	94. Prosenes
13. Penuel	54. Artistes	95. Sosomenos
14. Tycheros	55. Thymoleon	96. Philalethes
15. Pasiteles	56. Eustochos	97. Thaleros
16. ESORMON	57. Bianor	98. Polyaenos
17. Cratynter	58. Thryllumenos	99. Cratesimachos
18. Thrasymedes	59. Mellessen	100. Eunaemon
19. Evippos	60. Alypos	101. Diasemos
20. Cleotinus	61. Anochlos	102. Saphenus
21. Litoboros	62. Homognios	103. Bramoso
22. Apodemos	63. Epsephicos	104. Celanas
23. Bathybulos	64. Eutropos	105. Vistoso
24. Phrenedon	65. Coryphaeus	106. Polido
25. Zameles	66. Etoimos	107. Lustroso
26. Choronomos	67. Spudaeos	108. Chrestander
27. Leptologon	68. Eumestor	109. Spectabundo
28. Aglætos	69. Griphon	110. Philodulos
29. Megalonus	70. Emmenes	111. Paladino
30. Evemeros	71. Pathomachon	112. Comicello
31. Callophron	72. Anepsios	113. Regisato
32. Arthmios	73. Auloprepes	114. Arguto
33. Hypsegoras	74. Corosylos	115. Nicarchos
34. Autarces	75. Detalon	116. Marsidalio
35. Evages	76. Beltistos	117. Hedumenos
36. Atarbes	77. Horaeos	118. Agenor
37. Pamprosodos	78. Orthophron	119. Diaprepon
38. Gethon	79. Apsicoros	120. Stragayo
39. Holocleros	80. Philaplus	121. Zeron
40. Molin	81. Megaletor	122. Polyteles
41. Epitomon	82. Nomostor	123. Vocompos

124. Carolo	134. Edward	144. John
125. Endymion	135. Richard	145. Sir William
126. Sebastian	136. Sir Philip	146. William
127. Lawrence	137. Robert	147. Alexander
128. Olipher	138. George	148. Thomas
129. Quintin	139. James	149. Alexander
130. Goodwin	140. David	150. Walter
131. Frederick	141. Francis	151. Henry
132. Sir Jaspar	142. William	152. Sir Thomas
133. Sir Adam	143. Adam	153. Sir Thomas [1].

One of the author's many unrealized aims was a huge expansion of this toy.

...the aforesaid Sir Thomas purposeth, by God's assistance, to make mention of the illustrious families from thence descended, which as yet are in esteem in the countries of Germany, Bohemia, Italy, France, Spain, England, Scotland, Ireland, and several other nations of a warmer climate, adjacent to that famous territory of Greece, the lovely mother of this most ancient and honourable stem [2].

The sixteenth of the line was Esormon, a

soveraign Prince of Achaia. For his fortune in the wars, and affability in conversation, his subjects and familiars surnamed him 'Ωροχάρτος, that is [to] say, fortunate and well beloved. After which time, his posterity ever since hath acknowledged him the father of all that carry the name of Vrquhart... his wife Narfesia... was soveraign of the Amazons [3]...

The immediate object of the genealogy was to urge Cromwell

that the greatest State in the world stain not their glory by being the Atropos to cut the thred of that which Saturne's sithe hath not been able to mow in the progress of all former ages, especially in the person of him whose inward abilities are like to produce effects conducible to the State of as long continuance for the future [4].

In other words, Cromwell was desired to disencumber Cromarty from its creditors and to reinstate its ambitious proprietor.

---

1. 'Εχσκυβ., *Works*, 184-85.
2. Παντοχρον., *Works*, 174.
3. *Ibid.*, 156-157.
4. *Ibid.*, 152.

Urquhart's boasting was at heart generous and high-minded.   He
was prepared to give full value for the favors he asked, and never
doubted his ability to do so.   The 'Εκσκυβάλαυρον is in two parts.   In the first he outlines a
work on a universal language, a work of which he had already
written some part and lost it at the Battle of Worcester [1].   A
similar undertaking had been broached by Bishop Bedell in
1633, but never realized [2], and Urquhart anticipated the *Philosophical Language* of Bishop Wilkins of the Royal Society by
some fifteen years [3].   He shared Rabelais's love of words and
fertility in coining them.   He gave himself the pseudonym
" Parresiastes, " no doubt after the Parisians or " Parrhesiens, "
which means, according to Rabelais, " fiers en parler [4]. " It has
been pointed out that the modern chemical vocabulary is cons-
tructed on principles exactly similar to those which Urquhart
divulged more than a hundred years prior to its invention [5].   The
word was to him more than to Rabelais, more even than to Harvey, Nashe, or Sir Thomas Browne, the be-all and the end-all of
speech.   He thought Greek and Latin poor in vocabulary, and
wondered

why, after thousands of yeers continual practise in the polishing
of them by men of approved faculties, there is neither in them, nor
any other tongue hitherto found out, one single word expressive of
the vice opposite either to temperance or chastity in the defect, though
many rigid monks, even now-a-days, be guilty of the one, as Diogenes
of old was of the other.
But that which makes this disease the more incurable, is, that when
an exuberant spirit would to any high researched conceit adapt a
peculiar word of his own coyning, he is branded with incivility, if he
apologize not for his boldness with a *Quod ita dixerim, parcant Cicero-
nianae manes, ignoscat Demosthenis genius*, and other such phrases,

---

1. 'Εκσκυβ., *Works*, 190.
2. The reference to Bedell is made by G. Maitland in his introduction to
Urquhart's *Works*, xix-xx.
3. See *An Essay Towards a Real Character and a Philosophical Language*
(c. 600 pp., small Fol.), by John Wilkins, D. D., F. R. S. (London, 1668).
4. Παντοχρον., *Works*, 172 ; Rabelais, Bk. I, Ch. xvii.
5. By Hugh Miller, in *Scenes and Legends of the North of Scotland*, 154-55.

acknowledging his fault of making use of words never uttered by others, or at least by such as were most renowned for eloquence [1].

Failing to appreciate the lesson to be learned from those " renowned for eloquence, " he compares language with architecture, and deplores that it has been developed under kindred restraints. He concludes that

> The bonification and virtuification of Lully Scotus's hexeity, and albedineity of Suarez, are words exploded by those that affect the purity of the Latine diction ; yet if such were demanded, what other no less concise expression would comport with the neatness of that language, their answer would be, *altum silentium* ; so easie a matter it is for many to finde fault with what they are not able to amend [2].

The possibilities of his own language are infinite.

> First, there is not a word utterable by the mouth of man, which, in this language, hath not a peculiar signification by it self...
> Secondly, Such as will harken to my instructions, if some strange word be proposed to them, whereof there are many thousands of millions, deviseable by the wit of man, which never hitherto by any breathing have been uttered, shall be able, although he know not the ultimate signification thereof, to declare what part of speech it is ; or if a noune, into what predicament or class it is to be reduced, whether it be the signe of a real or notional thing, or somewhat concerning mechanick trades in their tooles or tearmes ; or if real, whether natural or artificial, complete or incomplete ; for words here do suppone for the things which they signifie, as when we see my Lord General's picture, we say, there is my Lord General.
> Thirdly, This world of words hath but two hundred and fifty prime radices...

. . . .

> Seven and twentiethly, In translating verses of any vernaculary tongue, such as Italian, French, Spanish, Slavonian, Dutch, Irish, English, or whatever it be, it affords you words of the same signification, syllable for syllable, and in the closure of each line a ryme, as in the original.

. . . .

> Seven and fiftiethly, The greatest wonder of all is, that of all the languages in the world, it is the easiest to learn ; a boy of ten yeers old

1. 'Εκσκυβ., *Works*, 195.
2. *Ibid.*, 195.

being able to attaine to the knowledge thereof, in three moneths space ;
because there are in it many facilitations for the memory, which no
other language hath but it self [1].

It has, in short, " sixty and three advantages above all other
languages, " and the author " might have couched thrice as many
more, of no less consideration then the aforesaid. "

The second part of the 'Εκσκυβάλαυρον has nothing to do with
the first. It is a history of the lives of a hundred and twenty
seven illustrious Scotsmen of the previous fifty years, written to
defend the good name of the country from aspersions cast upon it
by the Presbyterians. The best known of these heroes is the admirable Crichtoun. Urquhart's narrative of him is the longest of
them all, and is a thoroughly characteristic example of his independent writing [2].

The influence of Rabelais upon the style is, of course, dominant,
but it is that of Rabelais the technician, not the artist. The
humor which distinguishes Urquhart's great translation is almost
wholly absent, and he gives rein to the precepts of his theory of
language with no idea that he surpasses the Limosin scholar in the
excesses of his " verbocination, " or at least with no idea that the
practise is unbecoming. There is none of the salt of those irreverent and genial interruptions which render the most arduous
passages in Rabelais palatable. He borrows from the Limosin
the word *penitissim*, and the reader will recognize many other
Rabelaisiana, such as *hondersponderd*, *mountera cap*, *decumanal*,
Septembral juyce, etc., etc. The theme of the story is purely romantic, and it need scarcely be said that pure romance is not patient of
treatment in the grotesque style. The author admits in the chamber scene between Crichtoun and his lady that " To speak of her
hirquitalliency at the elevation of the pole of his microcosme, or
of his luxuriousness to erect a gnomon on her horizontal dyal, will
perhaps be held by some to be expressions full of obscoeneness [3], "
and so they are, not necessarily in themselves, but because they

---

1. 'Εxσxυβ., *Works*, 199-206.
2. *Ibid.*, 220-44.
3. *Ibib.*, 236.

violate the integrity of a supposedly idyllic passage. For the rest I know of no more spectacular display of sheer linguistic extravagance and originality than is sustained throughout this incomparable extract. The story does not ring true according to any ordinary canons, but its sincerity is unquestionable, and its very inchoate quality shows why it was possible for the author's mind to run so easily into the mold of *Pantagruel*. The fault of the creator was the translator's virtue.

The project of the language was set forth again as the first book of another conglomerate work called the *Logopandecteision*. That book was entitled, *Neudethaumata, or Wonders of the New Speech*. The other books are : *Chrestasebeia, or Impious Dealing of Creditors* ; *Cleronomaporia, or the Intricacy of a Distressed Successor or Apparent Heir* ; *Chryseomystes, or the Covetous Preacher* ; *Neleodicastes, or the Pitiless Judge* ; and *Philoponauxesis, or Furtherance of Industry*. These titles sufficiently indicate the chief scope of the whole, which was to bring home his plea that the government restore his estate. That done, not only will he work out the " New Speech, " but also undertake the improvement of his community in Scotland on a huge scale.

Urquhart is the only one of our writers who seems to have taken Rabelais on education and the conduct of public affairs seriously. The truth is, he took him over seriously. But for his creditors, says he,

I would ere now have banished all idleness from the commons, maintained several thousands of persons of both sexes, from the infant to the decrepit age, found employments proportionable to their abilities, bastant to afford them both entertainment and apparel in a competent measure ; by various multitudes of squameary flocks of several sizes, colours, and natures, educed out of the bowels of the ocean both far and neer, and current of fresh water streams, more abundance of wealth then that whole country had obtained by such a commodity these many yeers past ; erected ergastularies for keeping at work many hundreds of persons in divers kindes of manufactures ; brought from beyond sea the skillfull'st artificers could be hired for money, to instruct the natives in all manner of honest trades ; perswaded the most ingenious hammermen to stay with me, assuring them of ready coin for whatever they should be able to put forth to sale ; addicted the abjectest of the people to the servitritiary duty of digging for coals and

metals, of both which in my ground there is great appearance, and of
hitting of which I doubt as little, as of the lime and frees-tone quarries
hard at my house of late found out, which have not been these two
hundred yeers remarked ; induced masters of husbandry to reside
amongst my tenants, for teaching them the most profitable way, both
for the manner and season, of tilling, digging, ditching, hedging, dung-
ing, sowing, harrowing, grubbing, reaping, threshing, killing, milling,
baking, brewing, batling of pasture ground, mowing, feeding of herds,
flocks, horse, and cattel ; making good use of the excrescence of all
these ; improving their herbages, dayries, mellificiaries, fruitages ; setting up the most expedient agricolary instruments of wains, carts, slades,
with their several devices of wheels and axle-trees, plows and harrows
of divers sorts, feezes, winders, pullies, and all other manner of engines
fit for easing the toyl and furthering the work ; whereby one weak man,
with skill, may effectuate more then fourty strong ones without it ; and
leaving nothing undone that, by either sex of all ages, might tend to
the benefit of the labourer, or rather in applying most industriously the
outmost of their vertue to all the emoluments of a country farm, or
manual trade.

I would have encouraged likewise men of literature, and exquisite
spirits for invention, to converse with us for the better civilizing of the
country, and accommodating it with a variety of goods, whether honest,
pleasant, or profitable ; by vertue whereof, the professors of all sciences,
liberal disciplines, arts active and factive, mechanick trades, and
whatever concernes either vertue or learning, practical or theoretick,
had been cherished for fixing their abode in it.

I had also procured the residence of men of prime faculties for bodily
exercises, such as riding, fencing, dancing, military feats of mustering,
imbattleing, handling the pike and musket, the art of gunnery, fortifi-
cation, or any thing that in the wars belongeth either to defence or
assault, volting, swimming, running, leaping, throwing the bar, playing
at tennis, singing, and fingring of all manner of musical instruments,
hawking, hunting, fowling, angling, shooting, and what else might any
way conduce to the accomplishment of either body or minde, enriching
of men in their fortunes, or promoving them to deserved honours [1].

The Highlanders were therefore to receive the same educational
advantages as the son of Grandgousier, and Cromarty was to bask
in the sunlight of the prosperity which attended the reign of that
monarch in the Kingdom of the Butterflies. Grandgousier was
descended from Chalbroth, a giant of the time of Abel and Cain,

---

1. *Logopan.*, §§ 19-21, *Works*, 396-97.

and if his heredity was in some way responsible for the widom of his administration, Sir Thomas had taken care to give himself equal sanguinary qualifications.

Space does not admit of more than a summary review of the immortal translation. Its main aspects have been ably treated by Monsieur Lazare Sainéan [1], and I have drawn largely on his study for the following observations.

Cotgrave was, of course, the cornerstone upon which it was built. His *Dictionary* lacks only some thousand words [2] of providing a complete gloss to Rabelais, and he understood the spirit as well as the letter of his subject. With a profound knowledge of the "lingo of thieves and publicans" he combined the lore of the crafts, poetry, birds, flowers, proverbs, etc., etc. The solid merits of the *Dictionary* would require a volume to present. It contains everything from pedantic details like

Cope gorgée, *instead of* gorge coupée,

or

Hen hen hasch. *Feined words, wherewith* Rabelais *expresses a coughing,*

to droll and satirical definitions of proper names such as

Alcofribas. *A greedy glutton, a great devourer,*

or

Estrelin. *An easterling ; one of the east-parts, or of the Hansa-towns of Germany ; also a drunken huff-snuff, swaggerer, swash-Buckler.*

He corrects some of the misprints in Rabelais's text, though many escaped him, and he occasionally cites both a misprint and a correct form under the impression that both were correct. The most interesting point about him is this, that *confronted with doubtful forms, he is never at as loss to furnish an explanation.* It is a quality which, as Monsieur Sainéan suggests, Rabelais must have approved. The Master's affection for his scholarly people is

---

1. " Les Interprètes de Rabelais en Angleterre et en Allemagne, " *R. E. R.*, VII, 137 ff.
2. Sainéan gives a complete list of these, *op. cit.*, *R. E. R.*, VII, 147-58.

ever divided with that for Friar John, and Friar John, tireless of reiterating his ignorance of books, can yet quote classics or Scripture with a fine abandon. " Je ne suis pas clerc, " he says on these occasions, "les clercs le disent [1], " and Cotgrave occasionally reflects the same attitude.

The texts of Rabelais, Cotgrave, and Urquhart often represent an ascending scale of amplification. Thus

Rabelais.   ...abondance d'andouilles...   (Bk. I, Ch. iii).
Cotgrave.   Andouille.   *A link, or chitterling.*
Urquhart.   ...plenty of Links, Chitterlings and puddings.

It is well that Urquhart was without petty scruples in following Cotgrave to the letter when it pleased him to do so. Like other early translators, he frequently inserts the definition of an untranslatable or unfamiliar term into the text [2], and the effect is generally happy (Rabelais himself sometimes adopts a similar practise when using neologisms of which he is especially fond) [3]. The result is to reduce, though not to remove, the necessity of a commentary. The following is typical :

Rabelais.   ...es autres deslochoit les *spondiles* du col..., fendoyt les *mandibules*..., descroulloyt les *omoplates*, *sphaceloit* les greves, desgondoit les *ischies*, debezilloit les faucilles. Si quelqu'un se vouloit cacher..., faisoit voler la teste en pieces par la *commissure lamb-doïde*. (Bk. I, Ch. xxvii).
Cotgrave.   Spondyles.   *The knuckles, or turning joints, of the chine.*
Mandibules.   *The jaws.*
Omoplates.   *The shoulder-blades.*
Sphaceler.   *To mortify by inflammation.*
Ischie.   *The sciatica, or hip-gowt.*
Commissure lambdoïde... *Seame in the hinder part of the skull.*
Urquhart.   ...to others he unjointed the *spondyles* or knuckles of the neck..., cleft their *mandibules*, tore their jaws..., shook asunder their

---

1. Rabelais, Bk. V, Ch. xv.
2. Compare Florio's Montaigne, especially the medical terms ; see Sainéan, *op. cit., R. E. R.,* VII, 184.
3. E. g. *hippodromes*, " qui estoit le lieu où l'on promenoit et voltigeoit les chevaux ; " *microcosme*, " id est petit monde, c'est l'homme. " See Sainéan, *op. cit., R. E. R.,* VII, 181.

omoplates or shoulder-blades, *sphacelated* their shins..., inflamed their ankles, heaved off the hinges their *ishies*, their sciatica or hip-gout... If any offered to hide himself..., he made his head to fly in pieces by the *Lambdoidal commissure* which is a seame in the hinder part of the scull.

Monsieur Sainéan finds that where Urquhart is obscure it is often either because the *Dictionary* offers him no help or because he declines to avail himself of it.

Urquhart frequently retains French expressions in his text. Sometines, as in the case of puns, he has no other course. Thus,

In the like darknesse and mist of ignorance, are wrapped up these vainglorious Courtiers, and name transposers, who going about in their impresa's, to signifie *esperance* (that is, hope) have portrayed a sphere and birds pennes for peines : *Ancholie* (which is the flower colombine) for melancholy : ... a *corslet* for *non dur habit*, (otherwise *non durabit*, it shall not last) *un lit sans ciel*, that is, a bed without a testerne, for *un licencié*, a graduated person, as, Batchelour in Divinity, or utter Barrester at law... (Bk. I, Ch. IX).

Sometimes he wishes to preserve acoustic or other special values, as in : " nac petetin petetac tic torche lorgne " (Bk. I, Ch. XIX), " matagrabolising " (*Ibid.*), " retaconniculation " (Bk. I, Ch. III), " robidilardick " (*Ibid.*), " emberlucock " (Rab. *emburelucocquez*, Bk. I, Ch. VI), " coquecigrues " (Bk. I, Ch. XLIX), " incornifistibulating " (Bk. III, Ch. XXXVI), " philogrobolized " (Bk. II, Ch. x), etc.

At other times he seems to throw in a French word merely to please his whim. Thus he uses " humect " (Bk. I, Ch. v.), " lougarous " (Bk. I, Ch. VIII), " braguette " (Bk. I, Ch. XI), " botargos " (Bk. I, Ch. XXI), " andouilles " (*Ibid.*), " badot " (Bk. I, Ch. XVII), " clochepied " (Bk. I, Ch. XXIII), " brackmard " (Bk. I, Ch. XLIV), " cafard " (Bk. I, Ch. XLV), etc. Monsieur Sainéan has drawn attention to the naturalness of this rendering :

Rabelais. C'est *bien chien chié chanté* pour les discours. (Bk. III, Ch. XXXVI).

Urquhart. It is *Bien chien chié chanté*, well cacked, and cackled; shitten and sung in manner of Talk : ...

There is no consistency in his practise, for he sometimes translates words which one might expect he would have retained. Thus "maistre Mouche" becomes alternately "Mr. Mush" (Bk. III, Ch. xv) and "a fox" (Bk. II, Ch. xvi) ; "diable de Vauvert," "a terrible bustler and horrible coyle-keeper" (Bk. II, Ch. xviii) ; "diable de Biterne," simply "the devil" (Bk. II, Ch. xxvi), and so on.

There is a slight taint of gallicism in his proverbs, which he sometimes translates literally rather than logically. Thus

> *Rabelais.* ...escorchoyt le renard, disoit la patenostre du singe..., tournoyt les truies au foin..., saultoyt du coq à l'asne... (Bk. I, Ch. xi).
>
> *Urquhart.* ...He would flay the Fox, say the Apes Paternoster,... and turn the Hogs to the Hay,... leaped from the cock to the ass...
>
> *Rabelais.* A propos truelle... (Bk. I, Ch. xxxix).
> *Urquhart.* To the purpose of the truel...
>
> *Rabelais.* ...clerc jusques es dents... (Bk. I, Ch. xxvii).
> *Urquhart.* A Clerk even to the teeth.

It must be allowed, however, that such "transliterated" proverbs have a flavor all their own, which may have been nicely calculated.

Among Urquhart's gratuitous embroideries may be mentioned the terms of abuse used by the Cakemakers in Book I, Chapter xxv, the description of their fate in the next chapter but one, four additions to the Library of St. Victor, and lists in Book I, Chapter xii, and in the Prologue and Chapters xxvi, xxviii, and xxxviii of Book III. A final illustration may be given :

> *Rabelais.* Il en est veritablement quelque chose, force est que le confesse. Mais le grand effroy et vacarme principal provient du dueil et uloulement des Diables... (Bk. III, Ch. xxiii).
>
> *Urquhart.* I cannot, Goodly, deny, but that in these various things which I have rehearsed, there may be somewhat occasionative of the huge Yell and Tintamarre of the two engaged Bodies.
>
> But the most fearful and tumultuous Coil and Stir, the terriblest and most hideous Garboil and Hurry, the chiefest rustling Black

Sanctus of all, and most principal Hurly Burly, springeth from
the grievously plangorous howling and lowing of Devils...

The humor, the scholarship, the " parrhesia, " and the moral
attitude of Sir Thomas Urquhart were like Rabelais's own ; he
followed Grandgousier in his public ideals, the Lords of Kissebreech
and Suckfist in obscurantism, and Panurge in debt.   He termin-
ated his Gargantuan pedigree by dying, it is said, in a fit of
laughter on hearing of the restoration of Charles II.   The worst
that can be said of him is that his vivid imagination tended to
interchange the categories of the concrete and the abstract, the
possible and the impossible.   For the rest we need no other evidence but his translation to witness the greatness of his mind and
soul.   Rabelais was reincarnated in him, as he was also in Ben
Jonson, the chief differences between the two arising from the
presence in Jonson of a more independently creative talent. Monsieur Sainéan places Urquhart among the greatest of Pantagruelists :   certainly among those of England he stands alone
and supreme.

It remains to consider Peter Anthony Motteux, the translator
of Books IV and V, the *Pantagrueline Prognostication*, and the
Letters [1].   He was a Frenchman, born at Rouen in the year that
Urquhart is thought to have died, and came to England in 1685, to
rival his adoptive countrymen in their own language in the activities of the formidable Grub-street of that time.   He became editor, dramatist, and translator, and finally retired into the East
Indian trade.

He edited Urquhart's translation of Book III (which had not
been published before) in 1693, and the next year, having finished
his own rendering of Books IV and V, published the whole work in
five volumes.   It was reprinted in two volumes in 1708.   The
text was completely revised and annotated after Duchat by John
Ozell, and his version became the standard of the 18th century.
It was published six times from 1737 to 1843.

The best known accounts of Motteux's translation are probably

---

1. The best biography of Motteux is that by G. A. Aitken in the *Dict. Nat.
Biog.*

those of Charles Whibley[1]. Whibley is very hard on him. " Quick-witted, " " nimble, " " pert, " " vulgar, " " insensitive, " and " a tradesman ", are some of the epithets he uses, and evidence, alas, can be found to justify them all. He says of the age that " The romantic quality of Shakespeare and his contemporaries, faintly echoed under the first Stuarts, was forgottein in a timid classicism " ; that " it became at once a fashion and an ideal to write as you spoke ; and [that] the hacks of the day spoke with the accent of the coffee house[2]. " Peter Motteux was a hack. Whibley empha-sizes the influence of Scarron and his school, whose mission was the irreverent burlesquing of everything dignified or sacred. He points out that

slang, to the translator of Rabelais, is indispensable. The romance of Pantagruel and Panurge cannot be turned out of its own into any other tongue save by an artist in strange words. Urquhart was per-fectly equipped for the task, because his interest in oddly coloured speech never tired, and because, when he was himself at a loss, he made a liberal use of Cotgrave's Dictionary. Thus it was that his slang had ever a literary flavour ; it had already won the freedom of humane letters ; the dust of the street corner was not thick upon it. Motteux's slang was of another kind. It lacked literary association. The quickwitted Frenchman had picked it up in the gutter or the tavern ; he had caught it fresh-minted from the vulgar brains of his friends ; and, though it was lively enough to gain an instant laugh, it long since lost its humour... Nothing can be more impertinent than to interrupt the narrative of Rabelais with so foolish a catchword as " his name's Twyford. " To translate *maître d'eschole* by " the Busby of the place " is wofully to misunderstand the business of a translator. Still less excuse has Motteux, when, instead of the simple words " at dawn, " he indulges his fancy thus extravagantly : " when day, peeping in the East, made the Sky turn Black to Red, like a boiling Lobster. " The fact that he conveyed the image from *Hudi-bras*, where it was appropriate, to Rabelais, where it is a tiresome excrescence, does but heighten his sin [3]...

---

1. See the essay on Motteux in his *Literary Studies* (Macmillan, 1919), and his Introduction to Urquhart and Motteux's Rabelais (London, 1900), III, vii ff.
2. Rabelais, Transl. Urquhart and Motteux, ed. Whibley, III, xix-xx.
3. *Literary Studies*, 329-331.

It is conceded, on the other hand, that the translation has very solid merits of its own. Though it lacks dignity, it is always near the original, and when there is no chance of embroidery you may find passages which are no unworthy echo of the original prose [1].

Now Motteux had, I believe, more of a conscience than Whibley implies. In his preface to Book IV he displays a critical acumen in regard to his subject, of which, if we may allow the writer some little indulgence in his partiality for that portion of the romance which he is to render, a Dryden need not have been ashamed.

If uncommon Mirth, lively Wit, and deep Learning, wove into wholsom Satire, a bold, good, and vast Design admirably pursu'd, Truth set out in its true light, and a Method how to arrive to its Oracle, can recommend a Work, I am sure this has enough to please any reasonable Man. The three Books publish'd some time since, which are in a manner an entire Work, were kindly receiv'd :   Yet in the French they come far short of these two, which are also intire Pieces ; for the Satire is all general here, much more obvious, and consequently more entertaining... there was no small difficulty in doing Rabelais Justice...the obsolete Words and turns of Phrase, and dark Subjects, often as darkly treated, make the sense hard to be understood even by a Frenchman, and it cannot be easy to give it the free and easy Air of an Original ; for often what seems most common Talk in one Language, is what's often the most difficult to be made so in another ;... Far be it from me...to value my self upon hitting the Words of Cant in which my drolling Author is so luxuriant...

It was not less difficult to come up to the Authour's sublime Expressions. Nor would I have attempted such a Task, but that I was ambitious of giving a view of the most valuable Work of the greatest Genius of his Age, to the Mecœnas and best Genius of This... I'll not gravely insist upon its usefulness... I'll only add, that as Homer in his *Odysses* makes his Hero wander Ten Years through most parts of the then known World, so Rabelais, in a Three-months Voyage makes Pantagruel take a View of almost all sorts of People and Professions :   with this difference however between the Ancient Mythologist and the Modern, that while the *Odysses* has been compar'd to a setting Sun, in respect to the *Iliads*, Rabelais's last Work, which is this *Voyage to the Oracle of the Bottle*, (by which he means Truth) is justly thought his Masterpiece ; being writ with more Spirit, Salt, and Flame, than the First Part of his Works [2].

1. Rabelais, Transl. Urquhart and Motteux, ed. Whibley, III, xxii.
2. *Ibid.*, III, 20-24.

So much for Motteux's intentions ; what of his performance ?
Whibley's view is incontrovertible as far as it goes, but I believe
that it overemphasizes the shortcomings and understates the merits of a translation which at its best is the equal, and as a whole
but little the inferior of that of Urquhart.   Both works convey the
essential thing, that " certain Jollity of Mind pickled in the scorn
of Fortune. "   The scholar is more likely to be offended by the
improprieties of Motteux's slang than the layman, but for both the
offense has been somewhat mitigated by the passage of time.
Nearly two centuries and a half divide us from the language of
Will's, and though we may be able to recognize its vulgarities, they
have not that immediately jarring effect that the corresponding
ones of our own speech would have, and will, in the heat of the
narrative, escape many a reader altogether.   The argument is
impossible to illustrate with isolated citations, since it depends
upon the impression of the whole.   Let the unprofessional reader
think for a moment of Panurge in the storm, of the strange ways
of being akin in the country of Ennasin, of Pantagruel on the passing of heroes, or, if he will, of the whole of Books IV and V, and
ask himself candidly how many times he has ever had occasion to
remind himself that his interpreter in these high matters was Motteux and not Urquhart.   One may determine according to this
test how much or how little of what has been said in praise of
Urquhart should apply to his partner in the greatest contribution
that has been made to the lore of Rabelais in the English speaking
world.

b) *Critics and Imitators.*

There was no second edition of Urquhart's translation of Books
I and II of Rabelais for forty years after its publication.   In view
of its excellence this is somewhat surprising.   It is not impossible
that his publishers waited a few years for him to complete Book
III, or perhaps the whole work, not wishing to reprint only a portion of it, yet one would expect their scruples to have yielded
promptly had the demand been urgent.   The demand cannot have
been urgent.

But it was Urquhart and not Rabelais who was neglected. The French influence was strong at the time, and it may be supposed that a considerable number of the public who in other times might have had to depend upon a translation were then able to read their Rabelais in the original. If so the little regard paid to Urquhart would be partly, though by no means wholly, explained.

One admirer of Urquhart's work was his countryman, John Hall (1627-56), alias " J. de la Salle, " who wrote a dedicatory poem for the first edition. This is a eulogistic but discriminating criticism of Rabelais. It praises his learning, his humor, his " deep sense, " and " solid virtue. "

> For he was wise and Sovereignly bred
> To know what mankinde is, how't may be led :
> He stoop'd unto them, like that wise man, who
> Rid on a stick when's children would do so.
> For we are easie sullen things, and must
> Be laught aright, and cheated into trust,
> Whil'st a black piece of Flegme, that laies about
> Dull menaces, and terrifies the rout [1].

One can recognize the neo-classical age in the application of couplets to the prosy business of criticism, as well as in the emphasis on the moral and didactic values of its subject. This critic should be remembered who, notwithstanding the somewhat severe taste of his time, was able to find those values in Rabelais, and at the same time to enjoy what he calls his " wild disguise. " There were not many among the polite in the succeeding half century to share his enthusiasm [2] :   Rabelais was chiefly cultivated

---

1. Rabelais, Transl. Urquhart and Motteux, ed. Whibley, I, 4. On John Hall see *Dict. Nat. Biog.*

2. I have been referred at the eleventh hour by Mr. B. Jere Whiting to Edmund Gayton's *Pleasant Notes Upon Don Quixot* (London, 1654). Gayton clearly knew both his Rabelais and his Urquhart. He refers twice to Rabelais by name (pp. 34, 151), three times to " Garagantua " (pp. 33, 91, 269) ; uses the Urquhartian term " Nock-Andro " (p. 14 ; Urquhart's spelling is " Nockandrow. " — Bk. I, Ch. xiii) ; and conceives the pleasant fancy — which he expresses in the copious, breathless, and learned Rabelaisian manner — that the two volumes of " Don Quixot " were preserved from antiquity in the hollow tooth of Rabelais's hero (pp. 33-34 ; see below, Appendix F, p. 236). The book was preceeded by some verses by Anthony Hodges, in which Gayton is compared to Rabelais as a writer of wise and pleasant " Non-sence " (**2ʳ).

among the freer spirits of Grub Street. The latter had much to say about contemporary politics, and as political wranglers, can-whippers, and chirping mockers of women, pedants, lawyers, and whatever else the satirical muse can reasonably or unreasonably turn into sport, they could with obvious profit, and frequently did, call Rabelais into their councils.

There were, for example, two anonymous political tracts, published in 1660 and 1694 respectively, which seem to be related directly or indirectly in their general conception and in their scurrility to the Library of St. Victor. Both differ from the reflective and innocent *Musaeum Clausum* of Sir Thomas Browne [1], for they are local in scope and violently controversial. The first is entitled *Bibliotheca Fanatica* : or, *The Fanatic Library. Being a Catalogue of such Books as have been lately made, and, by the Authors, presented to the College of Bedlam* [2]. The following are some of the titles,

Canaan's Grapes ; being a taste of the virtues and fidelity of our Saints :

. . . .

But lately married : or a grave Reason why, amongst other Wares, he hath but for these two Years traded in Horns ; by Nicholas Gold, Rump Merchant.

. . . .

Lucri bonus est odor ex re qualibet ; a Treatise written in Defence of his seizing on the Boy's Close-stool Pan, and reserving the Contents for his own Profit, because the Lad was so profane to carry it on a Sunday ; by Alderman Atkins, Shit-breeches.

. . . .

Fistula in Ano, and the Ulcer of the Rump ; wherein is shewn, that there is no better Way to cure such Distempers, than a Burning, or Cauterising ; by the Rump-confounding Boys of the City of London.

The other work is *A Catalogue of Books, Of the newest Fashion, To be sold by Auction, at the Whigs Coffee-House, at the Sign of*

---

1. See above, pp. 109 f.
2. Reprinted in *Harl. Misc.*, VII, 141-44.

the Jackanapes, in Prating-Alley, near the Deanery of St. Paul's [1].
It contains these titles, among others :

Asperius nihil est humili, &c. A new-invented mathematical instrument,
by the help of which one may discover, that, the higher a jackanapes
climbs, the more he shows his arse...

. . . .

Asinus ad Lyram : An argument in law, proving, That killing of
horses is downright murder. Published as a caution to prevent the
effusion of christian blood...
In dubiis tutior pars. Or, the broad way to save a man's bacon, and
damn his soul.

John Phillips, one of the two renegade nephews of Milton,
is said by Charles Whibley to have written an imitation of the
prognostication of Pantagruel [2]. Whibley no doubt refers to
Montelion, 1660 ; *or the Prophetical Almanack : being a True
and Exact Account of all the Revolutions that are to happen in the
world this present year*, 1660, *till this time twelvemonth, by Montelion, knight of the Oracle, a well-wisher to the Mathematicks*, the
authorship of which is ascribed to Phillips by Sir Sidney Lee [3].
It was written, according to the latter, " in ridicule of the anti-
monarchical views and astrological almanacs of William Lilly. "
I have been unable to examine the text, and have, therefore, no
idea of how closely it may follow Rabelais.   Tom Brown, we shall,
see, also wrote a mock almanac, no doubt with the example of
Pantagruel in his mind, for he was a professed Rabelaisian, though
none of its details seems to be borrowed.

Another work of John Phillips is *Speculum Crape-Gownorum*
(1682), an attack on the pulpit, " largely borrowed from Eachard's
Grounds and Occasions of the Contempt of the Clergy [4]. " It ends
with a sermon on a text from *Gargantua*, which, being an all too
faithful parody of dull, repetitious sermonizing, is itself insuffer-
ably dull [5].

---

1. Reprinted in *Harl. Misc.*, XII, 257-62.
2. *Camb. Hist. of Eng. Lit.*, IX, 295.
3. *Dict. Nat. Biog.*, under John Phillips, 1631-1706.
4. *Dict. Nat. Biog.*
5. Phillips evidently read Rabelais in French, for his translation of the pas-

There are a few echoes of Rabelais in the writings of Samuel Butler. He must have read Rabelais in French, for he alludes to portions of his work which were not translated until after his death. He died in 1680, aged about sixty-eight, and some time, probably late, in his career wrote a collection of " characters, " which was first published in 1759 under the title of *The Genuine Remains.*

The character of " An Herald " recalls Rabelais on the colors and dress of Gargantua. The Herald

professes Arms not for use, but Ornament only, and yet makes the basest Things in the World, as Dogs-Turds and Women's Spindles, Weapons of good and worshipful Bearings... He makes Pedigrees as 'Pothecaries do Medecines, when they put in one Ingredient for another that they have not by them... [1]

Rabelais speaks of

ces glorieux de court, et transporteurs de noms, leszqelz, voulens en leurs devises signifier *espoir*, font pourtraire une *sphere* ; des *pennes* l'oiseaulx, pour *poines* ;... [etc., etc.]... et un *estront de chien*, c'est un *tronc de céans*, où gist l'amour de m'amye [2].

Butler's character of " A Catchpole, " or bailiff (not included in the *Remains* of 1759) was almost certainly suggested by the Chicanous of Rabelais. The Catchpole

...eats his bread, not with the sweat, but the blood of his brows, and keeps himself alive, like those that have issues, by having holes made in his skin ; for it is part of his vocation to be beaten, when it falls in his way, and sometimes kil'd if occasion serve [3].

It will be remembered that four chapters of Book IV of Pan-

---

sage he used for his text does not agree with that of Urquhart. It is, in his words, " Rabelais, *Chap.* 32. *Vertu nescio quo. The* [n] Grandgousier *sending to know what the matter was, found that some of his people had taken certain Simnels from the Subjects of* Picrochol. " — *Speculum Crape-Gownorum* (London, 1682), 25.

1. *Characters*, ed. Waller, 76.
2. Bk. I, Ch. ix.
3. *Characters*, 204.

tagruel (Ch. xii-xvi) are devoted to describing how the catchpoles live by being beaten.

The influence of Rabelais is traceable in *Hudibras* [1], though it is less obvious than that of Cervantes, which accounts for the plan of its rather slight story. That it owed something also to the *Satire Ménippée* was noticed by Voltaire, and the influence of Scarron's *Virgile Travesti* has been suggested by W. F. Smith [2]. The Puritan knight is, of course, a conscious travesty of Don Quixote. He is the soul of degradation, fat, dirty, perverse, mean, and suscipious. He is as vile as Panurge, and quite as learned, but is unredeemed by the affable wit of that character. The poem is grotesque satire, with this essential difference from the type perfected by Rabelais, that the point of view of the writer is devastatingly unsympathetic to the object of his attack. Rabelais introduces but few characters so evil as to be beyond redemption, or at least beyond understanding, and such as he does are symbolical, not realistic. All of his main characters, and all of the minor ones who are individualized to any extent, have some claim upon our sympathies. *Hudibras*, on the other hand, is a story of dog eat dog, or more accurately, dirty dog eat dirty dog.

It is clear, however, that the poem gave plenty of scope for the emulation of Rabelais in the invention of monstrous imagery. It is perhaps surprising that so little borrowing is actually to be found.

The ostentation of learning by Hudibras, by the squire Ralpho, and by the astrologer Sidrophel, is to be referred partly, though by no means narrowly, to Rabelais *passim*. Dr. Johnson wrote in the *Lives of The English Poets*, " If the French boast the learning of Rabelais, we need not be afraid of confronting them with Butler [3]. "

1. Pt. I of *Hudibras* was published in 1663, Pt. II in 1664, and Pt. III in 1678. A spurious edition of Pt. I had appeared in 1662. See *Camb. Hist. of Eng. Lit.*, VIII, 82, and *Dict. Nat. Biog.*

2. Voltaire, *Lettres sur les Anglais*, No. xxii, *Œuvres Complètes*, Paris, 1876-78, V, 38 ; W. F. Smith, *Camb. Hist. of Eng. Lit.*, VIII, 72-73.

3. *Lives of the English Poets*, ed. Hill, I, 212.

Of Hudibras,

> ...'tis known he could speak Greek
> As naturally as pigs squeek :
> That Latin was no more difficile,
> Than to a blackbird 'tis to whistle...

. . . .

> For Hebrew roots, although they're found
> To flourish most in barren ground,
> He had such plenty, as suffic'd
> To make some think him circumcis'd...

. . . .

> He was in logic a great critic,
> Profoundly skill'd in Analytic ;
> He could distinguish, and divide
> A hair 'twixt south, and south-west side ;
> On either side he would dispute,
> Confute, change hands, and still confute [1].

The poet makes him a mouthpiece of satire when he says that

> He'd undertake to prove by force
> Of argument a man's no horse ;
> He'd prove a buzzard is no fowl,
> And that a Lord may be an owl ;
> A calf an Alderman, a goose a Justice,
> And rooks Committee-men or Trustees [2].

The goose-justice argument was probably suggested by Rabelais's Judge Bridoye [3].

Hudibras speaks ever in tropes,

> And when he happen'd to break off
> I' th' middle of his speech, or cough,
> H' had hard words, ready to show why,
> And tell what rules he did it by... [4]

---

1. Pt. I, Canto I ; text according to *Hudibras*, ed. Nash (New York, 1874), 37-38.
2. *Ibid.*, 38.
3. Rabelais, Bk. III, Ch. XL, XLI.
4. *Hudibras*, Pt. I, Canto I, ed. Nash, 38-39.

His language is

> A Babylonish dialect,
> Which learned pedants much affect;
> It was a parti-color'd dress
> Of patch'd and piebald languages... [1]

A mathematician, he

> ...by geometric scale,
> Could take the size of pots of ale;
> Resolve, by sines and tangents straight,
> If bread or butter wanted weight;
> And wisely tell what hour o' th' day
> The clock does strike, by Alegebra [2].

He is an admirer of commentators, having " read ev'ry text and gloss over, " and

> ...as occasion serv'd, would quote;
> No matter whether right or wrong [3].

He knows (notice the probable allusion to Rabelais, Bk. IV, Ch. LV, LVI)

> Where Truth in person does appear,
> Like words congealed in northern air [4].

He is said to be as expert in school divinity as Alexander Hales Thomas Aquinas, or Duns Scotus,

> For he a rope of sand could twist
> As tough as learned Sorbonist [5].

Now Ralpho's

> ...knowledge was not far behind
> The knight's, but of another kind...

. . . .

1. *Hudibras*, Pt. I, Canto i, ed. Nash, 39.
2. *Ibid.*, 40.
3. *Ibid.*, 41.
4. *Ibid.*, 41.
5. *Poetical Works*, ed. Bell, I, 49, n.   These lines were altered in the edition of 1674.

For mystic learning wondrous able
In magic, talisman, and cabal,
Whose primitive tradition reaches,
As far as Adam's first green breeches...

. . . .

He'd extract numbers out of matter,
And keep them in a glass, like water,
Of sov'reign pow'r to make men wise...

. . . .

He had First Matter seen undressed :
He took her naked, all alone,
Before one rag of form was on.
The chaos, too, he had descry'd,
And seen quite thro', or else he ly'd... [1]

He was, in short, familiar with all the lore of the Rosicrucians.
Sidrophel, the astrologer, possesses similar endowments, and
recalls, of course, Her Trippa in Rabelais.

He had been long t'wards mathematics,
Optics, philosophy, and statics,
Magic, horoscopy, astrology,
And was [an] old dog at physiology...

. . . .

He made an instrument to know
If the moon shine at full, or no ;
That would, as soon as e'er she shone, straight
Whether 'twere day or night demonstrate ;
Tell what her d'ameter to an inch is,
And prove that she's not made of green cheese.

. . . .

With lute strings he would counterfeit
Maggots, that crawl on dish of meat ;
Quote moles and spots on any place
O' th' body, by the index face ;
Detect lost maidenheads by sneezing,
Or breaking wind of dames, or pissing ; [etc., etc.] [2]

_____

1. *Hudibras*, Pt. I, Canto i, ed. Nash, 57-63.
2. Pt. II, Canto iii, ed.. cit., 260-63.

Like a certain academician of the Quintessence he knew

> How many scores a flea will jump,
> Of his own length, from head to rump,
> Which Socrates and Chaerephon
> In vain assay'd so long agone... [1]

Hudibras, it will be remembered, consults him in regard to his prospects of success with the widow, a matter akin to that which Panurge brought before Her Trippa in Rabelais [2].

The beard of Hudibras, like that of Rabelais's Panurge, is tawny [3]. His horse is large, has but one eye, " though some say none, " and its ribs show " like furrows. " Its tail is long enough to drag in the dirt, and its mettle such that not even the steed of Julius Caesar,

> ...who, as fame goes,
> Had corns upon his feet and toes,

trod more lightly upon the ground [4]. Such a nag in general was the Rozinante of Don Quixote ; but it also resembles the " meschante jument, " the " jument borgne, " of the Chicanous of Rabelais [5]. It further suggests the mare of Gargantua in its size, in its implied speed, and in that it is explicitly compared to the horse of Caesar [6].

Butler, finally, like Rabelais, draws extensively upon the classics for illustration and ornament.

The two most conspicuous aspects of *Hudibras* are the travesty of *Don Quixote* and the political satire of which it is the vehicle. The style throughout is that of travesty. Now travesty, it may be said without hesitation, is the lowest and most malicious form of humor. It is the art of making the sublime ridiculous, and no more than that. Such excellences as it may possess depend upon

---

1. Pt. II, Canto III, ed. Nash,, 265 ; *cf.* Rabelais, Bk. V, Ch. XXII.
2. Pt. II, Canto III.
3. Pt. I, Canto I, ed. cit., 46 ; Rabelais, Bk. III, Ch. XXVIII.
4. Pt. I, Canto I, ed. cit., 54.
5. Rabelais, Bk. IV, Ch. XII and XIII.
6. Rabelais, Bk. I, Ch. XVI. This and the references in notes 3 and 5 were made by W. F. Smith, *Camb. Hist. of Eng. Lit.*, VIII, 75.

a certain consistency in the lower style substituted for that of the work ridiculed. It readily degenerates into mere facetiousness, and at its best is inferior to the higher and related form of parody, which, reversing the method, may be defined as the art of making the ridiculous sublime. Though travesty is a recurrent motive in Rabelais, his work as a whole is a colossal parody. Whatever similarities may be found between the Hudibrastic and the Rabelaisian humor, the difference in spirit is fundamental. That difference may be summarily, but not unjustly, illustrated by comparing Butler's figure of the dawn turning from black to red like a boiling lobster [1] with Rabelais's remark, which may have inspired it, that the lobster is " cardinalized " by boiling [2]. Butler's figure degrades the dawn ; Rabelais's dignifies the lobster, and is therefore, quite apart from its legitimate satire, superior. This opinion does not involve the denial that man, not to mention the cosmos, may be, as Butler saw them, wholly absurd, nor even the denial that Butler represented their absurdity with more fluent, learned, amusing, and altogether unanswerable illustrations and arguments than any other English writer, except possibly Swift. It is based upon the proposition that a convincing illusion of man, absurd as he is, and whatsoever may be represented in his likeness, as partaking of heaven as well as of earth, is a greater artistic achievement than an equally convincing illusion that he is a jackass, — greater by as much as the one conception is remote from and difficult to reconcile with the other, and by as much again as the less plausible is impatient of proof.

The English Rogue, Part I, by Richard Head, was published in 1665, and Parts II to IV, by Francis Kirkman, followed in '71, '74, and '80. It is, as the reader will recall, a kind of modern counterpart of *Mandeville's Travels*, with the difference that it contains the element of humor and a good deal of ribaldry. The complete title is *The English Rogue : described in the Life of*

---

1. *Hudibras*, Pt. II, Canto II, ed. Nash, 218 :
   " And like a lobster boil'd, the morn
   From black to red began to turn. "
2. Rabelais, Bk. I, Ch. XXXIX.

Meriton Latroon, a Witty Extravagant. Being a Compleat History of the most Eminent Cheats of both Sexes. Two authors of commendatory verses, " N. D. " and " M. Y., " compare it to *Guzman, Buscon, Francion,* and Rabelais [1]. As regards the last, I can state with some confidence that the work contains no trace whatever of his influence.

Rabelais is cited in his capacity of prevaricator by John Eachard in his *Grounds & Occasions of the Contempt of the Clergy and Religion* (1670) :

It is usually said by those that are intimately acquainted with him, that Homer's *Iliad* and *Odyssey* contain, mystically, all the Moral Law for certain, if not a great part of the Gospel (I suppose much after that rate that Rabelais said his *Gargantua* contained all the Ten Commandments) [2]...

It has been suggested that Robert South, the great Restoration Divine, owes a passage in one of his sermons to Panurge on debt and debtors in Rabelais, Book III, Chapter III. The connection is tenuous, if it exists at all, and is impossible to prove [3].

John Oldham (1653-83) was a worthy though very minor Rabelaisian. A B.A. of Oxford, he taught for a living, first in a school at Croyden, and later as a private tutor, and died of smallpox at the age of thirty in a chaplaincy newly granted him by the Earl of Kingston. His poetry won the praise of Rochester, Sedley, Waller, and Dryden, but brought him no corresponding worldly advantages [4].

He is chiefly remembered for the fiery quality of his Satires on the Jesuits, which were inspired by the discovery of the Popish Plot. Juvenal was his model, and he assailed the Papists with bitterness and power. It is clear that the thought in these poems was that of the man in the street, not that with which their educa-

---

1. *The English Rogue* [1665], I, XI, XVIII.
2. *Crit. Essays and Lit. Fragments,* ed. Collins, 249.
3. See the passage beginning " And this it is, that shews the rare and distinguishing excellency of gratitude... " through " ...it must and will make him still greater. " — South, *Sermons Preached Upon Several Occasions* (Oxford, 1842), I, 228-30.
4. See *Dict. Nat. Biog.*

ted author might have engaged a Jesuit in private controversy. The tone is literary and political, scarcely judicial. On the literary side, if Juvenal lent him something of the sting of his invective, Rabelais taught him as much in the art of the grotesque. Of the Pope he says, in Satire III :

> Whate'er he says esteem for holy Writ,
> And Text Apocryphal, if he think fit :
> Let arrant Legends, worst of Tales and Lies,
> Falser than *Capgraves*, and *Voragines*,
> Than *Quixot, Rabelais, Amadis de Gaul* ;
> If sign'd with sacred Lead and Fisher's Seal
> Be thought Authentic and Canoncial... [1]

Like Rabelais he asserts his pretensions to veracity with zeal :

> Believe what e'er I have related here,
> As true, as if 'twere spoke from Porph'ry Chair,
> If I have feign'd in aught, or broach'd a Lie,
> Let worst of Fates attend me, let me be
> Pist on by Porter, Groom, and Oyster-whore,
> Or find my Grave in Jakes, and Common-shore [2] ...

The following, from *Satyr IV*, though the closed couplets give it an epigrammatic flavor which is foreign to the manner of Rabelais, is otherwise a highly Rabelaisian conception :

> *Hey Jingo, Sirs !* What's this ? 'tis *Bread* you see ;
> *Presto be gone !* 'tis now a Deity.
> Two grains of Dough, with Cross, and stamp of Priest,
> And five small words pronounc'd, make up their *Christ*.
> To this they all fall down, this all adore,
> And strait devour, what they ador'd before ;
> Down goes the tiny *Saviour* at a Bit,
> To be digested, and at length beshit :
> From Altar to Close-Stool, or Jakes prefer'd,
> First Wafer, then a God, and then a — [3].

The exuberant boldness of such invention shows that, while these satires are really open invectives, the invective is not that

---

1. *Works* (London, 1722), I, 39.
2. Satire IV, *Works*, I, 78.
3. *Ibid.*, 75-76.

of a mere water-drinking Protestant. Oldham, in fact, wrote a eulogy of Charles I, paid numerous tributes to Charles II, and made repeated ironical references to the dissenters. It has even been thought that he may at last have joined the church. His pæons to drink are as energetic as his abusive pieces, and have a lyric quality which the hoarse muse of Rabelais might have envied.

For example,

> Make me a Bowl, a mighty Bowl,
> Large as my Capacious Soul,
> Vast, as my Thirst is ; let it have
> Depth enough to be my Grave ;
> I mean the Grave of all my Care,
> For I intend to bury 't there,
> Let it of Silver fashion'd be,
> Worthy of wine, worthy of Me... [1]

Oldham once tried his hand at grotesque description in prose in a fragment called the *Character Of a certain Ugly Old P—*, first printed in 1684 [2]. It contains allusions both open and veiled to Rabelais, and is otherwise worthy of perusal. It will be found in Appendix D below [3].

Tom Brown is familiar to every student of the Restoration, if only as the author of a certain quatrain on Dr. Fell, and he takes a conspicuous place among the English Rabelaisians. He was the son of a prosperous farmer of Shropshire, and having matriculated at Oxford, where he gained an extensive if not very profond scholarship and a taste for dissipation, gravitated, after an interval of school-mastering, toward London and Grub street [4]. He was several times incarcerated for debt, and on one occasion barely escaped serious punishment for writing a lampoon on Louis XIV after the Peace of Ryswick. Toward the end of his life he came under the patronage of the sixth Earl of Dorset,

---

1. *An Ode of Anacreon Paraphrased,* — *Works*, II, 102-03. See also *A Dithyrambick*, II, 183-90.
2. " P — " probably stands for " Priest. "
3. P. 223.
4. See *Dict. Nat. Biog.*

but his unbridled tongue brought about an estrangement, and threw him again upon his own resources. He lived by a prolific output of pamphlets, satires, lampoons, and translations. He died of his excesses in 1704, repentant of his sins, requesting his bookseller to expurgate subsequent editions of his works. It does not appear that his wish was respected. The best known of his writings are the *Amusements Serious and Comical* and the *Letters from the Dead*, published in 1700 and 1702 respectively. His collected works appeared in 1707-08, and were reprinted seven times in the course of the century.

Tom Brown turned for literary models to the verse satirists and epigrammatists of antiquity, for he found in them the very breath of the town which was his element ; but he also cultivated Lucian and Rabelais. Rabelais, indeed, was forever upon his tongue. He alludes to the observation of Rondibilis that every married man is a potential cuckold [1], twice mentions how Friar John and Gargantua put themselves to sleep by singing psalms [2], and cites the Friar's remark that the very shadow of an abbey steeple is fertile [3]. One of his *Letters from the Dead* is from " François Rabelais to the Physicians of Paris, " and others are imitative of *Pantagruel*, Chapter xxx. He writes a long version in couplets of an anecdote told by Panurge, composes a prognostication distantly akin to the *Pantagrueline*, and scatters grotesque imagery and abuse of a Rabelaisian flavor throughout his work. Extracts from some of his imitations will be found in Appendix E below [4].

Now Rabelais, taken in his entirety, is the most unaffected of human beings, bold and reckless to a degree, but in a manner entirely congruent with the spirit of the circles, both high and humble, in which he moved. Bald speech came naturally to him, as well as highly ornamented speech ; neither was proper to the English Restoration. On the contrary its expression most char-

---

1. In " A Consolatory Letter to Mr. H——, on his being a Cuckold, " — *Amusements*, ed. Hayward, 182.
2. In a letter " To my Lady —— that married an old decrepit Widower, " — *Amusements*, ed. Hayward, 181, and in another from " Pindar of Thebes to Tom Durfey, " *Ibid.*, 243.
3. In a letter " To a young Lawyer that dabbled in poetry ", — *Ibid.* 209.
4. Pp. 229 ff.

acteristically took the form of subtle and elegant irony. Rabelais's irony is often subtle, but quite as often it is the irony of
saying that black is white or that chalk is cheese. He was therefore, like Sir Wilful in Congreve's play, something of a stranger
among everyday Augustans, and was taken up not only for those
of his ideas which happened to coincide with their own, but also
as a kind of monster invoked to tease their jaded taste. Nothing,
they might have said, could really shock them, not even the cult
of Pantagruel.

Familiarity, however, may breed both affinity and contempt,
and these things are apparent in the treatment of Rabelais which
we find in Tom Brown. Brown's way was to apply the general
and elastic satire of Rabelais to the local and temporary affairs
of London, or vice versa, to imitate his general satire in the Grub
Street language. Neither method could conceivably produce
anything worthy of comparison to the original. Not only, on the
one hand, were Augustan personalities too obtrusive and too
narrow for the development of anything so humane, but, on the
other, the language, as observed above with regard to the translation of Motteux, was unduly restricted in its connotations. In
the drawing room it was correct, in the coffee house, cant ; each
institution had its formulas, which agreed in principle, and they
were observed by all and sundry.

On the other hand, it would be idle to blame Tom Brown for
not being another Rabelais, if by so doing one failed to appreciate
his masterly journalistic ease and the patness and fluency of
his criticisms of the little world that he knew.

The first extract in the appendix is from the prognostication
(*A Comical View*, etc.)[1]. The work was, as its title proclaims,
to be " Continued Weekly " (the predictions cover three weeks,
and were published together), and the fact is significant. Rabelais's prognostications were originally for a year, and in later
editions, " pour l'an perpetuel. "

Brown's poem, *A match for the Devil*[2], is an illustration of the

---

1. Pp. 229 ff.
2. *Works*, 1715, IV, 63-69.

fundamental change which Rabelais suffers when treated in couplets [1]. Rabelais's anecdote has a human interest equal to that of the events in relates, for its characters are individualized and speak in everyday language. No moral is pointed. The poet, however, is sententious, and his persons and language mere forms. The contrast is apparent from the following passages. Rabelais writes thus of the return of the laborer to his wife after his perilous bargain with the fiend to meet him in a scratching bout :

Le Laboureur retournant en sa maison estoit triste et pensif. Sa femme, tel le voyant, cuydoit qu'on l'eust au marché desrobbé. Mais entendant la cause de sa melancholie, voyant aussi sa bourse pleine d'argent, doulcement le reconforta et l'asceura que de ceste gratelle mal aulcun ne luy adviendroit. Seulement que sus elle il eust à se poser et reposer. Elle avoit ja pourpensé bonne yssue. " Pour le pis (disoit le Laboureur) je n'en auray qu'une esraffade : je me rendray au premier coup et luy quitteray le champ. — Rien, rien, dist la vieille ; posez vous sus moy et reposez : laissez moy faire. Vous m'avez dict que c'est un petit Diable : je le vous feray soubdain rendre, et le champ nous demourera. Si c'eust esté un grand Diable, il y auroit à penser [2].

Brown renders this as follows.

> The wretched Farmer homeward goes,
> And dreads his future endless Woes.
> His Cares, his Dunns, his Wants, his Wife,
> And all the Banes of happy Life,
> Would now afford him vast Content,
> Could he the unequal Match prevent.
> His prying Turtle quickly guest
> Some care uncommon fill'd his Breast.
> Husband and Wife, sometimes relate
> Their Cares and Bus'ness, tho' they hate.
> Nor always *Nature's* Call deny,
> And tho' both loath, yet both comply.

---

1. Compare Prior's version of the story of Hans Carvel, which he adapted from La Fontaine, who, in turn, had it from Rabelais. It is further evidence of the incompatibility of Rabelais and couplets, if such were needed, though it is an admirable poem. It is printed in *The Shorter Poems of Matthew Prior*, ed. Francis Bickley (The Abbey Classics, No. XIX), 60-63. See Rabelais, Bk. III, Ch. xxviii.
2. Rabelais, Bk. IV, Ch. xlvii.

Her wheedling Tongue soon found the Means
To make the Wretch disclose his Pains.
He tells the Combat and the Laws,
And magnifies his monst'rous Paws.
   Pish ! Is this all that Plagues your Mind ?
An easy Remedy I'll find.
You to your Wife's Advice submit,
And we'll the Devil himself out-wit.
Come, turn about, — and leave your Moans, —
These husbands are such very Drones. —
He sigh'd, obey'd, and did his best ;
His Task perform'd he went to rest.

The *Letters from the Dead* is a collection of eighty two letters, mostly from the dead to the living, but some also from the living to the dead.   The dead include many figures of classical antiquity, such as Hannibal, Pindar, and the Cumean Sybil ; figures from modern history, like James II, Louis XIV, and Catherine de Medicis; various authors, including Rabelais, Dryden, Prior, and Mrs. Behn ; and other persons of divers interests, Nell Gwyn, Bully Dawson (a famous Restoration bully), Madam Cresswell (a famous bawd), etc. The ultimate source of this travesty of the Homeric underworld is, of course, Lucian ; but Tom Brown, like Bishop Hall and the dramatist Webster, both of whom broached the same theme, drew his immediate inspiration from Chapter xxx of *Pantagruel*. In both Rabelais and Brown we have the most flippant travesty, though the latter develops his at greater length and with a larger proportion of detail.   Investigation might well disclose the joint influence of the sixth book of Scarron's *Virgile Travesti*, for Scarron is the outstanding master of travesty in the century, and Brown held him in the highest regard.

   The first letter, one of the best, is from " Mr. Joseph Haines, of Merry Memory, to his Friends at Will's Coffee House in Covent Garden[1]. "   Mr. Haines apologizes for his presumption in attempting to write of that which has occupied the talents of " Homer, Virgil, Dante, Don Quevedo, and many more, " and describes most accurately the means of his descent into the shades.   Having

---

1. *Amusements*, ed. Hayward, 211-28.

entered a grotto and so passed on to the Styx, he is rebuked by
Charon, for he has no money. After some delay " an honest
teller of the Exchequer and a clerk of the pay office " defray his
fare, and Charon, his demands satisfied, becomes communicative.
He beguiles the crossing with a story about an Irishman ! This
is auscipious, and before long Mr. Haines begins to discover friends
and to feel at home. For instance " my friend Nokes, with that
gaiety and openness which became him so well at the playhouse,
' Joe, ' says he, 'I'll give thee thy welcome to Hell.' With
that he carried me to a little blind coffee house..." Their conversation runs in this wise :

" And who do you take this worthy person to be, " says Mr. Nokes.
" But that I am in this lower world, " cried I, " I durst swear it is the
very individual quaker that sells his herb-snuff at the Rainbow coffee-
house. " " Damnably mistaken, " says Mr. Nokes, " before George,
this is no less a man than the great Cyrus, the first founder of the Persian monarchy [1]. "

The letter includes a description of Diogenes as a fop, which
is clearly after Rabelais, for the Cynic in Lucian retains his traditional character [2].

The letter from " François Rabelais to the Physicians of Paris [3] "
is in the form of a brief autobiography. Some of the main facts,
such as birthplace, choice of profession, and identity of patrons,
and the serenely humorous tone, are quite in order. On the other
hand the confessions are those of the legendary, not the real,
Curé de Meudon. Thus he had an " inclination...to lewdness, "
he " lived luxuriously, " he " composed the history of Gargantua
and Pantagruel for the ignorant. " That is journalism, not
scholarship.

A final extract is included in the Appendix from his work, namely
the letter from " Beau Norton to his Brothers at Hippolito's in
Covent-Garden [4]. " It is a view of the present state of numbers

---

1. *Amusements*, ed. Hayward, 216.
2. *Ibid.*, 217-19. See Lucian, *Dialogues of the Dead*, Nos. 1, 11, 16, 27.
3. Below, pp. 231 ff.
4. Below, pp. 234 ff.

of the great departed, a continuation of the theme of the letter
of Mr. Haines. While it contains no borrowing from Rabelais
it is the closest imitation of any portion of Rabelais's work that
Brown wrote. More of the characters here belong to antiquity
than in the letter of Mr. Haines, and the local satire is less obtrusive.

It would be easy to draw up an array of superficial resemblances
between the thought of Tom Brown and that of Rabelais in regard
to women, cuckolds, the church, medecine, drink, and other
matters ; but for reasons already given it would be superfluous
and misleading. Enough has been said to indicate that the
minds of the two men met at many points, and that the contact
was fruitful.

Rabelais, to repeat, was something of an exotic among the
Augustans. Whatever the failings of their arbiters, exoticism
was not one of them. Dryden, to whom one naturally looks for
a representative opinion, says no word of him, and his silence
is eloquent. Sir William Temple, however, who has an almost
equal right to speak for the literary aristocracy which he adorned,
is explicit on Rabelais and aware of his power. " Rabelais, "
he says, in his essay *Of Poetry* (1690),

seems to have been the Father of the Ridicule [sic], a Man of Excellent and
Universal Learning as well as Wit ; and tho' he had too much Game given
him for *Satyr* in that Age, by the Customs of Courts and of Convents,
of Processes and of Wars, of Schools and of Camps, of Romances and
Legends, Yet he must be Confest to have kept up his Vein of Ridicule
by saying many things so Malicious, so Smutty, and so Prophane, that
either a Prudent, a Modest, or a Pious Man could not have afforded,
tho' he had never so much of that Coyn about him ; and it were to be
wished that the Wits who have followed his vein had not put too much
Value upon a Dress that better Understandings would not wear, at least
in publick, and upon a compass they gave themselves which other Men
would not take. The Matchless Writer of *Don Quixot* is much more to
be admired for having made up so excellent a Composition of Satyr or
Ridicule without those Ingredients, and seems to be the best and highest
Strain that ever was or will be reached by that Vein [1].

---

1. *Critical Essays of the Seventeenth Century*, ed. Spingarn, III, 101-02. In
Temple's *Essay Upon The Ancient and Modern Learning* (1690) he includes
Rabelais among the " great Wits " of modern times. — *Ibid.*, III, 66.

One should observe that it is as *satirist* that Temple both praises
and blames him : he is the " Father of Ridicule. " How much
of his subject the critic failed to penetrate, and how seriously he
misunderstood what he imbibed, are apparent from the rest of
the argument, in which he confuses Rabelais's humor with quite
different types. He continues, without interruption, as follows :

It [the vein of ridicule] began first in Verse with an *Italian* Poem,
called *La Secchia Rapita*, was pursued by *Scarron* in *French* with his
Virgil Travesty, and in *English* by Sir *John Mince, Hudibras*, and *Cotton*, and with greater height of *Burlesque* in the *English* than, I think,
in any other Language. But let the Execution be what it will, the
Design, the Custom, and Example are very pernicious to Poetry, and
indeed to all Virtue and Good Qualities among Men, which must be
disheartened by finding how unjustly and undistinguish't they fall under
the lash of Raillery, and this Vein of Ridiculing the Good as well as the
Ill, the Guilty and the Innocent together. ' Tis a very poor tho' common Pretence to merit, to make it appear by the Faults of other Men.
A mean Wit or Beauty may pass in a Room, where the rest of the Company are allowed to have none ; ' tis something to sparkle among Diamonds, but to shine among *Pebbles* is neither Credit nor Value worth the
pretending.

Another critic was Thomas Rymer. In his well known attack
on *Othello* in *A Short View of Tragedy* (1692), he condemns the
crudeness of the language used by Iago to inform Brabantio of
the escape and marriage of Desdemona. " Brabantio was not
in Masquerade, " he says, " was not *Incognito* ; Jago well knew
his rank and dignity, " etc., etc.

Rymer did not object to ribaldry as such, and attacks that of
Iago only because he believes it to be out of place. He finds
ribaldry perfectly proper in the mouth of Rabelais's Friar John,
and quotes his words in support in the following passage :

After King *Francis* had been taken Prisoner at *Pavia, Rabelais* tells
of a Drunken bout between *Gargantua* and Fryer *John*, where the valiant
Fryer, bragging over his Cups, amongst other flights, says he, *Had I
liv'd in the days of Jesus Christ, I would ha' guarded* Mount Olivet *that
the Jews should never ha' tane him. The Devil fetch me, if I would not
have ham string'd those Mr. Apostles, that after their good Supper ran
away so scurvily and left their Master to shift for himself. I hate a Man*

*should run away, when he should play at sharps. Pox on't, that I shou'd
not be King of* France *for an hundred years or two. I wou'd curtail all
our French Dogs that ran away at* Pavia.

This is address, this truly Satyr, where the preparation is such that
the thing principally design'd falls in as it only were of course.

But *Shakespear* shews us another sort of address ; his manners and
good breeding must not be like the rest of the Civil World. *Brabantio*
was not in Masquerade... [etc.] [1].

This view of Rabelais, could it be separated from the heresy
which inspired its utterance, would be unexceptionable. As it
is, posterity will regard it forever as a lucky accident incidental to
an unlucky one, and will therefore, regardless alike of its rightness
and of the commendable method and zeal which brought it to
light, deny that it can be a credit to its author.

Rymer had studied Rabelais deeply, for he is fond of invoking
his example. Elsewhere in the *Short View* he condemns the
French opera, finding that it is nothing but an instrument invented
to flatter " the Grand Monarch. "

All flattery to him is insipid unless it be prodigious... All must be
monstrous, enormous, and outragious to Nature, to be like him, or give
any Eccho on his Appetite.

Were *Rabelais* alive again, he would look on his Gargantua as but
a Pygmy [2].

Again, in the attack on Othello, he ridicules the scene in which
the Duke attempts to reconcile Brabantio to Desdemona's marriage. The two " cap sentences, " he says, in a fashion that
reminds him both of *The Rehearsal* and of Panurge in Rabelais.

Panurge [he says], sadly perplexed, and trying all the means in the
World to be well advised in that knotty point *whether he should Marry
or no*, Amongst the rest consults *Raminigrobis* [sic], an old Poet, as one
belonging to *Apollo*, and from whom he might expect something like

---

1. *Critical Essays of the Seventeenth Century*, ed. Spingarn, II, 227. Rymer
quotes from Rabelais, Bk. I, Ch. xxxix.
2. *Critical Essays of the Seventeenth Century*, II, 214.

an Oracle. And he was not disappointed.   From *Raminigrobis* he had
this Answer :

> Prenez la, ne la prenez pas.
> Si vous la prenez, c'est bien faict.
> Si ne la prenez en effect,
> Ce sera œuuré par compas.
> Guallopez, mais allez le pas.
> Recullez, entre y de faict.
> > Prenez-la, ne.
> Take, or not take her, off or on :
> Handy dandy is your Lot.
> When her name you write, you blot.
> 'Tis undone when all is done,
> Ended ere it is begun.
> Never Gallop whilst you Trot ;
> Set not forward when you run,
> Nor be single, tho' alone.
> Take, or not take her, off or on [1].

The age, then, possessed one critic who praised Rabelais's
decorum, that quality of which every reader has felt the effect,
and which few have known how to describe. Rymer, whatever
his faults, was one of these few, the first in the history of English
criticism.

The passages quoted from Rymer and Motteux, though by far
the most significant, were not the only eulogies of Rabelais in
their time.   Motteux's editions of '93 and '94 were accompanied
by a considerable quantity of light-hearted verse from the pens
himself and his friends, which recommend both the original and the
translation to the favor of the reader [2].   The names of Motteux's
friends are undistinguished, but their efforts are readable, and if
the judgements expressed are occasionally wide of the mark, one
may remember that critical truth is never the primary motive of
eulogistic writing.   The most amusing of the collection are perhaps
the Hudibrastics of Alexander Oldis [3].

---

1. *Critical Essays of the Seventeenth Century*, ed. Spingarn, II, 230-31. See
Rabelais, Bk. III, Ch. xxi.
2. See Rabelais, Transl. Urquhart and Motteux, ed. Whibley, III, 26-31, and
Regis, *Garg. und Pant.*, II, 1396-1400.
3. See Regis, *Garg. und Pant.*, II, 1397-99.

CHAPTER V

THE AGE OF QUEEN ANNE

Swift, Bentley, Pope, Arbuthnot, Addison, Budgell, Young.

It happens that in the first quarter of the 18th century one great writer and one less great valued and to some extent imitated the writings of Rabelais. The spirit of the time was even less agreeable to Pantagruelism than that of the preceding period had been. The anti-Rabelaisian forces considered in the foregoing chapter were still operative, and, in addition, the language, both in literature and in the drawing room, had been mostly purged of the coarseness which had marked it since the Restoration. Such different men as Sir William Temple, Jeremy Collier, and Steele, are representative of the movement toward a more ladylike standard of speech. It was therefore as a matter of personal taste and perhaps as something of a protest against the prevailing fashions, certainly not as a concession to them, that Swift and his good friend Arbuthnot cultivated Rabelais.

Swift cites him often, and apparently from memory, in his fugitive writings. Thus in *The Examiner* of December 7th to 14th, 1710, he recalls " the story of a giant in Rabelais, " alluding, as the context indicates, to Bringuenarilles [1]. Addressing Bolingbroke in 1714, he complains of the displacement of the Primate and Chancellor of Ireland with the following illustration :

The poor dead Queen is used like the giant Lougarou in Rabelais. Pantagruel took Lougarou by the heels, and made him his weapon to kill

---

1. *Prose Works*, ed. Scott, IX, 119.

twenty other giants ; then flung him over a river into the town, and killed two ducks and an old cat [1].

He wrote some sarcastic manuscript notes in a copy of *The Freeholder* (No. 31, April 6th, 1716) opposite an essay by Addison in such a way that the text and the notes together form a dialogue. He invokes Rabelais the prevaricator.

Addison. What greater instances could His Majesty have given of his love to the Church of England, than those he has exhibited by his most solemn declarations ; by his daily example ; and by his promotions of the most eminent among the clergy to such vacancies as have happened in his reign.
Swift. Most undeniable truth, as any in Rabelais [2].

Bolingbroke wrote to Swift on March 17th, 1719, in answer to a letter now lost, as follows :

There never was a better application than yours of the story of Picrochole. The storks will never come, and they must be porters all their lives. They are something worse ; for 1 had rather be a porter than a tool, I would sooner lend out my back to hire, than my name [3].

Mr. F. Elrington Ball seems to be right in saying that " Swift had evidently applied to the position of the Pretender and his party the following passage from... Rabelais ([Bk.] I, [Ch.] XLIX) " :

Ainsi s'en alla le pauvre cholericque [Picrochole] ; puis, passant l'eau au Port Huaulcx et racontant ses males fortunes, fut advisé par une vieille lourpidon que son royaulme luy seroit rendu à la venue des cocquecigrues. Depuis ne sçait on qu'il est devenu. Toutesfoys, l'on m'a dict qu'il est de present pauvre gaignedenier à Lyon, cholere comme davant et tousjours se guemente à tous estrangers de la venue des cocquecigrues, esperant certainement, selon la prophetie de la vieille, estre à leur venue réintegré en son royaulme [4].

---

1. Letter to Bolingbroke dated Dublin, Sept. 14th, 1714, *Correspondance*, ed. Ball, II, 239.
2. Addison's essay is entitled *Answer to a celebrated Pamphlet, entitled " An Argument to prove the Affections of the People of England to be the best Security of the Government ; etc. "* — Repr. with Swift's notes in *Prose Works*, IX, 375-376; the present quotation is from p. 376.
3. *Correspondence*, III, 28.
4. *Ibid.*, III, 28, n. 1.

In *An Answer to a Paper, called " A Memorial... "* (March 25th, 1728 ?) Swift thus addresses his opponent, Sir John Browne :

For as to your scheme of raising one hundred and ten thousand pounds, it is as vain as that of Rabelais ; which was, to squeeze out wind from the posteriors of a dead ass [1].

A Meditation upon a Broomstick contains the following echo of two passages in Rabelais :

...[the broom is] now, at best, but the reverse of what it was, a tree turned upside down, the branches on the earth, and the root in the air.....
But a broomstick, perhaps, you will say, is an emblem of a tree standing on its head ; and pray what is man, but a topsyturvy creature, his animal faculties perpetually mounted on his rational, his head where his heels should be, grovelling on the earth [2] !

The trees on the Isle des Ferremens in Rabelais (Bk. V, Ch. ix) seemed to Pantagruel and his men to be " animaux terrestres, "

...en ce qu'elles ont la teste, c'est le tronc, en bas ; les cheveux, ce sont les racines, en terre ; et les pieds, ce sont les rameaux, contremont : comme si un homme faisoit le chesne fourchu.

Pantagruel tells in Book IV, chapter xxxii, how Antiphysie (" laquelle de tout temps est partie adverse de nature ") proves her children superior to those of Physie (" c'est nature ").

Avoir les pieds en l'air [she says], la teste en bas, estoit imitation du créateur de l'Univers :   veu que les cheveulx sont en l'home comme racines, les jambes comme rameaux.   Car les arbres plus commodement sont en terre fichées sus leurs racines que ne seroient sus leurs rameaux. Par ceste demonstration alleguant que trop mieulx et plus aptement estoient ses enfans comme une arbre droicte, que ceulx de Physis, les quelz estoient comme une arbre renversée.

The earliest of Swift's important works in which the influence is discernible is indeed the one which marks the beginning of his career as a prose writer, *A Tale of A Tub.*   He tells us himself that

---

1. *Prose Works*, VII, 114.
2. *Ibid.*, I, 333-334.

the greater part of it was written in 1696 [1]. It was published anonymously in 1704, in the author's thirty seventh year.

The story is, as everybody knows, an allegorical satire on the sects of Christianity. It begins in Section II. Three brothers, Peter, Martin, and Jack, representing the Papists, the Church of England, and the Dissenters, inherit at their Fathers' death three coats, which are the Christian religion. They are admonished by the will to wear them continually, and to make no change in their cut, as they might be tempted to do in deference to changing fashions. It is not long before they are led to a series of increasingly gross violations of that injunction, and they are at pains each time to overcome their scruples by the discovery of hidden meanings in its simple phraseology. The author digresses upon critics, digressions, madness, ears, and other matters, sometimes for whole chapters. The numerous subjects treated are outlined in the " Analytical Table " at the beginning. The title is explained in the " Author's Preface. " The work was conceived, it seems, by " the grandees of Church and State " as a means of diverting the wits, " lest these gentlemen, during the intervals of a long peace, should find leisure to pick holes in the weak sides of Religion and Government [2]. " It was suggested by the practise of seamen, who " have a custom, when they meet a whale, to fling him out an empty tub by way of amusement, to divert him from laying violent hands upon the ship. " The author was chosen, then, his " genius being conceived to lie not unhappily that way " to make game by writing *A Tale of A Tub*, which should serve until a vaster project to occupy the disturbers might be perfected. An outline is given of that design as follows :

It is intended, that a large Academy be erected, capable of containing nine thousand seven hundred forty and three persons ; which, by modest computation, is reckoned to be pretty near the current number of wits in this island. These are to be disposed into the several schools of this academy, and there pursue those studies to which their genius most inclines them. The undertaker himself will publish his proposals with all convenient speed ; to which I shall refer the curious reader for a more par-

---

1. In the " Apology " to the *Tale*, *Prose Works*, I, 3.
2. *Prose Works*, I, 39-40.

ticular account, mentioning at present only a few of the principal schools. There is, first, a large Paederastic School, with French and Italian masters.   There is also the Spelling School, a very spacious building :   the School of Looking-glasses :   the School of Swearing :   the School of Critics :   the School of Salivation :   the School of Hobby-horses :   the School of Poetry :   the School of Tops :   the School of Spleen :   the School of Gaming :   with many others, too tedious to recount.   No person to be admitted member into any of these schools, without an attestation under two sufficient persons' hands, certifying him to be a wit.

Swift here anticipates his own Academy of Lagado in *Gulliver's Travels*, and recalls Rabelais's academy of La Reine Quinte [1].   One will notice et once certain revealing tricks of style.   Thus the number of the wits is enormous, exact, and ironical.   The schools of the Academy form an imposing list, the satire of which consists in the grouping of unlikes.

Necessity is the mother of invention, and Peter, the eldest brother is a notable inventor (Section IV).   In that capacity he is reminiscent of Rabelais's Messere Gaster [2].   Gaster, of course, stands for hunger, Peter for religious superstition.   Peter invented the game of land speculation, many times buying and selling " a large continent, lately said to have been discovered in *Terra Australis Incognita*, " which represents purgatory [3].   He also invented a " sovereign remedy for the worms, especially those in the spleen " (a satire on penance and absolution) ; " a whispering-office, for the public good, and ease of all such as are hypochondriacal, or troubled with the colic " (the confessional) ; " an office of insurance for tobacco-pipes " (indulgences) ; " puppets and raree-shows " (ceremonies and processions) ; a " famous universal pickle " (holy water) ; and so forth.   Gaster's inventions in Rabelais are, of course, more various in scope and less narrowly satirical.

The following passage is distinctly reminiscent of Rabelais's Bishop Homenaz in praise of the Decretals [4], and its tone and symbolism further recall the chapters on the Ringing Island [5].

---

1. Rabelais, Bk. V, Ch. xxi, xxii.
2. Rabelais, Bk. IV, Ch. lvii, lxi, lxii.
3. *Prose Works*, I, 79-81.
4. Rabelais, Bk. IV, Ch. xlix-liv.
5. Rabelais, Bk. V, Ch. i-viii.

But of all Peter's rarities, he most valued a certain set of bulls, whose race was by great fortune preserved in a lineal descent from those that guarded the golden fleece... the terrible roaring, peculiar to their lineage, was preserved ; as likewise that faculty of breathing out fire from their nostrils ; which, notwithstanding many of their detractors took to be a feat of art ; to be nothing so terrible as it appeared ; proceeding only from their usual course of diet, which was of squibs and crackers... Peter put these bulls upon several employs. Sometimes he would set them a roaring to fright naughty boys, and make them quiet. Sometimes he would send them out upon errands of great importance ; where, it is wonderful to recount, and perhaps the cautious reader may think much to believe it, an *appetitus sensibilis*, deriving itself through the whole family from their noble ancestors, guardians of the golden fleece, they continued so extremely fond of gold, that if Peter sent them abroad, though it were only upon a compliment, they would roar, and spit, and belch, and piss, and fart, and snivel out fire, and keep a perpetual coil, till you flung them a bit of gold ; but then, *pulveris exigui jactu*, they would grow calm and quiet as lambs [3].

One of Rabelais's chapters is entitled " Comment, par la Vertu des Decretales, Est l'Or Subtilement Tiré de France en Rome. " Bishop Homenaz, having reached a climax in his eulogy, is moved to physical reactions like those of Peter's bulls.

Icy commença Homenaz rocter, peter, rire, baver et suer ; et bailla son gros, gras bonnet à quatre braguettes à une des filles, laquelle la posa sus son beau chef en grande alaigresse, apres l'avoir amoureusement baisé, comme guaige et asceurance qu'elle seroit premiere mariée [1].

The " bonnet à quatre braguettes " is, of course, the mitre, an insigne which Peter is fond of displaying.

In the height of his fits, (as it is usual with those who run mad out of pride,) he would call himself God Almighty, and sometimes monarch of the universe. I have seen him (says my author) take three old high-crowned hats, and clap them all on his head three story high, with a huge bunch of keys at his girdle, and an angling-rod in his hand. In which guise, whoever went to take him by the hand in the way of salu-tation, Peter with much grace, like a well-educated spaniel, would present them with his foot ; and if they refused his civility, then he would raise it as high as their chaps, and give them a damned kick

1. *Prose Works*, I, 81-83.
2. Rabelais, Bk. IV, Ch. LIII.

on the mouth, which hath ever since been called a salute. Whoever walked by without paying him their compliments, having a won derful strong breath, he would blow their hats off into the dirt [1].

The salutation required by Peter is precisely that offered by the Papimanes to Pantagruel and his men, for they regard them as proxies of the Holy Father.

Adoncques s'agenouillerent devant nous, et nous vouloient baiser les pieds. Ce que ne leurs voulusmes permettre, leur remontrans que au Pape, si là de fortune en propre personne venoit, ilz ne sçauroient faire d'advenaige. " Si ferions, si respondirent ilz. Cela est entre nous ja resolu. Nous luy baiserions le cul sans feuille, et les couilles pareille-ment... [2] "

A mildly Rabelaisian fondness of Swift for piling up epithets is apparent in a passage in Section VI about Peter's brother Jack (so named after Calvin), who has turned reformer.

And now the little boys in the streets began to salute him with several names. Sometimes they would call him Jack the bald ; sometimes, Jack with a lantern ; sometimes, Dutch Jack ; sometimes, French Hugh ; sometimes, Tom the beggar ; and sometimes, Knocking Jack of the North. And it was under one, or some, or all of these appelations, (which I leave to the learned reader to determine,) that he has given rise to the most illustrious and epidemic sect of Æolists [3] ...

Section VIII describes the Æolists, who include all pretenders to inspiration. It was clearly inspired by Rabelais's Isle de Ruach [4]. Swift's chapter is considerably longer, and is highly ingenious. The satire is more economical (indeed one may take the original for pure nonsense and not be aware of any deficiency), though he was evidently anxious to make the most of its comic possibilities. A lengthy quotation seems justified.

The learned Æolists maintain the original cause of all things to be wind, ...man is in the highest perfection of all created things, as having, by the great bounty of philosophers, been endued with three dis-

---

1. *Prose Works*, I, 84-85.
2. Rabelais, Bk. IV, Ch. xlviii.
3. *Prose Works*, I, 101.
4. Rabelais, Bk. IV, Ch. xliii.

tinct *animas* or winds, to which the sage Æolists, with much liberality, have added a fourth...

In consequence of this, their next principle was, that man brings with him into the world, a peculiar portion or grain of wind, which may be called a *quinta essentia*, extracted from the other four... This, when blown up to its perfection, ought not to be covetously hoarded up, stifled, or hid under a bushel, but freely communicated to mankind. Upon these reasons, and others of equal weight, the wise Æolists affirm the gift of BELCHING to be the noblest act of a rational creature. To cultivate which art, and render it more serviceable to mankind, they made use of several methods. At certain seasons of the year, you might behold the priests among them, in vast numbers, with their mouths gaping wide enough against a storm. At other times were to be seen several hundreds linked together in a circular chain, with every man a pair of bellows applied to his neighbor's breech, by which they blew up each other to the shape and size of a tun ; and for that reason, with great propriety of speech, did usually call their bodies, their vessels...

Now, their mysteries and rites were performed in this manner. ' Tis well known among the learned, that the virtuosos of former ages had a contrivance for carrying and preserving winds in casks or barrels, which was of great assistance upon long sea voyages, and the loss of so useful an art at present is very much to be lamented... [The Æolists] in honour of their founder's memory, have to this day preserved great numbers of those barrels, whereof they fix one in each of their temples, first beating out the top ; into this barrel, upon solemn days, the priest enters, where, having before duly prepared himself by the methods already described, a secret funnel is also conveyed from his posteriors to the bottom of the barrel, which admits new supplies of inspiration, from a northern chink or cranny. Whereupon, you behold him swell immediately to the shape and size of his vessel. In this posture he disembogues whole tempests upon his auditory, as the spirit from beneath gives him utterance, which, issuing *ex adytis et penetralibus*, is not performed without much pain and gripings. And the wind, in breaking forth, deals with his face as it does with that of the sea, first blackening, then wrinkling, and at last bursting it into a foam. It is in this guise the sacred Æolist delivers his oracular belches to his panting disciples [1] ...

Jack's abuse of his father's will (he used it " for a night-cap when he went to bed, and for an umbrella in rainy weather, " as well as for a panacea in sundry diseases) [2], his boorish tricks [3], his

1. *Prose Works*, I, 106-110.
2. *Ibid*, I, 131.
3. *Ibid.*, I, 134.

braying intonations [1], and his perverse love of punishment [2], all have their counterparts in *Gargantua and Pantagruel*. Thus:

When he had some roguish trick to play, he would down with his knees, up with his eyes, and fall to prayers, though in the midst of the kennel. Then it was, that those who understood his pranks, would be sure to get far enough out of his way, and whenever curiosity attracted strangers to laugh, or to listen, he would, of a sudden, with one hand, out with his gear, and piss full in their eyes, and with the other, all bespatter them with mud.

The passage is as near to Rabelais in spirit as any that could be cited, though the details are entirely original. Consider, for example, this pleasantry of Panurge.

Un jour, que l'on avoit assigné à tous les théologiens de se trouver en Sorbone pour examiner les articles de la foy, il feist une tartre bourbonnoise, composée de force de hailz, de *galbanum*, de *assa fœtida*, de *castoreum*, l'estroncs tous chaulx et la destrampit en sanie de bosses chancreuses, et, de fort bon matin, en gressa et oignit théologalement tout le treillis de Sorbone, en sorte que le diable n'y eust pas duré. Et tous ces bonnes gens rendoyent là leurs gorges devant tout le monde, comme s'ilz eussent escorché le regnard, et en mourut dix ou douze de peste, quatorze en feurent ladres, dix et huyct en furent pouacres, et plus de vingt et sept en eurent la verolle ; mais il ne s'en soucioit mie [3].

Jack enjoys being beaten.

He would stand in the turning of a street, and, calling to those who passed by, would cry to one, " Worthy sir, do me the honour of a good slap in the chaps. " To another, " Honest friend, pray favour me with a handsome kick on the arse ; " " Madam, shall I entreat a small box on the ear from your ladyship's fair hands ? " " Noble captain, lend a reasonable thwack, for the love of God, with that cane of yours over these poor shoulders [4]. "

Compare with this, Rabelais, Book IV, Chapter xvi, " Comment par Frere Jean est faict essay du naturel des Chicanous. " Thus,

---

1. *Prose Works*, I, 135. Cf. the voices of the Monagaux in Rabelais, Bk. V, Ch. iii.
2. *Ibid.* I, 136.
3. Rabelais, Bk. II, Ch. xvi.
4. *Prose Works*, I, 136.

" Par la sacre botte de sainct Benoist, dist frere Jan, presentement j'en sçauray la verité. " Adoncques descend en terre, mist la main à son escarcelle, et en tira vingt escuz au Soleil. Puis dist à haulte voix en presence et audience d'une grande tourbe du peuple Chiquanourroys : " Qui veut guaingner vingt escuz d'or pour estre battu en Diable ? — Io, io, io, respondirent tous. Vous nous affollerez de coups, monsieur, cela est sœur. Mais il y a beau guaing. " Et tous accouroient à la foulle, à qui seroit premier en date pour estre tant precieusement battu.

If the aspects of *A Tale of a Tub* just reviewed are rightly thought to be owing in large measure to Rabelais's example, so is much of *Gulliver's Travels* (1727).

The influences discernible in that work are many, but all of a piece. Swift was demonstrably familiar not only with Rabelais, but also with such works as the *Voyages Comiques* of Cyrano de Bergerac, *The Voyage of Domingo Gonzales to the World of the Moon* by Francis Godwin, *The Discovery of a World in the Moone* by Bishop Wilkins, the *History of Sevarambes* by D'Alais, and the *Journey of Jacques Sadeur to Australia* by Foigny [1], and one can scarcely suppose him to have been ignorant of *Robinson Crusoe* or of the *True History* of Lucian. The tempest which drives Gulliver upon the coasts of Brobdingnag has been found to have been taken almost literally from Samuel Sturmy's *Magazine or Compleat Mariner* [2]. For the general conception of the work, therefore, no single source need be argued.

The Rabelaisian elements in the *Voyage to Lilliput* are obvious. Thus Gulliver appears as a giant, and much is made of the discrepancy between his bodily proportions, with all that they imply, and those of the little folk who enslave and entertain him. His appetite, like Gargantua's, requires whole flocks to appease, his thirst whole hogsheads of liquor to slake [3]. Six scholars are retained to teach him the language, and three hundred tailors to make him a suit of clothes [4]. He is able to inundate the countryside

---

1. See the article on Swift by Richard Garnett and Thomas Seccombe in *Encycl. Brit.*, 13th ed.
2. Th. Borkowsky, " Quellen zu Swift's Gulliver, " *Anglia*, XV, 355.
3. *Gulliver*, Bk. I, Ch. I and II.
4. *Ibid.*, Ch. II.

when he urinates [1], as Gargantua did the city of Paris and the neighborhood of Ancenys, his mare the Gué de Vede, and Pantagruel the battlefield of the Dipsodes [2]. His body comes to no harm from the arrows which the minute warriors discharge against it [3]. The intellectual and practical genius of the people reminds us of the progressive subjects of Grandgousier, though they are by contrast sadly deficient in morality. Gulliver himself reflects, in this part of the work, the ideals of Rabelais's giant kings, for he refuses to indulge the hatred of the King of Lilliput against the King of Blefuscu. Political groups in Lilliput are divided on issues of high and low heels, and methods of opening eggs. Their bases of alignment are comparable to those of the belligerents in the famous war in *Gargantua* [4], both satirizing the triviality of political motives the world over.

As in *A Tale of A Tub*, Swift here makes the most of his comic situations, and delights in transcribing the Lilliputian language [5], as he does later the languages of Brobdingnag, Laputa, and the land of the Houyhnhnms. In so doing he recalls the gibberish of Panurge in three passages of Chapter ix of *Pantagruel*.

The *Voyage to Brobdingnag* introduces a giant king who is in every respect a peer of Grandgousier and his offspring, a statesman so virtuous that he can scarcely understand Gulliver's descriptions of the corrupt state of European politics. Upon Gulliver's offering to introduce him into the secrets of firearms, he loses all patience.

As for himself, he protested, that although few things delighted him so much as new discoveires in art or in nature, yet he would rather lose half his kingdom than be privy to such a secret, which he commanded me, as I valued my life, never to mention any more [6].

Swift's criticisms of life, as we follow them in the words of his traveller, are alternately straightforward and ironical. Like Dr.

---

1. *Gulliver*, Bk. I, Ch. i, cf. Ch. v.
2. Rabelais, Bk. I, Ch. xvii, xxxvi, xxxviii, and Bk. II, Ch. xxviii.
3. *Gulliver*, Bk. I, Ch. i ; cf. Rabelais, Bk. I, Ch. xxxvi, in which Gargantua mistakes artillery fire for the stings of gadflies.
4. Ch. xxv ff.
5. See for example the name of the Emperor of Lilliput, Ch. iii : " Golbasto Momaren Evlame Gurdilo Shefin Mully Ully Gue. "
6. *Gulliver*, Bk. II, Ch. vii.

Watson in *Sherlock Holmes*, Gulliver can understand the obvious or that which is carefully explained to him, but is deficient in perceiving subtleties. He is still more so in applying the moral lessons he learns to the conduct of his own life. This is how he describes the learning of the Brobdingnagians :

> The learning of this people is very defective, consisting only in morality, history, poetry, and mathematics, wherein they must be allowed to excel. But the last of these is wholly applied to what may be useful in life, to the improvement of agriculture, and a mechanical arts ; so that among us it would be little esteemed. And as to ideas, entities, abstractions, and transcendentals, I could never drive the least conception into their heads [1].

This attack on abstract sophistry anticipates the satire in the next voyage, and clearly agrees with the views of Rabelais. So does the observation that in Brobdingnag " to write a comment upon any law is a capital crime. "

Swift excels, as every critic has pointed out, not only in satire, but in circumstantial realism, an art of which Defoe is perhaps the outstanding master in English. The first two voyages of *Gulliver* illustrate this at its best. In them it is developed with such skill and the satire with such restraint, that they have remained favorites with children. In the last two voyages the satire becomes more preoccupying and the story more fantastic. Its details are still wrought with the utmost care, but the total effect is intentionally monstrous. The style, which is simple and even throughout the first two voyages, now runs to longer sentences and occasionally shows the heaping up of parallel constructions. A hint of this tendency occurs already toward the end of the account of Brobdingnag. The king

...was perfectly astonished with the historical account I gave him of our affairs during the last century, protesting it was only a heap of conspiracies, rebellions, murders, massacres, revolutions, banishments, the very worst effects that avarice, faction, hypocrisy, perfidiousness, cruelty, rage, madness, hatred, envy, lust, malice, or ambition, could produce [2].

---

1. *Gulliver*, Bk. II, Ch. VII.
2. *Ibid.*, Ch. VI.

This outburst is positively without parallel in the earlier part of the work.

The voyage to Laputa contains the famous account of the Academy of Projectors in Lagado [1], imitated from Rabelais's chapters on the Quintessence, and aimed at the Royal Society. The experiments are of the same kind as Rabelais describes [2]. Thus one worker " had been eight years upon a project for extracting sunbeams out of cucumbers, " another was endeavoring to " calcine ice into gunpowder, " and another " had contrived a new method for building houses, by beginning at the roof, and working downwards to the foundation ". One of Rabelais's doctors compounds human urine with horse dung as a medicine for prolonging the lives of kings and princes ; one of Swift's is busy reducing " human excrement to its original food. " Some of Rabelais's people plough the seashore with a yoke of foxes ; one of Swift's projectors " had found a device of ploughing the ground with hogs, to save the charges of ploughs, cattle, and labour. " One of Rabelais's cuts fire with a knife ; one of Swift's writes on the malleability of fire. Lagado is where the speculative habits of thought of the people at large, as described in Chapter II, are cultivated to the highest point of futility. Gulliver's imagination is stirred by their example and he invents on the spur of the moment a plan for the detection of political conspirators. The papers of all suspected persons should be seized, and

...might be delivered to a sett of artists, of dexterity sufficient to find out the mysterious meanings of words, syllables, and letters. They should be allowed to put what interpretation they pleased upon them, giving them a sense not only which has no relation at all to them, but even what is quite contrary to their true intent and real meaning ; thus, for instance, they may, if they so fancy, interpret a *sieve* to signify a *court lady*, a *lame dog* an *invader*, the *plague* a *standing army*, a *buzzard* a *great statesman*, the *gout* a *high priest*, a *chamber-pot* a *committee of grandees*, a *broom* a *revolution*, a *mouse-trap* an *employment*, a *bottomless-pit* a *treasury*, a *sink* a *court*, a *cap and bells* a *favourite*, a *broken reed* a *court of justice*, an *empty tun* a *general*, a *running sore* an *administration* [3].

---

1. *Gulliver*, Bk. III, Ch. v.
2. Rabelais, Bk. V, Ch. xxi, xxii.
3. *Gulliver*, Bk. III, Ch. vi, text of first edition, *Works* viii, 199, n. 2.

The reader will recognize here an identity of method and similarity of tone with Rabelais's satire on heraldry [1].

Swift, like Tom Brown and others, follows Rabelais and Lucian in a burlesque of the Homeric underworld. The governor of Glubbdubdrib possesses necromantic power, and summons many illustrious figures from among the dead to converse with Gulliver [2]. Alexander assures Gulliver " upon his honour that he was not poisoned, but died of a fever by excessive drinking " ; Homer, it seems, was not blind ; and Aristotle " freely acknowledged his own mistakes in natural philosophy. "   The satire is severe upon tyrants, commentators, flatterers, and modern historians.   Rabelais's burlesque occurs in Book II, Chapter xxx, but he also remarks in the first chapter of *Gargantua* that " emperors, kings, dukes, princes, and popes " are probably descended from junk peddlers, and Gulliver more or less confirms his suspicions.

I desired the Governor would call up a dozen or two of kings with their ancestors in order for eight or nine generations.   But my disappointment was grievous and unexpected, for instead of a long train with royal diadems, I saw in one family two fiddlers, three spruce courtiers, and an Italian prelate.   In another, a barber, an abbot, and two cardinals [3].

Another echo of the same chapter is Gulliver's speculations about what he would do if he were immortal.   Rabelais says,

...je cuyde que sois descendu de quelque riche roy ou prince au temps jadis ; car oncques ne veistes homme qui eust plus grande affection d'estre roy et riche que moy :   afin de faire grand chere, pas ne travailler, poinct ne me soucier, et bien enrichir mes amis, et tous gens de bien et de sçavoir [4].

Gulliver says,

I would first resolve by all arts and methods whatsoever to procure myself riches...In the second place, I would from my earliest youth apply myself to the study of arts and sciences, by which I should

---

1. Rabelais, Bk. I, Ch. ix.
2. *Gulliver*, Bk. III, Ch. vii, viii.
3. *Ibid.*, Ch. viii.
4. Rabelais, Bk. I, Ch. i.

arrive in time to excel all others in learning. Lastly, I would carefully
record every action and event of consequence that happened... my
choice and constant companions should be a set of my own immortal
brotherhood... I would provide them with convenient lodges round
my own estate, and have some of them always at my table, only ming-
ling a few of the most valuable among you mortals, whom length of
time would harden me to lose with little or no reluctance, and treat
your posterity after the same manner [1].

Some brief remarks by Gulliver upon the whimsicality and vices
of women may be mentioned in passing as expressing one of the
two opposed Rabelaisian moods toward the sex [2].   In addition to
the catalogues of parallel constructions (one of which has been
quoted) [3], one notices also a Rabelaisian etymology [4], an example of

1. *Gulliver*, Bk. III, Ch. x.
2. The wife of the Prime Minister of Laputa deserts him for the pleasures of
the town of Lagado (Ch. ii). An Academician of Lagado, studying " ways and
means of raising money without grieving the subject, " proposes to tax women
" according to their beauty and skill in dressing... But constancy, chastity, good
sense, and good nature were not rated, because they would not bear the charge
of collecting " (Ch. vi).
3. Above, p. 164. Compare : " Their outward garments were adorned with
the figures of suns, moons, and stars, interwoven with those of fiddles, flutes,
harps, trumpets, guitars, harpsichords, and many other instruments of music,
unknown to us in Europe. " — Ch. ii. " It is allowed, that senates and great
councils are often troubled with redundant, ebullient, and other peccant humours,
with many diseases of the head, and more of the heart ; with strong convulsions,
with grievous contractions of the nerves and sinews in both hands, but especially the right ; with spleen, flatus, vertigos, and deliriums ; with scrofulous
tumours full of foetid, purulent matter ; with sour frothy ructations, with canine
appetites and crudeness of digestion, besides many others needless to mention.
This doctor therefore proposed, that upon the meeting of a senate, certain physicians should attend at the three first days of their sitting, and at the close of
teach day's debate, feel the pulses of every senator ; after which, having
maurely considered, and consulted upon the nature of the several maladies, and the
methods of cure, they should on the fourth day return to the senate house, attended
by their apothecaries stored with proper medecines ; and before the members
sat, administer to each of them lenitives, aperitives, abstersives, corrosives,
restringents, palliatives, laxatives, cephalalgics, icterics, apophlegmatics, acous-
tics, as their several cases required ; and according as these medecines should
operate, repeat, alter, or omit them at the next meeting. " — Ch. vi. " ...the
breed of discoverers, witnesses, informers, accusers, prosecutors, evidences,
swearers, together with their several subservient and subaltern instruments... "
— Ch. vi. " How great a share in the motions and events of courts, councils
and senates might be challenged by bawds, whores, pimps, parasites, and buf-
foons ! " — Ch. viii.
4. The etymology of *Laputa*, Ch. ii.

precision where precision is superfluous [1], the use of gibberish [2], and one paragraph containing a display of professional jargon [3].

Long sentences and catalogues are most conspicuous in the *Voyage to the Houyhnhnms* [4]. Here the attack on the vices of society at large is unrelenting, and, as in the earlier voyages, includes vocational satire (e. g. of lawyers [5], doctors [6], and aristocracy [7]). A medecine made of dung and urine is mentioned as popular among the Yahoos [8], again recalling the invention of Rabelais's chemist. The vices of these filthy creatures, their gluttony, drunkenness, spleen, lust, and thievishness are described with a grossness that is almost hyper-Rabelaisian [9]. A final illustration of the influence on Swift's style may be given. Gulliver is explaining to the Houyhnhnm his master the economic situation of England.

I replied that England (the dear place of my nativity) was computed to produce three times the quantity of food, more than its inhabitants are able to consume, as well as liquors extracted from grain, or pressed out of the fruit of certain trees, which made excellent drink, and the same proportion in every other convenience of life. But, in order to feed the luxury and intemperance of the males, and the vanity of the females, we sent away the greatest part of our necessary things to other countries, from whence, in return, we brought the materials of diseases, folly, and vice, to spend among ourselves. Hence it follows of necessity, that vast numbers of our people are compelled to seek their livelihood by begging, robbing, stealing, cheating, pimping, forswearing, flattering, suborning, forging, gaming, lying, fawning, hectoring, voting, scribbling, star-gazing, poisoning, whoring, canting,

---

1. " May your celestial Majesty outlive the sun, eleven moons and a half. " — Ch. ix.

2. E. g. " Ickpling gloffthrob squutserumm blhiop mlashnalt zwin tnod-balkuffh slhiophad gurdlubh asht. " — Ch. ix. For translation see preceding note.

3. See p. 166. n. 3

4. The lists range from a dozen to thirty odd terms : see for example the quotation below. Other examples may be found in *Prose Works*, VIII, 252, 255, 265, 288, 305.

5. End of Ch. v.

6. Middle of Ch. vi.

7. End of Ch. vi.

8. Ch. vii.

9. Ch. i, vii, viii.

libelling, freethinking, and the like occupations : every one of which
terms, I was at much pains to make him understand [1].

One will notice the sly inclusion of " voting " in this list.

A delightful appreciation of the *Voyage to the Houyhnhnms*,
and of Rabelais also, in passing, was written by Bentley in a pamphlet entitled *Critical Remarks Upon Gulliver's Travels* [2]. He
argues playfully and with rich learning that the Houyhnhnms have
actually existed. He invents a description of " the Stedes Coun-
trye, " which he pretends to cite from Chaucer [3] ; mentions the
noble descendants of the race that belonged to Achilles, Alexander,
Caesar, Caligula, and other heroes ; draws attention to the doctrines of Virgil and Ausonius that the souls of Houyhnhnms are
admitted to the Elysian Fields ; and calls Lucretius, Pliny, and a
number of other writers to witness their chastity, good sense, and
other special virtues [2]. He writes that :

The last of the true *Houyhnhm* Race, which resided in *Europe*, lived
about the Middle of the *sixteenth Century* ; and was not less famous,
for the Honours conferred on him in *France* ; than for having enjoyed
the Friendship of the greatest Wit of his Time, the learned *Rablais*.
History, indeed, leaves it uncertain, by what means the Intimacy
began between them : Whether *Pantagruel*, in his coasting Voyage,
touched at that Island, and brought him away from his native Country ;
or, whether *Rablais* himself, (who was the *Gulliver* of that Age, and
almost as celebrated for the Poignancy of his Wit, and the Extensiveness
of his Genius as the *British Voyager*,) having visited that Country, pre-
vailed with that *Houyhnhm* to accompany him into *Europe*.
However, thus much is well attested, that the University of *Orleans*
made him a Compliment of the Degree of *Doctor in Physick*, by the
Name of *Joannes Caballus*, M. D. and it is universally agreed by the
Learned, that the Custom of conferring honorary Degrees, which, at
present, is in so great Practice and Repute with our Universities, was
at first introduced and recommended by this single Circumstance.
Altho' it is generally doubted, whether many of our *Modern Honorary
Graduates*, have as much Knowledge of Languages, as good a Capacity,
or half as much Integrity as that noble Animal [4].

---

1. Ch. vi.
2. *Critical Remarks Upon Gulliver's Travels*, 3d ed., Dublin, 1735 [pp. 1-24].
3. It is not a bad imitation of Chaucer's manner (*Critical Remarks, etc.*, 8-9).
4. *Critical Remarks, etc.*, 23.

Richard Bentley was by no means the only contemporary who thought of Rabelais when he thought of Swift. Pope and Gay wrote Swift a letter on October 22d of the year following the publication of *Gulliver*, containing the first draft of certain well known lines in the *Dunciad*. " Your name is in it, " says Pope, " with some others, under a mark of such ignominy as you will not much grieve to wear in that company. Adieu, and God bless you, and give you good health and spirits.

> Whether thou choose Cervantes' serious air ;
> Or laugh and shake in Rabelais' easy chair,
> Or in the graver gown instruct mankind,
> Or, silent, let thy morals tell thy mind [1]. "

Lord Bathurst wrote him on September 9th, 1730, gaily chiding him for his shortcomings as correspondent, and threatens, unless he mends his ways, to

...take your works to pieces, and show you that they are all borrowed or stolen. Have you not stolen the sweetness of your numbers from Dryden and Waller ?...And in your prose writings,...they are only some little improvements upon the humour you have stolen from Miguel de Cervantes and Rabelais [2].

These are almost exactly the words used by Lady Mary Wortley Montague, as reported by Spence.

Swift has stolen all his humour from Cervantes and Rabelais [3].

An " Epitaph Proposed For Dr. Swift " (1745) begins :

Hic jacet Democritvs ille neotericvs, Rabelaesius noster, Ionathan Swift [4]...

Voltaire realized both that the two men were alike and that they were unlike, but though he appreciated Swift, he scarcely did justice

---

1. *Correspondence of Swift*, III, 427.
2. *Ibid.*, IV, 163.
3. Joseph Spence, *Anecdotes... of Mr. Pope, etc.* (1819, 2d ed., London, 1858), 176.   The date of this remark is 1740-41.
4. *Poems of Swift*, ed. Browning, II, 400.

to Rabelais in drawing his distinction[1]. Coleridge's epigram, on
the other hand, is faultless : " Anima Rabelaisii habitans in sicco. "

No critic, indeed, can well overlook the influence of Rabelais
upon Swift, and one is not surprised to find that its extent has
sometimes been exaggerated.   Swift outlined his literary aims with
the utmost clarity in a famous letter to Pope, written on the occasion of his revising *Gulliver* for the press, and taken with all that
his statement implies, they are as different from Rabelais's as possible.   Rabelais writes to make people laugh, to give pleasure, and
to cure the sick [2].   His romance, as he tells us in the Prologue to
Gargantua, is to contain wisdom, like the Silenes to which Alcibiades
compares Socrates in the *Symposium*, — " entendement plus que
humain, vertu merveilleuse, couraige invincible, sobresse non
pareille, contentement certain, asseurance parfaicte, deprisement
incroyable de tout ce pourquoy les humains tant veiglent, courent,
travaillent, navigent et bataillent. " Swift confines himself to
" deprisement. "

...the chief end I propose to myself in all my labours is to vex the world
rather than divert it ; and if I could compass that design without
hurting my own person or fortune, I would be the most indefatiguable
writer you have ever seen, without reading. ... I have ever hated all
nations, professions, and communities, and all my love is toward
individuals !

His writing was certainly an instrument in the spread of wisdom,
but it achieved its goal by an approach which is outwardly one-
sided.   It has, indeed, probably diverted more readers than have
ever opened a volume of Rabelais, but again with a difference.   The
diversion offered, while one does not really enjoy it the less for the
purpose it serves, is but bait on the hook of his satire, and the hook

---

1. He speaks of " l'ingénieux docteur Swift, qu'on appelle le Rabelais d'Angleterre. Il a l'honneur d'être prêtre comme Rabelais, et de se moquer de tout
comme lui ; mais on lui fait grand tort, selon mon petit sens, de l'appeler de ce
nom... M. Swift est Rabelais dans son bon sens et vivant en bonne compagnie.
Il n'a pas, à la vérité, la gaieté du premier, mais il a toute la finesse, la raison, le
choix, le bon goût, qui manquent à notre curé de Meudon. " — *Dictionnaire
Philosophique* (Librairie des Bibliophiles), II, 292-293.   Saintsbury thinks that
this passage is unjust to both men ; see his *History of Criticism*, II, 516-17.
   2. See the Epistle to Odet preceding Book IV.

is terribly sharp. " The secret of [his] success...is the writer's marvellous imperturbability in paradox, his teeming imagination and his rigid logic [1]." It is only "teeming imagination" that he shares with Rabelais, who is neither imperturbable, nor, in any strict sense, logical. It is significant in the latter regard that Swift makes the physical measurements of Lilliput and Brobdingnag consistent in every detail, while the monstrous proportions of the giants in Rabelais are notoriously elastic. Rabelais has been praised for his characterizations ; Swift never once created a character who can be disengaged from the story :   even Gulliver is no exception. Rabelais, it has been said, lived laughing and died laughing ; Swift affected gravity.

One can understand, therefore, why Swift emulated Rabelais so little in the matter of style. If you are to vex mankind you must speak simply, for nobody will go out of his way to be scolded. That is why Swift makes little or no reference to the classics or to other learned sources, and why his vocabulary is so plain. He abhors cant, whether vulgar or erudite, as he makes clear in three outspoken passages [2], and one may recall the observations of Gulliver that he chooses " to relate plain matter of fact in the simplest manner and style, " that the admirable Brobdingnagians never multiply words, and that the poetry of the Houyhnhnms is marked by a fine propriety [3].   Hazlitt thought that while Rabelais loved absurdity, Swift hated it.   It seems more likely that he loved absurdity but respected a strict set of literary scruples in its use.   Had he not loved absurdity he could scarcely have loved Rabelais, and so might have agreed with Pope.

Pope's attitude toward Maitre François was not unlike that of

---

1. Article on Swift by Richard Garnett and Thomas Seccombe, *Encycl. Brit.*, 13th ed,

2. He condemns " cut out for a court, " " a pardoning planet, " " clapt up, " " left in the lurch, " " the mob, " " outed, " " a great beauty, " " went roundly to work, " in some " Short Remarks on Bishop Burnet's History, " — *Prose Works*, X, 329 ; and the following words :   omniscience, omnipresence, ubiquity, attribute, beatific vision, eccentric, idiosyncracy, and entity, in " A Letter to a Young Gentleman Lately enter'd into Holy Orders, " — *Ibid.*, III, 202.   His theory of linguistic propriety is expressed in " A Proposal for Correcting, Improving and Ascertaining the English Tongue, " — *Ibid.*, XI, 1-21.

3. *Gulliver*, Bk. IV, Ch. xii ; Bk. II, Ch. vii ; and Bk. IV, Ch. ix.

a cat lover toward dogs. The cat lover may be challenged to admit that dogs have some good qualities, but if he does so it is with reluctance, for he knows in his heart that they are dirty, ill mannered, demonstrative, and otherwise obnoxious. The cat lover speaks twice in Spence's *Anecdotes... of Mr. Pope*.

1) Dr. Swift was a great reader and admirer of Rabelais ; and used sometimes to scold me for not liking him enough. Indeed there were so many things in his works, in which I could not see any manner of meaning driven at, that I could never read him over with any patience [1].

2) Rabelais had written some sensible pieces, which the world did not regard at all.— " I will write something, (says he,) that they shall take notice of " : and so sat down to writing nonsense. — Every body allows that there are several things without any manner of meaning in his Pantagruel. Dr. Swift likes it much, and thinks there are more good things in it than I do. — Friar John's character is maintained throughout with a great deal of spirit. — His concealed characters are touched only in part, and by fits : as for example, though the King's Mistress be meant in such a particular, related of Gargantua's mare ; the very next thing that is said of the mare, will not, perhaps, at all apply to the Mistress [2].

These passages speak for themselves, especially in that Pope should trouble himself at all about such a sophistry as the association of the mare and the mistress. It can only have been his devotion to his good friend the Dean and a sincere desire to please him that inspired the incongruous image of the latter in the *Dunciad* laughing and shaking in Rabelais's easy chair [3], though Warburton supposed that this was good criticism [4]. Pope mentions *Gargantua* impartially in *A Key to the Lock* (1714) [5] ; but in a letter to

1. Joseph Spence, *Anecdotes... of Mr. Pope, etc.*, ed. Singer (London, 1858), Sect. IV, 106. This remark is dated between 1734 and 1736.
2. *Ibid.*, Sect. V, 156 ; date between 1737 and 1739.
3. See above, p. 169.
4. " The *easy chair* suits his age [Swift was sixty one when the lines were first published] :   *Rab'lais' chair* marks his character :   and he fills and possesses it as the heir and successor of that original genius. " — Warburton, 1751 ; cit. in Pope's *Works*, ed. Croker, Elwin, and Courthope (London, 1882), IV, 313, n.
5. " I shall now...desire the reader to compare this key with those upon any other pieces,... in particular with the keys to Petronius Arbiter, Lucian's true History, Barclay's Argenis, and Rabelais's Gargantua ; and I doubt not he will do me the justice to acknowledge, that the explanations here laid down, are

Parnell, composed jointly with Gay, Jervas, and Arbuthnot (between January and March, 1716 ?), catches himself, such is human frailty, actually Pantagruelizing.   His part of the letter contains this paragraph :

When a man is conscious that he does no good himself, the next thing is to cause others to do some.   I may claim some merit this way, in hastening this testimonial from your friends above-writing :   their love to you indeed wants no spur, their ink wants no pen, their pen wants no hand, their hand wants no heart, and so forth (after the manner of Rabelais ; which is betwixt some meaning and no meaning) ; and yet it may be said, when present thought and opportunity is wanting, their pens want ink, their hands want pens, their hearts want hands, &c., till time, place, and conveniency, concur to set them a-writing, as at present, a sociable meeting, a good dinner, warm fire, and an easy situation do, to the joint labour and pleasure of this epistle [1].

Dr. John Arbuthnot, a third and important member of the Scriblerus Club, shared Swift's rather than Pope's view of Rabelais and grotesque satire.   So much is to be inferred from *The Memoirs of Martinus Scriblerus*, probably written in 1714, the year of the club's heyday, though it was not printed until 1741, six years after the Doctor's death.   Pope may have had some hand in its composition, but Arbuthnot was the only other member of the Club besides Swift who could conceivably have written it.

The aim of the club, as expressed by Pope, was " to have ridiculed all the false tastes in learning, under the character of a man of capacity enough, that had dipped into every art and science, but injudiciously in each [2]. "   Of the *Memoirs* only the first book was completed, though the impetus behind it is evident also in *Gulliver*.   Warburton understood that Cervantes was the model of the work [3] ; certainly much of the satire agrees with that in *Don Quixote*,

reduced as naturally, and with as little violence, both from the general scope and bent of the work, and from the several particulars ... " — *Works*, X, 496-97.
1. Cit. in *The Works of Oliver Goldsmith*, ed. Gibbs (London, 1884-86), IV, 168. For date see *Ibid.*, 166, n. 2.
2. Cit. Aitken in *The Life and Works of John Arbuthnot* (Oxford, 1892), 57.
3. " Mr. Pope, Dr. Arbuthnot, and Dr. Swift projected to write a satire, in conjunction, *on the abuses of human learning* ;   and to make it the better received, they proposed to do it in the manner of Cervantes (the original author of this species of satire) under the history of some feigned adventures. " — Warburton, Cit. Aitken, *op. cit.*, 307, n. 1.

and the simple and incisive style is on the whole more Cervantic
than Rabelaisian.   On the other hand the story, like *Gargantua*
and unlike *Don Quixote*, deals with the birth, education, and early
maturity of the hero, and the two narratives proceed in somewhat
parallel fashion.

Thus both Martinus and Gargantua have lengthy genealogies,
the one being found on " a skin of the true Pergamenian Parchment, " the other on a piece of elm bark [1].   The utterances of
both on their first appearance in the world are recorded.   Gargantua cried " A boire ! A boire ! " Martinus " uttered the voice
of nine several animals ; he cried like a calf, bleated like a sheep,
chattered like a magpie, grunted like a hog, neighed like a foal,
croaked like a raven, mewed like a cat, gabbled like a goose, and
brayed like an ass [2]. "

The costuming and education of each is described.   Rabelais
ridicules the scholastic curriculum, Arbuthnot the exclusive authority of the classics.   Gargantua plays at two hundred and sixteen
games [3] ; Chapter V of the *Memoirs* is " A Dissertation upon Play-
things. "   The squire Gymnast perfects Gargantua in various acro-
batic and military exercises ; the *Memoirs* tell " Of the Gymnas-
tics, in what exercises Martinus was educated... [4] "

Martinus's pedantic tutor Crambe answers to Thubal Holoferne
and Jobelin Bridé in Rabelais. His " treatise of syllogisms " is a
parody of the sophist logic.   He argues thus with Cornelius whether there can be such a thing as " the idea of an universal Lord
Mayor. "   Crambe affirms the proposition, but

Cornelius told him, that he was a lying rascal ; that an *universale*
was not the object of imagination, and that there was no such thing in
reality, or *à parte rei*.   " But I can prove, " quoth Crambe, " that
there are clysters *a parte rei*, but clysters are *universales* ; *ergo*.   Thus
I prove my minor.   *Quod aptum est inesse multis*, is an *universale* by
definition... [5] "

---

1. *Memoirs*, Ch. I (*Life and Works of Arbuthnot*, 311) ; Rabelais, Bk. I, Ch. I.
2. Rabelais, Bk. I, Ch. VI ; *Memoirs*, Ch. I (*Life and Works of Arbuthnot*, 315).
3. Rabelais, Bk. I, Ch. XXII.
4. Rabelais, Bk. I, Ch. XXIII ; *Memoirs*, Ch. VI.
5. *Memoirs*, Ch. VII (*Life and Works of Arbuthnot*, 334).

Compare this with Janotus vs. Maistre Jousse Bandouille :

Ha! dist Janotus, baudet, baudet, tu ne concluds poinct *in modo et figura.* Voylà de quoy servent les propositions et *parva logicalia. Pannus pro quo supponit* ? — *Confuse,* dist Bandouille, *et distributive.* — Je ne te demande pas, dist Janotus, baudet, *quo modo supponit,* mais *pro quo*; c'est, baudet, *pro tibiis meis* [1]...

Crambe, like many of Rabelais's people, is a player upon words.

Who [he asks] is not governed by the word *led* ? Our nobleman and drunkards [note the juxtaposition] are pimp-led, physicians and pulses fee-led, their patients and oranges pil-led, a new married man and an ass are bridle-led [2]...

One might mention also the Rabelaisian satire on the administration of the law in Martinus's litigation after his marriage to half of a pair of Siamese twins [3], and that on research in the chapter " Of the Discoveries and Works of the great Scriblerus [4]. " Satire dominates in the *Memoirs* as in *Gulliver* ; indeed they might have been written by Swift, who was no doubt the immediate inspiration of his gifted and sympathetic colleague.

Addison adapted Rabelais's chapters about how Pantagruel and his crew heard certain frozen words (Bk. IV, Chs. LV, LVI) in *The Tatler* (No. 254, Thurşday, Nov. 23d, 1710). His adaptation is free and spirited, but since he felt called upon to designate his source one would rather he had come nearer the truth than to have named the " Journal " of Sir John Mandeville, whom he calls " our renowned Countryman. " Surely it is Nemesis that since Addison's day the authorship of the " Voiage and Travaile " of

1. Rabelais, Bk. I, Ch. xx.

2. *Memoirs,* Ch. viii (*Life and Works of Arbuthnot,* 341).

3. *Memoirs,* Ch. xiv, xv, esp. the latter, which deals with Dr. Pennyfeather for Scriblerus, vs. Dr. Leatherhead for Prince Ebn-Hai-Paw-Waw, the black prince of Monopotapa. Compare Baisecul vs. Humevesne in Rabelais, Bk. II, Ch. x-xiii.

4. *Memoirs,* Ch. xiv [orig. Ch. vii]. The satire is like that in Rabelais's catalogue of the Library of St. Victor (Bk. II, Ch. vii) and in his chapters on the Quintessence (Bk. V, Ch. xxi and xxii), though it is slightly less grotesque.

that fictitious character has been settled upon a Frenchman. A well known legendary anecdote of the life of Rabelais, the source of the expression in present French, " un quart d'heure de Rabelais, " was retailed by a certain Eustace Budgell in the *Spectator* of Thursday, January 24th, 1712. These matters would scarcely be worth mentioning were they not the only scraps of evidence I have found in the fugitive literature of the time of any interest in Rabelais outside the orbit of the famous Club. The *Spectator*, except in this paper, has yielded none ; and no more has the *Tatler*[1].

We have unhappily to conclude this view of the generation named for Queen Anne by noticing a forthright and lugubrious anathema of the Master, a shabby recognition indeed of one who had lent inspiration to the greatest of its representatives. Rabelais has survived, of course, all critical " spitters in the dish " throughout the ages, and will doubtless do so always. Those who value most in him the revolutionary element will perhaps rejoice to count the obstacles which have accumulated in the past against his immortality, but the more conservative cannot but find them disturbing. Edward Young, echoing Sir William Temple, exposes himself as follows :

There are some prose satirists of the greatest delicacy and wit ; the last of which can never, or should never, succeed without the former. An author without it, betrays too great a contempt for mankind, and opinion of himself, which are bad advocates for reputation and success. What a difference is there between the merit, if not the wit, of Cervantes and Rabelais ? The last has a peculiar art of throwing a great deal of genius and learning into frolic and jest ; but the genius and the scholar is all you can admire ; you want the gentleman to converse with in him :   he is like a criminal who receives his life for some services ; you commend, but you pardon too. Indecency offends our pride,

---

1. Monsieur Jacques Boulenger includes Adrian Beverland, with date 1714, in a list of English writers who are said to have cited or imitated Rabelais (*Rabelais à Travers les Ages*, 22). The Latin *De Peccato Originali* of Beverland was published in 1679, and was freely adapted and expanded, rather than translated, into French in 1714 by Jean Frédéric Bernard as the *Etat de L'Homme dans le Péché Originel.* The latter contains in Chapter III " Les fruits du Mariage, Conte en prose imité de Rabelais " (pp. 127 ff.), and elsewhere refers to him (Ch. II, § 12, p. 90). I can find no mention of his name, no allusion to his work, nor any trace of his influence, in the original Latin.

as men ; and our unaffected taste, an judges of composition : nature has wisely formed us with an aversion to it ; and he that succeeds in spite of it, is, aliena venia, quam sua providentia tutior [1].

---

1. Preface to the satires, *Poetical Works*, II, 61. The satires were published in 1728 as *The Universal Passion*.

CHAPTER VI

THE AGE OF THE NOVEL

Lord Chesterfield, Henry Fielding, Thomas Amory, Oliver Goldsmith,
Charles Churchill, Samuel Johnson, Tobias Smollett, Laurence Sterne.

The gaiety which marks the age of Queen Anne was menaced by
certain phases of the succeeding generation, though it was by no
means suppressed. The language after Temple and Addison is
wanting in the gentlemanly profanity which the taste of many of
their contemporaries still tolerated, the moralistic bent of the great
mind of Dr. Johnson not infrequently caused him to qualify his
praise of humorous writers, and melancholy was celebrated by the
poets. Thus, though Rabelais's name in world literature was securely established, his English reputation in the middle of the
eighteenth century was bound to be somewhat circumscribed. His
last two important imitators were, as a matter of fact, reckless,
and his critics, on the whole, cautious.

A few disciples occur in the next century, such as the admirable
Peacock, the pedestrian Southey, the American Leland, and very
possibly others. Byron, had he been a novelist, Dickens, had he
lived in the Renaissance, might have given us something Rabelaisian. Smollett and Sterne are the last of those in whom the
influence has any great significance for English literature as a
whole.

Lord Chesterfield wrote patronizingly in a letter to his son, dated
December 5th, 1749 :

If you will please people, you must please them in their own way ;...
Rabelais first wrote a most excellent book, which nobody liked ; then,

determined to conform to the public taste, he wrote *Gargantua* and *Pantagruel*, which everybody liked, extravagant as it was [1].

Fielding objected to Rabelais on moral grounds. He makes a conventional acknowledgment of his greatness in the Invocation which introduces Book XIII of *Tom Jones* [2], but he considered him inferior to Swift [3], and damned him outright in the *Covent Garden Journal* of February 4th, 1752:

There are some...[he says], who, though not void of these talents [i. e. of wit and humor], have made so wretched a use of them, that, had the consecration of their labours been committed to the hangman, no good man would have regretted their loss ; nor am I afraid to mention Rabelais, and Aristophanes himself, in this number. For, if I may speak my opinion freely of these two last writers, and of their works, their design appears to me very plainly to have been to ridicule all sobriety, modesty, decency, virtue, and religion, out of the world [4].

Fielding's name has been frequently mentioned beside that of Rabelais by his critics, though I cannot discover any traces of Rabelaisian influence in his writings, not even in those which are grotesquely satirical, such as *Jonathan Wild* or *Tom Thumb the Great*. Robert Lloyd prefers Fielding to Swift and Rabelais (1763), of the latter of whom he calls him the

...favourite child,
Who, less eccentrically wild,
Inverts the misanthropic plan,
And, hating vices, hates not man [5].

1. *Letters*, ed. Mahon, I, 370.
2. " First, Genius ; thou gift of Heaven ; ...Come, thou that hast inspired thy Aristophanes, thy Lucian, thy Cervantes, thy Rabelais, thy Molière, thy Shakespear, thy Swift, thy Marivaux, fill my pages with humour ... " — *Works*, ed. Maynadier, V, 262.
3. Booth in *Amelia* is certainly speaking for Fielding when he says to a charlatan author " that Dr. Swift hath been generally allowed, by the critics in this kingdom, to be the greatest master of humour that ever wrote. Indeed, I allow him to have possessed most admirable talents of this kind ; and, if Rabelais was his master, I think he proves the truth of the common Greek proverb — that the scholar is often superior to the master. " — *Amelia*, Bk. VIII, Ch. v, *Works*, VIII, 225.
4. *Works*, XI, 257.
5. From the poem " The Cobler of Cripplegate's Letter, " published in *The*

It is enlightening to learn that Rabelais was a misanthrope !
" Courtney Melmoth " observed (1776) that Fielding shared the
opinion of Horace, Rabelais, Lesage, Cervantes, and Swift that
" *laughing* satire was the likeliest to succeed [1]. " Thomas Love
Peacock, insisting that a novel in order to last must contain essential wisdom (for " mere amusement " will " certainly not pass to
posterity "), finds that the writers who have " led fancy against
opinion with a success that no other names can parallel " are Cervantes, Rabelais, Swift, Voltaire, and Fielding [2]. George Meredith
associates roughly the same group : " O for a breath of Aristophanes, Rabelais, Voltaire, Cervantes, Fielding, Molière ! [3] " If
the great novelist found Rabelais immoral, he has himself been so
regarded by large sections of the public. One learns, for example,
that in 1894 a certain New York bookseller was forced into litigation before he could sell copies of *Tom Jones*, Rabelais, or *The
Decameron* [4].

Rabelais was known to the author of *The Life and Opinions of
John Buncle Esquire* (1756), for he makes that hero on one occasion
dine " at Catarric on a hot pigeon-pye just drawn, and ale of one
ear, that is, admirable, as Rabelais means by the phrase, ' We had
wine of one ear ', alluding to the one shake of the head to the right
shoulder, when a thing is excellent [5]. " Scholars are not agreed upon
the interpretation of " vin à une aureille, " but the one accepted
by Thomas Amory was once thought admissible [6]. Whether he
was right or wrong, it argues something more than a casual acquaintance with Maître François that he fastened upon such an
unfamiliar idiom.

A careful perusal of this strange and lengthy novel (it is at least
four fifths as long as the whole of *Gargantua and Pantagruel*) has

St. James's Magazine, May, 1763 ; cit. in *Fielding The Novelist*, by F. T. Blanchard, 172, from Anderson's *Works of The British Poets* (London, 1795), X, 676.
  1. *Liberal Opinions* (London, 1776), III, v ; cit. Blanchard, *op. cit.*, 207.
  2. C. Van Doren, *Life of T. L. Peacock*, 135-36 ; cit. Blanchard, *op. cit.*, 364.
  3. *Essay on the Comic Spirit*, 1877 ; cit. Blanchard, *op. cit.*, 454.
  4. See *The Critic* (New York), XXIV, 444 ; cit. Blanchard, *op. cit.*, 493.
  5. *The Life and Opinions of John Buncle Esquire*, Intro. E. A. Baker (London :
Routledge, Library of Early Novelists), 339.
  6. The expression occurs in Rabelais, Bk. I, Ch. v. See note by Clouzot
and Sainéan, *Œuvres de Rabelais*, ed. Lefranc, I, 64, n. 103.

failed to bring to light any particle of Rabelaisian influence upon it, and yet Hazlitt wrote as follows :

The soul of Francis Rabelais passed into John [sic] Amory, the author of *The Life and Adventures* [sic] *of John Buncle*. Both were physicians, and enemies of too much gravity. Their business was to enjoy life. Rabelais indulges his spirit of sensuality in wine, in dried neats'-tongues, in Bologna sausages, in botargos. John Buncle shows the same symptoms of inordinate satisfaction in tea and bread-and-butter. While Rabelais roared with Friar John and the monks, John Buncle gossiped with the ladies, and with equal and uncontrolled gaiety. These two authors possessed all the insolence of health, so that their works give a fillip to the constitution ; but they carried off the exuberance of their natural spirits in different ways. The title of one of Rabelais' chapters (and the contents answer to the title) is, " How they chirped over their cups. " The title of a corresponding chapter in *John Buncle* would run thus : " The author is invited to spend the evening with the divine Miss Hawkins, and goes accordingly ; with the delightful conversation that ensued [1]. "

Certainly *John Buncle* is a healthy book, a discursive and highly diverting one. It contains one passage not unworthy of the robustious vein of *Pantagruel* [2], and Amory's miscellaneous erudition sometimes appears to surpass Rabelais's own : it is at least its equal on the common ground of medecine [3], and it embraces many matters which Rabelais never touches, such as metallurgy and the higher mathematics [4]. Saintsbury says that " It is impossible to conceive Rabelais as being for one moment ignorant of the ludicrous side of his thoughts or words ; if we laugh we always laugh with, never at him ; ... In Amory, on the other hand, there is no secondary meaning whatever. His greatest absurdities are set down with an ultra-scientific matter-of-factness, without the very slightest touch of tongue in cheek or wink in eye [5]. " He has drawn what may be the right distinction. We laugh, to be sure,

---

1. *John Buncle*, Intro., v.
2. The description of Jack Gallaspy, *John Buncle*, 290-92.
3. See, for example, the episode of Dr. Stanvil, *John Buncle*, 431-34 , also .358 ff.
4. See *John Buncle*, 374 ff., and 353 ff.
5. *The Peace of The Augustans*, 151.

with Rabelais ; but who shall say that Thomas Amory was not aware
of the ludicrousness of marrying seven wives, of carrying on a
courtship over the intricacies of the calculus [1], of thinking it sufficient, once and for all, to observe that he had a great many children [2] ?   Dry humor may, of course, be as dry as the desert, and
so is the greater part of *John Buncle*.   One may, however, believe
in the author's humorous intention, and enjoy his better pages,
without subscribing to the comparison drawn by Hazlitt.

Goldsmith says little of Rabelais, but that little indicates that
he valued him.   Thus he mentions him beside Cervantes as one of
those authors whose meaning suffers in a translation, however
good [3] ; alludes, somewhat loosely, to a volume in the Library of
St. Victor [4] ; refers to " Rabelais's bedchamber [5] ; " says that the
pseudonym Panurge was adopted by one of his contemporaries [6] ;

---

1. *John Buncle*, 353 ff.

2. *Ibid.*, 285.

3. In a notice of *Satirical Letters*, translated from the German of G. W. Ra-
bener (*Monthly Review*, August, 1757), — *Works*, ed. Gibbs, IV, 284.

4. *Enquiry into the present state of Polite Learning in Europe*, 1759, Ch. ii,
— *Works*, III, 474.   See Rabelais, Bk. II, Ch. vii.   Goldsmith's words are :
" But the wiser part of mankind would not be imposed upon by unintelligible
jargon, nor, like the knight in Pantagruel, swallow a chimera for a breakfast,
though even cooked by Aristotle. "   The title of Rabelais's imaginary volume
is :   " Quæstio subtilissima, utrum Chimera, in vacuo bombinans, possit come-
dere secundas intentiones ? et fuit debatuta per decem hebdomadas in concilio
Constantiensi. "   I am indebted for this note to Professor C. H. C. Wright.

5. Letter xxx of the *Letters from a Citizen of the World* is dated May 2d, 1760,
and entitled " The Proceedings of the Club of Authors. "   A poet is introduced
who reads a realistic description of a poverty stricken author asleep in his garret.
" ' There, gentlemen, ' cries he, ' there is a description for you ; Rabelais's bedchamber is but a fool to it.' " — *Works*, III, 114.   The exact meaning is obscure
to me.

6. Goldsmith's poem *The Haunch of Venison* was written c. 1771, published
posthumously in 1776.   Of two guests invited to share the haunch

> The one is a Scotchman, the other a Jew ;
> They both of them merry, and authors like you :
> The one writes the *Snarler*, the other the *Scourge* ;
> Some think he writes *Cinna* — he owns to Panurge.

J. W. M. Gibbs's note reads :   " Prior and Forster say this Scotchman is
'Parson Scott,' who was a paid writer in support of the North Ministry.   He
wrote in the *Public Advertiser* with the signatures Panurge and Anti-Sejanus ;
and it was he who unsuccessfully offered to pay Goldsmith to induce him to
write for the North faction. " — *Works*, II, 49.

and attributes to Rabelais a remark to the effect that " the moments in which a reckoning is mentioned [are] the most melancholy of our lives[1]. "

Charles Churchill invokes " Eternal Truth " in his poem *The Ghost*, exhorting her to eschew the " strumpet air " which she assumes in Rabelais, and to

> ...come in sacred vesture clad,
> Solemnly dull, and truly sad[2]!

It is odd, but perhaps worth recording, that Garrick compared the humor of Dr. Johnson with that of Rabelais, to the detriment of the latter. " Rabelais, " he told Boswell, " and all other wits are nothing compared with him. You may be diverted by them ; but Johnson gives you a forcible hug, and shakes laughter out of you, whether you will or no[3]. " Johnson admitted one evening at the Reynolds's that he recognized himself in a volume of *Modern Characters from Shakespeare* which had just been published (1778), in which he was hit off by the line of Celia in *As You Like It* :

> " I must borrow Garagantua's mouth " [sic].

He was put to the awkward necessity of explaining its application for the benefit of Sir Joshua's daughter.

Why, Madam, [said he], it has a reference to me, as using big words, which require the mouth of a giant to pronounce them. Gargantua is the name of a giant in *Rabelais*.
Boswell. But, Sir, there is another amongst them for you :

> " He would not flatter Neptune for his trident,
> Or Jove for his power to thunder. "

Johnson. There is nothing marked in that. No, Sir, Gargantua is the best.

---

1. In *A Description of Various Clubs*, first published in the *Busy Body* (October 14th, 1759), reprinted with some omissions in his collection of *Essays*, 1765 ; *Works*, I, 252.
2. Bk. II, ll. 161-68, probably written in the early fifties, *Poetical Works*, ed. Hannay and Tooke, II, 63. I am grateful to Mr. Theodore Spencer for this reference.
3. Boswell's *Life*, ed. Hill, II, 231. The remark belongs to the year 1773.

Boswell continues,

Notwithstanding this ease and good humour, when I, a little afterwards, repeated his sarcasm on Kenrick, which was received with
applause, he asked " *Who* said that ? " And on my suddenly answering, *Gargantua*, he looked serious, which was a sufficient indication that he did not wish it to be kept up [1].

It was noticed above that Johnson found the learning of Samuel
Butler the equal of that of Rabelais [2].   It appears on the whole
that the great romance preoccupied him but little ; yet fortunately we are able to record his expressed opinion of its quality.
How judicial, how Johnsonian, are his words !

Nor could the licentious *Rabelais* himself forbear to ridicule this
impious dotage [the belief in astrology], which he does with exquisite
address and humour, where, in the fable which he so agreeably tells
from *Æsop*, of the man who applied to *Jupiter* for the loss of his hatchet,
he makes those, who, on the poor man's good success, had projected
to trick *Jupiter* by the same petition, a kind of astrologick atheists,
who ascribed this good fortune, that they imagined they were now all
going to partake of, to the influence of some rare conjunction and con-
figuration of the stars.   *Hen, hen, disent ils—Et doncques, telle est au
temps present la revolution des Cieulx, la constellation des Astres,
& aspect des Planètes, que quiconque Coignée perdra, soubdain de-
viendra ainsi riche ?*—Nou. Prol. du IV. Livre [3].

Of the first of the two novelists who imitated Rabelais Saintsbury writes as follows :

For sheer nastiness nobody of genius except Swift (for that of Rabelais, and still more certain things in Cervantes himself, fall out of
real comparison) has ever come near Smollett [4].

Readers of *The Adventures of An Atom* will probably subscribe
to Saintsbury's view.   This work is a grotesque satire of the
conduct of public affairs in England from the beginning of the

---

1. Boswell's *Life*, ed. Hill, III, 255-56.   Date 1778.
2. Above, p. 134.
3. From his note on *King Lear*, Act I, Sc. II, ll. 128 ff., *Johnson on Skakes-
peare, Essays and Notes*, ed. Raleigh, 156-57.
4. *The Peace of The Augustans*, 131.

Seven Years War to the date of its publication, 1769, its chief purpose being, as Scott says, "besides that of giving the author the opportunity to raise his hand, like that of Ishmael, against every man,...to inspire the horror of continental connexions [1]." Chatham, Bute, and other statesmen are ruthlessly bespattered with filth, the King himself most of all. All are represented as personages in a fictitious history of Japan, as told to the author, alias Nathaniel Peacock, by the Atom. The acridity of the satire and the writer's bland manner of embroidering enormities suggest Swift throughout. Smollett drew on Rabelais for the same kind of material as Swift in *A Tale of A Tub* and *Gulliver*.

The Atom thus describes how he came to be part of the person of Nathaniel Peacock.

It was in the era of Foggien, one thousand years ago, that fate determined I should exist in the empire of Japan, where I underwent a great number of vicissitudes, till, at length, I was inclosed in a grain of rice, eaten by a Dutch mariner at Firando, and, becoming a particle of his body, brought to the Cape of Good Hope. There I was discharged in a scorbutic dysentery, taken up in a heap of soil to manure a garden, raised to vegetation in a sallad, devoured by an English supercargo, assimilated to a certain organ of his body, from which, at his return to London, being diseased in consequence of impure contact, I was again separated with a considerable portion of putrefied flesh, thrown upon a dunghill, gobbled up and digested by a duck ; of which duck your father, Ephraim Peacock, having eaten plentifully at the feast of the cordwainers, I was mixed with his circulating juices, and finally fixed in the principle part of that animalcule which, in process of time, expanded itself into thee, Nathaniel Peacock [2].

The emperor in whose reign the story begins, Got-ham-baba

was rapacious, shallow, hot-headed, and perverse ; in point of understanding, just sufficient to appear in public without a slavering bib ; inbued with no knowledge, illumed by no sentiment, and warmed with no affection, except a blind attachment to the worship of Fakku-basi, which seemed indeed to be a disease in his constitution. His heart was meanly selfish, and his disposition altogether unprincely.

---

1. *Select Works of Tobias Smollett*, Prefatory Memoir by Sir Walter Scott, I, 21.
2. *Ibid.*, II, 474.

Of all his recreations, that which he delighted in most, was kicking the breech of his cuboy, or prime minister, an exercise which he every day performed in private [1].

The cuboy, Fika-kaka, like Rabelais's *chicanous*, gladly submits to this physical chatisement.

He presented his posteriors to be kicked as regularly as the day revolved ; and presented them not barely with submission, but with all the appearance of fond desire : and truly this diurnal exposure was attended with such delectation as he never enjoyed in any other attitude.

To explain this matter I must tell thee, Peacock, that Fika-kaka was from his infancy afflicted with an itching of the podex, which the learned Dr. Woodward would have termed *immanis* αἰδοίων *pruritus* [2].

The thirteenth chapter of *Gargantua* is invoked in connection with this disease, Smollett being evidently anxious to surpass Rabelais on his own ground.

Be that as it may, certain it is, all the most eminent physicians in Japan were consulted about this strange tickling and tingling, and among these the celebrated Fansey, whose spirit afterwards informed the body of Rabelais. This experienced leech, having prescribed a course of cathartics, balsamics, and sweeteners, on the supposition that the blood was tainted with a scorbutical itch, at length found reason to believe that the disease was local. He therefore tried the method of gentle friction : for which purpose he used almost the very same substances which were many centuries after applied by Gargantua to his own posteriors : such as a nightcap, a pillow-bier, a slipper, a poke, a panier, a beaver, a hen, a cock, a chicken, a calf-skin, a hare-skin, a pigeon, a cormorant, a lawyer's bag, a lamprey, a coif, a lure ; nay, even a goose's neck, without finding that *volupte merifique au trou du cul*, which was the portion of the son of Grangousier. In short, there was nothing that gave Fika-kaka such respite from this tormenting titillation as did smearing the parts with thick cream, which was afterwards licked up by the rough tongue of a boar-cat. But the administration of this remedy was once productive of a disagreeable incident. In the mean time, the distemper gaining ground, became so troublesome, that the unfortunate quanbuku was incessantly in the fidgets, and ran about distracted, cackling like a hen in labour [2].

---

1. *Works*, II, 476.
2. *Ibid.*, II, 478.

One should observe in the paragraph that follows how Smollett has caught Rabelais's colloquial and learned manner.

> The source of all this misfortune was the juxtaposition of two atoms quarreling for precedency, in this the cuboy's seat of honour. Their pressing and squeezing, and elbowing and jostling, though of no effect in discomposing one another, occasioned all this irritation and titillation in the posteriors of Fika-kaka. What! dost thou mutter, Peacock? dost thou presume to question my veracity? Now, by the indivisible rotundity of an atom, I have a good mind, caitiff, to raise such a buzzing commotion in thy *glandula pinealis*, that thou shalt run distracted over the face of the earth, like Io when she was stung by Juno's gad-fly! What! thou who hast been wrapped from the cradle in visions of mystery and revelation, and swallowed impossibilities like lamb's wool, and digested doctrines harder than iron three times quenched in the Ebro! thou to demur at what I assert upon the evidence and faith of my own consciousness and consistency!—Oh! you capitulate! well, then beware of a relapse—you know a relapsed heretic finds no mercy [1].

The only relief that Fika-kaka could find was osculation of the affected part by his inferiors. Skill in the performance of the act became the means of high promotion to many, those with black beards being chiefly honored.

It is unnecessary to attempt an analysis of the whole satire. The adjectives which the Atom applies to the emperor read like Swift, but when he says of a certain individual that " his elocution [is] more discordant than the braying of fifty asses [2], " or that the teeth of the multitude " chattered so loud, that the sound was heard at the distance of half a league [3], " we think rather of Rabelais. Both furnish precedent for the Atom's habit of digressing (on breeches [4], satire [5], and other subjects), and for the type of the satire on the church [6]. If Swift owed much to Rabelais in grotesque invention, Smollett owed still more to Swift. Rabelais's

1. *Works*, II, 478.
2. *Ibid.*, II, 483.
3. *Ibid.*, II, 515.
4. *Ibid.*, II, 487.
5. *Ibid.*, II, 490.
6. The Japanese are said to worship " Fakku-basi, or the white horse ";
see their creed, *Works*, II, 484.

influence comes to him less directly than indirectly, and in general consists simply of an impulse toward the extreme and the monstrous. His style, like Swift's, is consistently precise and elegant, and while he uses more polysyllabic words from the Latin than that author, he does so rather to sharpen the logic of his expression than to enrich its rythmic or acoustic patterns. It is the type of humorous prose of the century, and its tricks were inherited by such men as Thomas Love Peacock, Dickens, and Thackeray, to mention no more.

It might be argued that the opening chapters of *Peregrine Pickle* owe something to the example of Gargantua's education and to the vandalism of Panurge, but in default of evidence that borrowing occurs it is wisest to pass them by in silence. The central tradition of realistic prose narrative had by the generation of Smollett moved too far away from Rabelais to be affected by his technique, or at least by any of its elements except those he shares with all great realists.   Even T. L. Peacock, while he thrills to the Pantagruelistic *joie de vivre*, and delights to quote Rabelais's text, is but little indebted to it in form or organic matter.

One might say the same of the strictly narrative portions of Sterne's *Tristram Shandy* but that none of that strange work *is* strictly narrative. It seems that Sterne might have given us his charming scenes and such people as the Shandys, Dr. Slop, and Corporal Trim, without the prodigious wealth of accidentals which the story is made a pretext for him to display, and which are, to be sure, of equal if not superior interest.   There are narrative and descriptive passages which would appear to owe no more to the example of Rabelais than to that of Cervantes or Fielding, but Sterne's flow of invention jumps so readily and unexpectedly from one mode of expression to another that any one, measured in pages, forms but a small portion of the whole.   He repeatedly calls attention to his own jumpiness, saying, for example, "—But this is neither here nor there—why do I mention it ?   —Ask my pen, —it governs me,—I govern not it [1], " or " I begin with writing

---

1. *The Life and Opinions of Tristram Shandy*, Bk. VI, Ch. VI (Oxford, 1921), 381. Arabic numerals refer to pages in this edition unless otherwise specified.

the first sentence—and trusting to Almighty God for the second [1]. "
What we actually find is that the example of both Rabelais the
realist and Rabelais the eccentric is apparent at every turn, and
that it is a fundamental and shaping influence.

It was at Jesus College, Cambridge, in the early thirties, that
Sterne began to cultivate Maître François and certain closely
related authors, led to them, it appears, by his friend John Hall
Stevenson. The latter, according to Mr. Walter Sichel, " came
of a good Durham family and by a chance inherited the South
Yorkshire castle of Skelton, near Saltburn-by-the-Sea. He was
a handsome madcap and hypochondriac, with more wit, says
Sir Walter Scott, than grace, a dilettante born : dilettante as
viveur, as author, as confirmed valetudinarian, as an eccentric
in would-be fashion, but this dilettantism must be qualified. He
was a dilettante in everything but delicacy, for the delicate was
foreign to a mind which in this respect eventually added to his
friend's degeneration. A confirmed roué and an ardent booklover,
he plied a cynical tongue, which concealed, Sterne assures us, a
kindly heart and many good actions [2]. "

Hall Stevenson named Skelton " Crazy Castle, " and used there
to gather together a convivial group of " demoniacs, " local
squires and parsons, including the now Reverend Laurence Sterne,
his neighbor in the country, for out-of-door sports and the pleasures
of well nourished and well moistened conversation.

> Some fell to fiddling, some to fluting,
> Some to shooting, some to fishing,
> Others to pishing and disputing [3].

This was in the fifties. It seems certain, according to Mr. Wilbur
L. Cross, that these gatherings were partly emulative of those of
the wanton Hell-Fire Club founded in the middle of the decade
by Sir Francis Dashwood [4]. That club met at Medmenham Abbey,
an ancient Cistercian monastery situated on the Thames between

1. *Shandy*, Bk. VIII, Ch. ii, 493.
2. Walter Sichel, *Sterne, A Study*, 21.
3. From Hall Stevenson's *Crazy Tales*, cit. W. L. Cross, *The Life and Times of Laurence Sterne* (Oxford and New Haven, 1925), I, 121.
4. W. L. Cross, *op. cit.*, I, 119-21.

Great Marlow and Henley, to celebrate the black mass, and it would appear also to indulge in promiscuous fornication and other forms of strenuous debauchery. They supposed that their pursuits were Rabelaisian, and accordingly inscribed the motto of the Abbé de Thelème over their portals, " Fay ce que vouldras. " The institution came to an end during a celebration of the " mass " when John Wilkes the politician liberated a baboon which all took to be the devil in person. An entertaining account of the members and of that incident may be found in Charles Johnstone's *Chrysal, or The Adventures of A Guinea* (1760-65) [1].

The " Demoniacs " of Crazy Castle had also, of course, the example of Rabelais before them. Each owned a nickname, that of the Rev. Robert Lascelles being " Pantagruel " or " Panty. " Sterne was " the Black Bird, " Stevenson " Cousin Anthony [2], " and Dashwood, who sometimes joined them, " the Privy Counsellor [3]. "

It is sufficient to have mentioned the gatherings at Skelton and to have noticed that their jesting was merry. The *Crazy Tales* of Hall Stevenson (1762) represent the productions it inspired, and are worthy of perusal by those interested in the background of Sterne's literary career. As it happens, they nowhere recall Rabelais.

That author, however, was decidedly Sterne's favorite. He refers to Rabelais in his correspondence in such a way as to make clear that he thought of himself as his successor in humorous writing [4].

---

1. *Chrysal or the Adventures of a Guinea* by Charles Johnstone, ed. E. A. Baker (London : Routledge, Library of Early Novelists), III, Ch. xix-xxvii. The incident of the baboon occurs in Ch. xxi.

2. See Paul Stapfer, *Laurence Sterne, sa personne et ses ouvrages* (Paris, 1870), 17.

3. See W. L. Cross, I, 121.

4. Thus Sterne warns his friend the Rev. John Blake against the wiles of a set of marriage mongers with whom he has become involved (1758) as follows : " The whole appears what I but too shrewdly suspected, a contexture of plots against your fortune and person, grand mama standing first in the *dramatis personae*, the Loup Garou, or raw head and bloody bones, to frighten Master Jackey into silence, and make him ło to bed with Missy, *supperless* and in peace — " (cit. W. L. Cross,, I, 111. Loupgarou occurs in Rabelais, Bk. II, Ch. xxix). Answering one who attacked his bawdiness, after the publication of Books I and II of *Tristram Shandy*, he writes : " I... deny I have

Bishop Warburton, Voltaire, and several other contemporaries seconded him in this opinion [1]. But if that evidence were wanting the text of his published writings would be amply conclusive.

The earliest of these, *A Political Romance* (January, 1759), better known by its later title, *The History of a Good Warm-Watch-Coat*, while it owes nothing in particular to Rabelais's example, called forth the inevitable comparison in the *Key* which Sterne himself supplied [2].

Tristram Shandy, the first two volumes of which appeared in 1760, is hugely indebted to Rabelais throughout. It is well to understand at the outset, however, that it is also demonstrably indebted in various degrees to a couple of dozen other authors, greater and lesser, including Erasmus, Bishop Hall, Cervantes, Burton, Swift, Locke, Arbuthnot, and three French imitators of Rabelais namely, Béroalde de Verville, Guillaume Bouchet, and N. Des Lauriers, alias "Bruscambille. [3]"

Sterne no doubt had considerable difficulty with the French of

gone as far as Swift : he keeps a due distance from Rabelais ; I keep a due distance from him " (cit. W. L. Cross, I, 174). Books III and IV were unmercifully attacked. Sterne wrote to Stephen Croft : " If my enemies knew that by this rage of abuse and ill-will, they were effectually serving the interests both of myself, and works, they would be more quiet — but it has been the fate of my betters, who have found, that the way to fame, is like the way to heaven — through much tribulation — and till I shall have the honour to be as much maltreated as Rabelais and Swift were, I must continue humble ; for I have not filled up the measure of half their persecutions " (cit. W. L. Cross, I, 248).

1. Warburton called him " the English Rabelais " by way of recommendation to the bench of bishops. Horace Walpole said he did not believe the latter had ever heard of the French humorist (see W. L. Cross, I, 194). " Voltaire, reserving the place of honour for Swift, called Sterne 'le second Rabelais d'Angleterre' " (remark by Lewis Melville, *The Life and Letters of Laurence Sterne*, I, 293 ; see Voltaire, *Œuvres Complètes*, 1876-78, VII, 369). For notice of four eulogistic reviewers of *Tristram Shandy* who compared the author to Rabelais see W. L. Cross, I, 188, 262, and II, 36, 105.

2. " Every Man turn'd the Story to what was swimming uppermost in his Brain ; — so that, before all was over, there were full as many Satyres spun out of it, — and as great a Variety of Personages, Opinions, Transactions, and Truths, found to lay hid under the dark Veil of its Allegory, as ever were discovered in the thrice-renowned History of the Acts of *Gargantua* and *Pantagruel*. " — cit. W. L. Cross, I, 166.

3. On the multiplicity of Sterne's sources see W. L. Cross, I, 128 ff. and John Ferriar, *Illustrations of Sterne, passim.*

Rabelais, in any case the text he chiefly read and quoted was the translation of Urquhart and Motteux as revised and annotated after Duchat by Ozell. Of this the earliest edition was published in 1737, and the only other before *Tristram Shandy* in 1750 ; but I have found no evidence as to which of the two he used. He draws on Ozell not only for the text, but occasionally also for material contained in the introduction and notes. Thus a Latin quotation on the title page of *Shandy*, Book III, is taken from Motteux's Life of Rabelais prefixed by Ozell to the first of his five volumes [1].

In Chapter xix of that book Sterne thus invokes three of his favorite authors in an order and in words which seem to belie his true preferance :

By the tombstone of Lucian—if it is in being—if not, why then by his ashes !   by the ashes of my dear Rabelais, and dearer Cervantes [2] !

The next chapter contains a reference to " Didius, the great church lawyer " and " his code *de fartendi et illustrandi fallaciis*, " the title of which seems to be an adaptation of " *Ars honestè* far-tandi (pettandi) *in societate*, per M. Ortuinum, " which is the seventeenth item in the catalogue of the Library of St. Victor [3].

The Author's Preface to *Tristram Shandy*, which is inserted in the same book between Chapters xx and xxi, contains this quotation from Rabelais's Book III, marked with inverted commas, but not labelled with its author's name :

for what hindrance, hurt, or harm doth the laudable desire of knowledge bring to any man, if even from a sot, a pot, a fool, a stool, a winter-

---

1. " Multitudinis imperitae non formido judicia ; meis tamen, rogo, parcant opusculis — in quibus fuit propositi semper, a jocis ad seria, a seriis vivissim ad jocos transire. — Joan. Saresberiensis, *Episcopus Lugdun.* " — *Shandy,* 142 ; see Ozell's Rabelais, 1737, I, cxx. Sterne has expanded and altered the original, which ends : " ...In quibus fuit propositi semper à nugis ad bona transire seria. " I am indebted for this reference to a MS. note in the Grenville copy of *Tristram Shandy* (see below, p. 247), title page of Vol. III.

2. *Shandy,* 171-72.

3. *Shandy,* 173 ; Rabelais, Bk. II, Ch. vii, — Ozell, II, 50.

mitten, a truckle for a pully, the lid of a goldsmith's crucible, an oil bottle, an old slipper, or a cane chair [1] ?

An explicit reference to Pantagruel and the island of Ennasin occurs in Chapter xxxii [2]. In Chapter xxxviii Tristram's father is said to have learned from Ambrose Paraeus the relation that exists between "the length and goodness of the nose" and "the flaccidity and softness of the nurse or mother's breast [3]." He may have taken the allusion to Paraeus from the Serées of Bouchet [4] or it may have come from Ozell's footnote to Rabelais, Book I, Chapter XL, which cites the name and the passage in Bouchet à propos of Friar John's similar explanation of why he himself has "such a goodly Nose [5]." Whether Bouchet was consulted or not, Sterne did have Rabelais in mind at the time (though Rabelais does not mention Paraeus), for in the final paragraph of the chapter he remarks that he has, among other tasks, "a dialogue between my father and my uncle Toby, upon the solution of Prignitz, Scroderus, Ambrose Paraeus, Ponocrates, and Grangousier to relate [6]," and in the next chapter but two alludes to the very page of Ozell on which Friar John's explanation and the corresponding footnote occur, as follows :

There is no cause but one, replied my uncle Toby—why one man's nose is longer than another's, but because that God pleases to have it so.—That is Grangousier's solution, said my father [7].

Book IV opens with Slawkenbergius's Tale about "the stranger"

---

1. Shandy, 179 ; quoted from Rabelais, Bk. III, Ch. xvi, — Ozell, III, 99. The original begins, "What Hindrance, Hurt, or Harm..." and ends, "an Oil Bottle, or old Slipper ? "
2. " Now, my great-grandfather's nose was for all the world like unto the noses of all the men, women, and children, whom Pantagruel found dwelling upon the island of Ennasin. — By the way, if you would know the strange way of getting akin amongst so flat nosed a people — you must read the book ; — find it out yourself, you never can. " — Shandy, 197 ; see Rabelais, Bk. IV, Ch. ix.
3. Shandy, 210-11.
4. Guillaume Bouchet, Les Serées, No. 24, ed. Roybet, IV, 65.
5. Ozell, I, 317, n. 14.
6. Shandy, 212.
7. Shandy, 216-17.

and his nose. The Promontory of Noses which " the stranger " is said to have visited may be a reminiscence of " the Fair of Noses " mentioned by Ponocrates in the passage on Friar John's nose already cited [1]. A reference occurs some pages beyond to " Pantagruel and his companions in quest of the oracle of the bottle [2]. "

The accidental circumcision of Tristram calls forth his remark in Book V, Chapter xxvi, that

> Fifty thousand pannier loads of devils—(not of the Archbishop of Benevento's—I mean of Rabelais's devils) with their tails chopped off by their rumps, could not have made so diabolical a scream of it, as I did—when the accident befell me [3]...

Parson Yorick always carries a volume of Rabelais about him, and being asked by Uncle Toby in Chapter xxviii " what a polemic divine is, " replies

> The best description, Captain Shandy, I have ever read, is of a couple of 'em, ...in the account of the battle fought single hands betwixt Gymnast and Captain Tripet ; which I have in my pocket [4].

Uncle Toby begs to hear it, and it is then said that Yorick " read, or pretended to read, as follows. " The next chapter consists of a quotation of Ozell's version of the burlesque duel in Rabelais, Book I, Chapter xxxv, with one or two unimportant alterations [5]. The solemn interjections of my uncle Toby, Mr. Walter, and Corporal Trim, are highly amusing.

Mr. Walter Shandy advises Uncle Toby how to govern his prospective bride in Book VIII, Chapter xxxiv.

> ...suffer her not [he says] to look into *Rabelais*, or *Scarron*, or *Don Quixote*—

---

1. *Shandy*, 221 ; Rabelais, Bk. I, Ch. xl, Ozell, I, 317. — Ponocrates says that Friar John has such a goodly nose " because... he came with the first to the Fair of Noses, and therefore made choice of the fairest and the greatest. "

2. *Shandy*, 239.

3. *Shandy*, 351.

4, *Shandy*, 355.

5. *Shandy*, 355-56 ; Ozell's Rabelais, I, 294-95.

—They are all books which excite laughter ; and thou knowest, dear Toby, that there is no passion so serious as lust [1].

A probable borrowing occurs in the second paragraph following, in which Mr. Walter warns the lover that it will be well for him to abate his passions during the courtship, lest the widow be given too sanguine an impression of his inclination for her, and pre-scribes blood letting " below the ears, according to the practise of the ancient Scythians, who cured the most intemperate fits of the appetite by that means. " The same prescription and the re-ference to the Scythians are made by the physician Rondibilis to Panurge in Rabelais, Book III, Chapter xxxi [2].

Sterne's tender heart is strikingly weighed against his gusto for Rabelais in a passage in *Shandy*, Book IX, Chapter xxiv. Tris-tram is talking to poor Maria, the mad woman he meets on the road to Moulins. Her alternate glances at him and at her little goat cause him to ask, " What resemblance do you find ? "—and he continues :

I do entreat the candid reader to believe me, that it was from the humblest conviction of what a Beast man is,—that I asked the ques-tion ; and that I would not have let fallen an unseasonable pleasantry in the venerable presence of Misery, to be entitled to all the wit that ever Rabelais scattered [3].

The following self-explanatory reference to *Gargantua* occurs in Book IX, Chapter xxv. Sterne is defending himself for having written " a chapter which has only nothing in it. "

—Why then was it left so ? And here without staying for my reply, shall I be called as many blockheads, numskulls, doddypoles, dunder-heads, ninnyhammers, goosecaps, joltheads, nincompoops, sh-t-a-beds —and other unsavoury appelations, as ever the cake-bakers of Lernè cast in the teeth of King Garangantua's [sic] shepherds — And I'll let them do it, as Bridget said, as much as they please ; for how was it possible they should foresee the necessity I was under of writing the 25th chapter of my book, before the 18th, etc. [4] ?

1. *Shandy*, 543.
2. Ozell's Rabelais, III, 210. I owe this reference to the annotator of the Grenville copy of *Tristram Shandy* (M S. note in Vol. VIII, 221).
3. *Shandy*, 578.
4. *Shandy*, 579 ; see Rabelais, Bk. I, Ch. xxv, Ozell, I, 255.

Sterne borrows a few names from Rabelais, e. g. "Agelastes" (one who never laughs)[1], "Kysarcius" (Rabelais's "Baise-cul[2]"),"Homenas[3]." The "Montero-cap,"the "constant wager" of Corporal Trim in Book VI, Chapter xxiv, is perhaps a reminiscence of that used for a wipe-breech by the youthful Gargantua[4] ; while the name Sterne gives to a tall man and a short man together in Book VII, Chapter vii, "Size-ace," undoubtedly derives from the following in Rabelais (Book V, chapter x) :

He told us that twenty chance Devils, very much fear'd in our Country, dwelt there in six different Stories, and that the biggest Twins or Braces of them were call'd Sixes, and the smallest Amb's-Ace[5] ...

Sterne also borrows the word "belute," meaning to spatter with mud, from Rabelais's "beluter[6]." The phrase "G-fol-re-ut" occurs in *Shandy*, Book VI, Chapter i, echoing Panurge in Rabelais, Book II, Chapter xxxi[7]; and "matter of Breviary," a favorite expression of Friar John, is used by Sterne in *Shandy*, Book VIII, Chapter viii[8].

So much for the material borrowed[9]. It forms a sufficiently

---

1. *Shandy*, Author's Preface (between chapters xx and xxi of Bk. III), 173. The word occurs as a plural is Rabelais, and is translated " Eavesdroppers, " but the French is supplied in a footnote with its etymology ; see Rabelais, The Epistle to Odet preceding Bk. IV, Ozell, IV, lxiv, and *Ibid.*, n. 3.

2. *Shandy*, Author's Preface, 173 ; Rabelais, Bk. II, Ch. x, Ozell, II, 100, *et al.* Ozell's translation is, of course, " Kissebreech. "

3. *Shandy*, Bk. IV, Ch. xxv, 286 ; the name in Rabelais is that of the Bishop of the Papimanes, Bk. IV, Ch. xlviii-liii. Sterne's Homenas is a clergyman.

4. *Shandy*, 411-12 ; Rabelais, Bk. I, Ch. xiii, Ozell, I, 197.

5. *Shandy*, 442 ; Ozell's Rabelais, V, 37.

6. *Shandy*, Bk. II, Ch. ix, 97. This is the earliest use of the word in English recorded by the Oxford Dictionary. The etymology given is *be* + ad. L. *lutum*, mud. Rabelais uses *beluter* most often to mean " to copulate " (Bk. III, Ch. xi, xix, xxvi ; Bk. IV, Ch. xliv), but once, at least, for " to kill [time] " (Bk. I, Ch. xxii). Sterne must have taken *beluted* from the French, for the translators always use a different word.

7. *Shandy*, 374 ; Ozell's Rabelais, II, 235.

8. *Shandy*, 499.

9. It may be mentioned here that " The Fragment " containing the story of the Notary in Sterne's *Sentimental Journey* (1768, ed. Francis Bickley, 182-90) is said to have been " in the old French of Rabelais's time ; and, for aught I know, might have been wrote by him " (p. 183). I cannot see that the " Fragment " or any other part of the *Sentimental Journey* is in any sense Rabelaisian.

revealing prologue to a consideration of the shaping influence
of Rabelais upon Sterne's art.

" Shandeism " is a slightly decadent offspring of " Pantagruelism. " Some attempt was made in the introductory chapter to
indicate what the second of the terms signifies, and we may hear
Sterne's own observations upon the first. Its implications are,
of course, too many for anyone to grasp who is not thoroughly
familiar with *The Life and Opinions of Tristram*. In one place
we hear of certain " good, honest, unthinking Shandean people, "
who include " Zeno, Cleanthes, Diogenes Babylonius, Dionysius
Heracleotes, Antipater, Panaetius, and Posidonius among the
Greeks ;—Cato and Varro and Seneca amongst the Romans ;
—Pantaenus and Clemens Alexandrinus and Montaigne amongst
the Christians [1]. " The effect of the list is to describe Sterne as
Shandean, not the individuals mentioned. How impressive,
how romantic, and how impertinent to call Zeno, Cato, Seneca,
and Montaigne "good, honest, and unthinking ! " And who, one
blushes not to ask, is Diogenes Babylonius ? " Anti-Shandeans "
are addressed, among other readers, in the Author's Preface [2],
but they are nowhere abused as Rabelais abuses those critics
whom he calls " spitters in the dish [3], " for Sterne had not a drop
of gall in his make-up. He follows Rabelais in grotesquely satirizing speculative thought, and, like him, does so chiefly with
reference to individual character and to exploit the opportunities
offered for sheer nonsensical invention. " True Shandeism, "
says he, " think what you will against it, opens the heart and lungs,
and like all those affections which partake of its nature, it forces
the blood and other vital fluids of the body to run freely through
its channels, makes the wheel of life run long and cheerfully
round [4]. " Here it is at one with the medecine of Rabelais. Rabelais indicates the curative value of *Pantagruel* for the toothache,
the pox, the gout, etc., in the Author's Prologue to Book II, and

---

1. *Shandy*, Bk. III, Ch. IV, 145.
2. *Shandy*, Bk. III, between Ch. XX and XXI, 173.
3. Rabelais, Bk. IV, Ancien Prologue. That prologue is omitted from Ozell's
translation.
4. *Shandy*, Bk. IV, Ch. XXXII, 307.

cites Hippocrates on the therapeutics of cheerfulness in the Ancient Prologue to Book IV.   The Epistle to Odet which follows
that Prologue asserts that his previous writings have in fact
fulfilled their promise.

You are not unacquainted, *most Illustrious Prince*, how often I have
been, and am daily press'd and required, by great Numbers of eminent
Persons, to proceed in the *Pantagruelian* Fables ; they tell me that
many languishing, sick, and disconsolate Persons perusing them, have
deceiv'd their Grief, pass'd their Time merrily, and been inspir'd with
new Joy and Comfort [1].

Following that Epistle comes the Author's Prologue, which
opens as follows :

Good People, God save and keep you :   Where are you ?   I can't
see you ; stay—I'll saddle my Nose with Spectacles—Oh, oh ! 'twill
be fair anon I see you.   Well, you have had a good Vintage, they say ;
this is no bad News to *Frank*, you may swear ; you have got an infallible
Cure against Thirst ; rarely perform'd of you, my Friends !   You,
your Wives, Children, Friends, and Families are in as good Case as
Heart can wish ; 'tis well, 'tis as I'd have it :   God be praised for it,
and if such be his Will, may you long be so.   For my part I am there-
abouts, Thanks to his blessed Goodness ; and by the means of a little
Pantagruelism, (which you know is a certain Jollity of Mind pickled
in the Scorn of Fortune) you see me now Hale and Cheery, as sound
as a Bell, and ready to drink, if you will [2].

Sterne echoes both the idea and the manner of this passage
in *Shandy*, Book VIII, Chapter III.

—Bonjour !—good morrow !—so you have got your cloak on be-
times !—but 'tis a cold morning, and you judge the matter rightly—'tis
better to be well mounted, than go o'foot—and obstructions in the
glands are dangerous—And how goes it with thy concubine—thy wife,
—and thy little ones o' both sides ?   and when did you hear from the
old gentleman and lady—your sister, aunt, uncle, and cousins—I hope
they have got better of their colds, coughs, claps, tooth-aches,
fevers, stranguries, sciaticas, swellings, and sore eyes [3].

---

1. Ozell's Rabelais, IV, LXI-LXII.
2. *Ibid.*, IV, LXVIII-LXIX.
3. *Shandy*, 494.   The style of this passage should be compared with that of
one cited above (p. 67) from *The Metamorphosis of Ajax* of Sir John Harington.

Sterne, like Rabelais, is ever conscious of the immediate presence of his reader, who is usually addressed as "Madam [1]," less often as "Sir [2]," occasionally as "your worship [3]," and once in the plural as "my lads [4]." His colloquial manner may be further illustrated by the frequent occurrence of the ethical dative [5], parenthesis [3], and interruptions [6], and by the faithful retention of the sometimes complicated form of the original in reported conversation [7]. He is fond of homely images and epithets [8].

There is scarcely sufficient common ground between Sterne's reading and that of Rabelais to warrant comparison. It is enough to observe that they delighted equally in miscellaneous lore, both learned and popular. Sterne, however, was an arch-dilettante and wanted the ripe scholarship of his master [9].

He displays the jargon of the art military again and again in connection with my uncle Toby [10], that of the law in connection

---

1. *Shandy*, 10, 19, 47, 54, etc.
2. *Shandy*, 25, 48, etc.
3. *Shandy*, 34, 396.
4. *Shandy*, 369.
5. E.g. " ...he might venture to foretell you to an hour when he should get to his journey's end. " — *Shandy*, 35.
6. See quotation below, pp. 203-04.
7. " So that in the midst of a dispute on the subject, in which, by the bye, he was frequently involved, — he would sometimes break off in a sudden and spirited Epiphonema, or rather Erotesis, raised a third, and sometimes a full fifth above the key of the discourse, — and demand it categorically of his antagonist, Whether he would take upon him to say, he had ever remembered, — whether he had ever read, — or even whether he had ever heard tell of a man, called Tristram, performing anything great or worth recording ? — No, — he would say, — Tristram ! — The thing is impossible. " — *Shandy*, Bk. I, Ch. xix, 52.
8. E.g. : " ...it so happened, that in 49 instances out of 50, the said head was compressed and moulded into the shape of an oblong conical piece of dough, such as a pastry-cook generally rolls up in order to make a pie of. " — *Shandy*, Bk. II, Ch. xix, 138. Also : " ...I mean good, honest, devilish tight, hard knots. " — *Shandy*, Bk. III, Ch. x, 151.
9. An interesting revelation of one of Sterne's meretricious albeit plausible pretentions to learning was made by Mr. Edward Bensley in a letter to the *Times Literary Supplement* of November 1, 1928. Sterne, it appears, did not, as has been supposed, consult the authorities he cites on the art military in Books II and III of *Shandy* in connection with my uncle Toby, but instead took his information almost verbatim from Chambers's *Cyclopaedia*.
10. *Shandy*, Bk. II, Ch. i, ii, iii, and xii, Bk. III, Ch. xxv.

with a certain contract between Mr. and Mrs. Walter Shandy[1], that of theology in a passage on the baptism of Tristram [2], and that of medecine in describing his birth, and again when he describes the bruised knees of the Abbess of Andouillets [3]. The cant of scholarship is parodied in certain Latin footnotes [4].

His preoccupation with words is like that of his own uncle Toby.

> Gentle critic ! when thou hast...considered within thyself how much of thy own knowledge, discourse, and conversation has been pestered and disordered, at one time or another, by this, and this only [i. e. " the unsteady uses of words "] :—What a pudder and racket in Councils about οὐσία and ὑπόστασις ; and in the Schools of the learned about power and about spirit ; about essences and about quintessences ; —about substances and about space.—What confusion in greater Theatres from words of little meaning, and as indeterminate a sense ! when thou considerest this, thou wilt not wonder at my uncle Toby's perplexities,—thou wilt drop a tear of pity upon his scarp and his counterscarp ;—his glacis and his covered way ;—his ravelin and his half-moon : 'Twas not by ideas,—by Heaven ; his life was put in jeopardy by words [5].

We have noticed certain names and words Sterne took from Rabelais : he manufactured plenty of the same stamp himself. Thus the name " Phutatorius " in the Author's Preface[6] is learnedly derived from the Greek verb Φυτεύω (metaph. to generate), and " Gastripheres " from γαστήρ + Φέρω (stomach + to carry) [6]. One may add " Monopulus," " Eugenius," " Somnolentius [7]," and " saint Paraleipomenon [8]. " His popular formations include " Hobby-Horsical [9], " " ink-shed [10], " " be-virtued, be-pictured,

---

1. *Shandy*, Bk. I, Ch. xv.
2. *Shandy*, Bk. IV, Ch. xxix.
3. *Shandy*, Bk. II, Ch. xix, and Bk. VII, Ch. xxi, respectively.
4. *Shandy*, Slawkenbergius's Tale, Bk. IV, 235, 236.
5. *Shandy*, Bk. II, Ch. ii, 79-80.
6. *Shandy*, Bk. III, between Ch. xx and xxi, 173.
7. *Shandy*, Bk. III, between Ch. xx and xxi, 173.
8. *Shandy*, Bk. III, Ch. xxxvi, 204.
9. *Shandy*, Bk. I, Ch. xxiv, 70, Bk. III, Ch. xiii, 165.
10. *Shandy*, Bk. II, Ch. ii, 79.

be-butterflied, befiddled [1], " " squirtical [2], " " corregiescity [3], " " devilesses [4], " " tristramed [5], " " τυπτω-ing [6]. "

Like Rabelais Sterne delights in lengthy catalogues. Thus some thirty parts of the body are enumerated in the " Excommunication " pronounced upon Obadiah for tying tight knots in Dr. Slop's bag : " 'May he be cursed in the hair of his head ! —May he be cursed in his brains, and in his vertex,' (that is a sad curse, quoth my father), 'in his temples, in his forehead...' " etc. [7] A long list of legal terms occurs in Book I, Chapter xv [8] ; a list of the garments of antiquity in Book VI, Chapter xix [9] ; and a list of the streets of Paris in Book VII, Chapter xviii [10].

Shorter groupings of parallel words and constructions illustrate not only his fondness for that feature of Rabelais's style, but also many of its characteristic patterns of rythm, sound, and sense, Thus he quotes the passage already noticed about " a sot, a pot, a fool, a stool, " etc., and echoes it in another place as follows :

What's wrong now !—Diable !—a rope's broke !—a knot has slipt !— a staple's drawn !—a bolt's to whittle !—a tag, a rag, a jag, a strap, a buckle, or a buckle's tongue, want altering [11].

It would be easy to multiply examples. In Book III, Chapter iv, he remarks that his (the author's) jerkin has been drubbed by the critics

pell-mell, helter-skelter, ding-dong, cut and thrust, back stroke and fore stroke, side way and long way [12].

In Chapter xxiv of the same Book he speaks of " a simple, single,

---

1. *Shandy*, Bk. II, Ch. iii, 81.
2. *Shandy*, Bk. III, Ch. viii, 149.
3. " ...the corregiescity of Corregio ". — *Shandy*, Bk. III, Ch. xii, 163.
4. *Shandy*, Bk. III, The Author's Preface, between Ch. xx and xxi, 175.
5. *Shandy*, Bk. III, Ch. xxxviii, 211.
6. " τυπτω-ing it, at Greek and Latin. " — *Shandy*, Bk. V, Ch. xlii, 369.
7. *Shandy*, Bk. III, Ch. xi, 159.
8. *Shandy*, 38.
9. *Shandy*, 403.
10. *Shandy*, 455.
11. *Shandy*, Bk. VII, Ch. viii, 444.
12. *Shandy*, 146.

silly affair [1]. " Rabelais in his Prologue to Book III, having accumulated in one sentence a hundred or more verbs to describe how Diogenes tumbled his tub, concludes it with the summary understatement that the Cynic " every way so bang'd it and belabour'd it, that it was ten thousand to one he had not struck the bottom of it out [2]. " Notice how Sterne recalls that sentence in *Shandy*, Book III, Chapter IV :

—you might have rumpled and crumpled, and doubled and creased, and fretted and fridged the outside of them all to pieces; —in short, you might have played the very devil with them [3]...

In Book III, Chapter XXXVI, occurs this vivid passage :

Now don't let Satan, my dear girl, in this chapter, take advantage of any one spot of rising ground to get astride of your imagination, if you can any ways help it ; or if he is so nimble as to slip on—let me beg of you, like an unbacked filly, to frisk it, to squirt it, to jump it, to rear it, to bound it—and to kick it, with long kicks and short kicks, till, like Tickletoby's mare, you break a strap or a crupper, and throw his worship into the dirt [4].

The mare in Rabelais

was, soon scar'd out of her seven Senses, and began to start, to funk it, to squirt it, to trot it, to fart it, to bound it, to gallop it, to kick it, to spurn it, to calcitrate it, to winse it, to frisk it, to leap it, to curvet it, with double Jirks, and Bum-motions ; insomuch that she threw down *Tickletoby*, though he held fast by the Tree of the Pack Saddle with might and main [5].

A final illustration of the breathless manner may be given. This time it is the manner of the popular orator, as in Rabelais's " discours. " Notice the grouping of expressions in pairs, threes, and fours.

Now—Ten thousand, and ten thousand times ten thousand (for

---

1. *Shandy*, 187.
2. Ozell's Rabelais, III, IX.
3. *Shandy*, 145.
4. *Shandy*, 203.
5. Rabelais, Bk. IV, Ch. XIII, Ozell, IV, 54.

matter and motion are infinite) are the ways by which a hat may be dropped upon the ground, without any effect.—Had he flung it, or thrown it, or cast it, or skimmed it, or squirted it, or let it slip or fall in any possible direction under heaven,—had he dropped it like a goose—like a puppy—like an ass—or in doing it, or even after he had done, had he looked like a fool—like a ninny—like a nincompoop—it had failed, and the effect upon the heart had been lost.

Ye who govern this mighty world and its mighty concerns with the engines of eloquence,—who heat it, and cool it, and melt it, and mollify it,—and then harden it again to your purpose—

Ye who wind and turn the passions with this great windlass, and, having done it, lead the owners of them, whither ye think meet—

Ye, lastly, who drive—and why not, Ye also who are driven, like turkeys to market with a stick and a red clout—meditate—meditate, I beseech you, upon Trim's hat [1].

Two elliptical aspects of Rabelais's style are the use of parenthesis and the subordination of several modifiers one to another, and both are found in Sterne. The first has already been mentioned, and is so common in both writers as to need no illustration. The second appears in this sentence of Rabelais :

Which in itself is to him so grievous for the cordial Affection wherewith he hath always cherished his Subjects, that more it cannot be to any mortal Man ; yet in this (above human Apprehension) is it to him the more grievous, that these Wrongs and sad Offences have been committed by thee and thine, who Time out of Mind, from all Antiquity, thou and thy Predecessors have been in a continual League and Amity with him, and all his Ancestors; which, even until this Time, you have as sacred together inviolably preserved, kept and maintained so well, that not he and his only, but the very barbarous Nations, the Poictevins, Bretons, Manceaux, and those that dwell beyond the Isles of the Canaries, and that of Isabella, have thought it as easy to pull down the Firmament, and to set up Depths above the Clouds, as to make a Breach in your Alliance ; and have been so afraid of it in their Enterprises, that they have never dared to provoke, incense, or indamage the one for Fear of the other [2].

Compare this with the following from *Shandy*, Book III, Chapter XI :

—By the golden beard of Jupiter—and of Juno (if her majesty wore

---

1. *Shandy*, Bk. V, Ch. VII, 332.
2. Rabelais, Bk. I, Ch. XXXI, Ozell, I, 276-77.

one) and by the beards of the rest of your heathen worships, which by
the bye was no small number, since what with the beards of your celestial gods, and gods aerial and aquatic—to say nothing of the beards
of town-gods and country-gods, or of the celestial goddesses your wives,
or of the infernal goddesses your whores and concubines (that is in case
they wore 'em)—all which beards, as Varro tells me, upon his word
and honour, when mustered up together, made no less than thirty
thousand effective beards upon the pagan establishment ;—every beard
of which claimed the rights and privileges of being stroken and sworn
by—by all these beards together then—I vow and protest, that of the
two bad cassocks I am worth in the world, I would have given the
better of them, as freely as ever Cid Hamet offered his—to have stood
by, and heard my uncle Toby's accompaniment [1].

A notable ellipsis has been pointed out in Rabelais by Huguet
in Book IV, Chapter XVII [2] : " Et estoit le noble Bringuenarilles
[says Rabelais] à cestuy matin trepassé, en facon tant estrange
que plus esbahir ne vous fault de la mort de Aeschylus. "   A
whole page of discussion growing out of the last phrase follows,
after which he begins again, " Plus de Anacréon poète.... "   Sterne,
since even the learned style of writing was much less highly
wrought in his day than it had been in the Renaissance, would
never have risked using such a very obscure construction, unless
humorously, and in that case would probably have called attention to it, and thereby simplified it, perhaps by repeating the
key phrase, " ne vous fault esbahir. "   Nevertheless his habits
of thought were decidedly elliptical, and he goes further than
Rabelais in the length of his interruptions, as for example when
he breaks a conversation between Mr. Walter and my uncle Toby
by ten chapters, the fifth and sixth of which respectively
terminate one book and begin another [3].

Occasional inversions of word order suggest the influence of
Rabelais [4], as also certain repetitions of words and phrases [5].

---

1. *Shandy*, 161.
2. *Étude sur la Syntaxe de Rabelais*, 438.
3. *Shandy*, Bk. I, Ch. XXI, 58, to Bk. II, Ch. VI, 90.
4. E.g. " — find it out yourself, you never can. " — Bk. III, Ch. XXXII, 197 ;
" ...translated shall a couple of volumes be. " — Bk. IV, Ch. I, 247 ; " he set
the corporal to work — and sweetly went it on. " — Bk. VI, Ch. XXI, 406.
5. The expression " Leave we... " is repeated three times in Bk. VI, Ch. XX,
405.

Grotesque ideas are rare in Sterne, the most conspicuous being a Rabelaisian affectation of precision, as when he says that Trim " bent forwards just so far, as to make an angle of 85 degrees and a half upon the plain of the horizon [1], " that Mr. Walter Shandy " must have reddened, pictorially and scientifically speaking, six whole tints and a half, if not a full octave above his natural color[2], " or that " the Antinosarians denied that a nose of 575 geometrical feet in length could be worn, at least by a middle-sized man [3]. "

I have described the Rabelaisian aspects of Sterne's work as conservatively as might be, and certain limitations should be indicated. The more fantastic of his mannerisms, such as his use of very short chapters (even of chapters with nothing in them), dashes, asterisks, index hands, and marbled pages, seem not to be owing to Rabelais at all, but to other writers. The shortness of the chapters and the violence of his method of digressing are doubtless chiefly accountable to Béroalde de Verville [4], Guillaume Bouchet, and N. des Lauriers (alias " Bruscambille [5] "). Professor Cross points out the connection that exists betweenh is typographical tricks and two works entitled An Essay towards the Theory of the Intelligible World (by " Gabriel John, " i. e.   Tom D'Urfey ?) and A Voyage Round the World (by John Dunton, 1691) [6].

The most fundamental difference between Sterne's humor and Rabelais's is the innuendo and periphrasis upon which so much of the former depends. This is related to his sentimentalism,

---

1. Shandy, Bk. II, Ch. xvii, 110.
2. Shandy, Bk. III, Ch. v, 146-47.
3. Shandy, Bk. IV, Slawkenbergius's Tale, 238-239.
4. The incident of the circumcision of Tristram Shandy (Bk. V, Ch. xvii) appears to have been inspired by the fiftieth chapter of Le Moyen de Parvenir of Béroalde. In each the chamber pot is missing, missing through the agency, in the one, and the neglect, in the other, of a woman, and in each, as a result, Sir Martin Wagstaffe is securely trapped. Each episode fills a very brief chapter, just over one 8° page in length.
5. See Le Moyen de Parvenir of Béroalde, 1610 (modern edition by Garnier Frères, Paris) ; Guillaume Bouchet, Les Sérees, 1584 ff. (modern edition by C. E. Roybet, Paris, 1873-82) ; and des Lauriers, Les Fantaisies de Bruscambille, 1612. " Bruscambille " was the author Mr. Walter Shandy was delighted to be able to purchase for three half-crowns (Shandy, Bk. III, Ch. xxxv).
6. W. L. Cross, The Life and Times of Laurence Sterne, I, 132.

and to the comparatively fastidious taste of his age. He continually belies a remark in Book IV, Chapter xxxii : " I shall not be
at all nice in the choice of my words [1], " for though he always
likes to be shocking, he generally prefers to pretend that he is
not [2].

Saintsbury argues that, without attempting to compare the
relative merits of the two writers, one can assert Sterne's task
to have been the harder :　it is harder, he says, to write an eccentric novel than an eccentric romance [3].　One wonders whether
the observation was worth the making.　The truth is that *Tristram Shandy* is not an eccentric novel ; it is not a novel at all.
It is a series of papers which, though they are written with a
more consistent and individual humor, have otherwise not a jot
more unity than the papers of Mr. Spectator.　Paul Stapfer effec-
tively anticipated any attempt to confuse Sterne's rank with that
of Rabelais when he said :　" Il y a du dieu dans Rabelais, — du
diable aussi :　dans Sterne il y a du singe [4]. "　The common
ground upon which the two great men meet as near rivals, and in
which the guidance of the earlier is most significant, is the representation of lively scenes and people by the use of informal
description, and of dialogue, with its accompanying facial and bodily
expression.　Nobody would wish to deny to Sterne the charm of
his people and of his droll animadversions upon life, but however
much his manner may be owing to Rabelais, he does not pretend
to speak with the same force and wisdom.　His quality is special,
and therefore, by definition, unrivalled.

---

1. *Shandy*, 307.
2. For example, the perfectly innocent request that the nurse makes of Tristram when the chamber pot is found to be missing is expressed thus : " — cannot
you manage, my dear, for a single time, to ＊＊＊＊ ＊＊＊ ＊＊ ＊＊＊ ＊＊＊＊＊＊ ? "
— *Shandy*, Bk. V, Ch. xvii, 345.
3. *The Peace of The Augustans*, 141.
4. *Laurence Sterne — Sa personne et ses ouvrages*, 143.

CHAPTER VII

CONCLUSION

It has been said that Gargantua ceased to embody the ideals of western civilization at the close of the sixteenth century [1]. The difference between the age which produced him and all succeeding ages is, indeed, marked. A living Gargantua would certainly have been as much out of place in a Restoration or Queen Anne drawing room, assuming he could squeeze through the door, as he would have been at home in a tavern of the Renaissance.

It is evident that the Elizabethans and their nearer descendants were in a better position than the Augustans or the novelists to produce Rabelaisian satire from life. For the same reason, while one would expect to find, and does find, that they were good textual critics of the great romance — witness Holyband and Cotgrave — they were lacking in the perspective necessary to its appraisal as a whole. That was first achieved in the second half of the seventeenth century, by John Hall, Motteux, Thomas Rymer, and others.

Rabelais's later influence in English literature has not proved

---

1. " Im 17., im 18. und auch noch manchmal in unserm Jahrhundert treffen hie und da die dem 16. Jahrhundert eigentümlichen Laute unser Ohr. Aber sie klingen fremd und befremdend. Im Zeitalter der Allongeperrüke, des Zopfes und des schwarzen Cylinders findet sich Gargantua nicht zurecht. Was soll der ungeschlachte Riese mit einem zimperlichen Marquisdegen, wenn er die schwere Keule zu schwingen gewohnt ist, was soll er mit den engen Kniehosen, wo seiner unentbehrlichen ' braguette ' ihr gebührendes Recht nicht würde, was soll er mit weissen Glacéhandschuhen, die ihn genieren würden, wenn er die Faust ballen wollte ? Er ist ein Kind des 16. Jahrhunderts und würde zum Zwerge verkümmern, wenn man ihn in die engen Schranken späterer Jahrhunderte einzwängen wollte. " — Heinrich Schneegans, *Gesch. d. Grot. Sat.*, 483.

less important than his earlier ; rather the contrary, as is apparent
when we compare the Elizabethan Rabelaisians with Swift or Sterne.
No English writer has attempted a completely bookish imitation,
certainly not Urquhart in his translation, and while it would be
wrong to overemphasize the difficulty of reconciling *Pantagruel* with
more modern thought, our imitators from the Restoration onward
show that it has not always been overcome. An apparent cycle
can be discerned in the course of the influence, which takes its
first effect in the heyday of Shakespeare, grows more powerful as
it meets opposing currents in more conservative times, and at last,
combined with the new romanticism, is consumed in a wild orgy
of scurrility, eccentricity, and sentimentalism.

Rabelais's contribution to the living English vocabulary — as
opposed to the extinct ones of Gabriel Harvey, Urquhart, and
others — while it would appear to have been substantial, is not
easy to measure. Whatever its extent, it must be regarded as important, for the very difficulty of isolating it proves how thoroughly
it has been assimilated.

The question arises whether Rabelais has given us a genuine,
that is, a self-propagating, tradition. A bastard tradition there
certainly is, which were better forgotten, that of the atheism,
obscenity, frivolity, cynicism, and the rest of the misunderstood
and misnamed virtues of the Curé de Meudon. There is probably
also a legitimate tradition, though in the period through Sterne the
evidence is insufficient to establish it. Thus, for example, it is
possible, but far from proven that Shakespeare received Rabelaisian ideas from Ben Jonson. Pope was in contact with the Pantagruelism of Swift, but he also read *Pantagruel* itself, and was affected by neither. Smollett and Sterne imbibed Rabelais through
Swift, as well as at the fountain head, but to what extent it would
be impossible to say. And if we have had no tradition, neither,
except for the shortlived Scriblerus Club, have we ever produced
anything like an authentic school. Even of this one the acknowledged master was Cervantes and not Rabelais, while the more
ostensibly Rabelaisian " Demoniacs " and " Medmenhamites "
were sociable rather than primarily literary groups.

Englishmen, then, have turned to Rabelais as individuals, and, generally, except for some of the denouncers, without reference to his nationality.   His name has been coupled with that of Aristophanes, Lucian, or Cervantes, oftener than with that of Molière.

His legacy has been on the whole healthy.   The reason, apart from his own great virtues, is because his vocabulary and the forbidding appearance, rather than the fact, of his learned eclecticism have deterred the many.   His high wisdom is simple, but most of those who pass for simple people have wanted both the simplicity and the perseverance to find it.   The parting words of Maître Æditue to Pantagruel and his men at the close of the eighth chapter of the Fifth Book are these :   " Amis, vous notterez que par le monde y a beaucoup plus de couillons que d'hommes, et de ce vous souvienne. "

APPENDIX A

SHAKESPEARE AND RABELAIS

Two details of the pedant in *Love's Labour's Lost* appear, as remarked above (p. 36), to have been borrowed from Rabelais, probably at hearsay. I have collected below a list of further parallels between the two authors, which, if we had other and sure evidence of substantial Rabelaisian influence in the plays, might possess considerable interest. Taken alone I do not regard them as highly significant. Many of them have been pointed out before, though not for example, the striking parallel to Portia's figure of the candle in *The Merchant of Venice*, but I have omitted numerous coincidences which other writers have thought worth bringing forward [1].

Love's Labour's Lost
1) See above, p. 36.
2) V, II, 585-86.

    Costard. ...He is a marvellous good neighbour, faith, and a very good bowler...

3) V, II, 612-14.

    Biron... thou hast no face.
    Holofernes. What is this ?
    Boyet. A cittern-head.

Rabelais, I, IV.
... aultres voisins, tous bons beuveurs, bons compaignons et beaulx joueurs de quille là. — (König, 217).

Rabelais, II, III.
Car elle avoit visaige de rebec. — (König, 217).

---

1. For the affirmative that Rabelais's influence is present in Shakespeare see : Regis, *Garg. und Pant.*, II, CLXXI ; König, *Ueber die Entlehnungen Shakespeare's*, 195 ff. ; Whibley, " Rabelais en Angleterre, " *R. E. R.*, I, 2-3 ; Jusserand, *Hist. Lit. du Peuple Angl.*, II, 716-17, 717, n. 1 ; Bourgeois, " Rabelais en Angleterre, " *R. E. R.*, III, 80-81 ; Upham, *The French Infl. in Eng. Lit.*, 237-40 ; Lee, *The French Renaissance in England*, 162-63 ; Sainéan, " Rabelaisian, " No. 34, *R. E. R.*, IX, 282-84 ; Boulenger, *Rabelais à Travers les Ages*, 20-21. For the negative see : W. F. Smith, " Rabelais et Shakespeare, " *R. E. R.* I, 217-21.

Romeo and Juliet
1) I, III, 41-43.
  Nurse... " Yea," quoth he, " dost thou fall upon thy face ? Thou wilt fall backward when thou hast more wit ; Wilt thou not, Jule ? "...

Rabelais, V, xxi.
Cela [their short heels] estoit la cause pourquoi elles, d'orenavant, à toutes rencontres d'hommes, seront moult subjettes et faciles à tomber à la renverse. — (König, 217).

Two Gentlemen of Verona
1) I, i, 156-58.
  Proteus. Go, go, be gone, to save your ship from wreck, Which cannot perish having thee aboard, Being destin'd to a drier death on shore.

Rabelais, IV, xxiv.
Car tes destinées fatales ne sont à perir en eau. Tu seras hault en l'air certainement pendu, ou bruslé guaillard comme un pere. — (König, 214).

Comedy of Errors
1) III, ii, 21-23.
  Luciana. Alas, poor women ! make us but believe, Being compact of credit, that you love us ; Though others have the arm, show us the sleeve...

Rabelais, III, iii.
...vos crediteurs priront Dieu que vivez,... d'autant que plus ayment la manche que le braz, et la denare que la vie. — (Smith, *R. E. R.*, I, 218).

2) III, ii, 116-26.
  Dromio S. ...She is spherical, like a globe ; I could find out countries in her.
  Antipholus S. In what part of her body stands Ireland ?
  Dro. S. Marry, sir, in her buttocks ; I found it out by the bogs.
  Ant. S. Where Scotland ?
  Dro. S. I found it by the barrenness ; hard in the palm of her hand.
  [Etc., etc. for some thirty lines.]

Rabelais, III, xxviii.
Ta barbe, par les distinctions du gris, du blanc, du tanné et du noir, me semble une Mappemonde. Reguarde icy : voy là Asie ; icy sont Tigris et Euphrates. Voy là Afrique. Icy est la montaigne de la Lune. Vois tu les paluz du Nil ? Deçà est Europe. [etc.] — (Smith, *R. E. R.*, I, 219).

Henry IV, Part I
1) The relationship of Falstaff to Prince Hal.

Rabelais.
The relationship of Panurge to Pantagruel.

2) I, ii, 27-30.
  Falstaff. ...let not us that are squires of the night's body be called thieves of the day's beauty. Let us be Diana's foresters, gentlemen of the shade, minions of the moon...

Rabelais, *Pant. Prog.*, Ch. v.
A list of persons including hunters are said to be under the influence of the moon.

3) III, i, 59.

Hotspur. " ...Tell truth and shame the devil. "

Henry IV, Part II

1) I, ii, 50-54.

Falstaff. ...Well, he may sleep in security ; for he hath the horn of abundance, and yet the lightness of his wife shines through it ; and yet cannot he see, though he have his own lanthorn to light him.

2) III, ii, 111 ff.

Falstaff puns extensively upon the names of his recruits (for some 75 lines).

Merchant of Venice

1) IV, i, 184-201.

Portia. The quality of mercy is not strain'd.

It droppeth as the gentle rain from heaven

Upon the place beneath. It is twice blest :

It blesseth him that gives and him that takes.

[Etc., etc.]

2) V, i, 90-91.

Portia. How far that little candle throws his beams !

So shines a good deed in a naughty world.

Rabelais, III, xxxvi.

...faisons honte au diable d'enfer, confessons verité. — (Smith, *R. E. R.*, I, 219.)

Rabelais, III, end of xiii.

[*Pantagruel*]. L'aultre [porte de songes] est de corne, par laquelle entrent les songes certains, vrays et infaillibles ; comme, à travers la corne, par sa resplendeur et diaphanéité, apparoissent toutes especes certainement et distinctement. — Vous voulez inferer, dist frere Jean, que les songes des coquz cornuz, comme sera Panurge, Dieu aidant et sa femme, sont tousjours vrays et infaillibles. — (König, 215.)

Rabelais, IV, ix.

The punning on names by the people of L'Isle Ennasin occupies most of the chapter.

Rabelais, IV, iv.

...la sentence des Stoïciens, lesquelz disoient troys parties estre en benefice : l'une du donnant, l'aultre du recepvant, la tierce du recompensant : et le recepvant tresbien recompenser le donnant quand il accepte voluntiers le bienfaict, et le retient en soubvenance perpetuelle. — (König, 218-19. König says the source of this passage is Seneca. Lib. I, *de beneficiis*, cap. i-ii.)

Rabelais, IV, xxvi.

Macrobe... eulx vivens [i.e. Demons et Heroes], tout bien abonde en ce lieu... — Il y a, dist Pantagruel, de l'apparence en ce que dictes. Car, comme la torche ou la chandelle, tout le temps qu'elle est vivente et ardente, luist es assistans, esclaire tout autour, delecte un chascun, et à chascun expose son service et sa clarté, ne faict mal ne desplaisir à personne ;... Ainsi est il de ces ames nobles et insignes.

As You Like It

1) III, ii, 237-39.
   Celia. You must borrow me Gargantua's mouth first. 'Tis a word too great for any mouth of this age's size.

Shakespeare is alluding almost certainly to the popular hero. No allusion to Rabelais could have been understood by the audience at large.

Twelfth Night.

1) II, iii, 21-24.
   Sir Andrew... In sooth, thou wast in very gracious fooling last night [Sir Andrew was drunk], when thou spok'st of Pigrogromitus, of the Vapians passing the equinoctial of Queubus...

Sir Andrew's words might be a confused recollection of Picrochole, the opponent of Grandgousier in *Gargantua* ; and of Gargantua's passing the Gué de Vede in Ch. xxxvi, or, as W. F. Smith suggests (*R. E. R.*, I, 220-21), of the speech of Baisecul in Bk. II, Ch. xi, beginning : " Mais à propos passoit entre les deux tropicques six blans, vers le zenith et maille, par autant que les mons Riphees avoyent eu celle année grande sterilité de happelourdes,... " (etc., etc.)

Troilus and Cressida.

1) I, iii, 85 ff.
   Ulysses' long comparison of an army without a commander to the heavenly bodies deprived of the government of Sol.

Rabelais, III, iii.
Panurge compares at length credit in human economics to the force which controls the heavenly bodies. — (König, 204-05.)

2) III, iii, 145-50.
   Ulysses. Time hath, my lord, a wallet at his back,
   Wherein he puts alms for oblivion,
   A great–sized monster of ingratitudes.
   Those scraps are good deeds past, which are devour'd
   As fast as they are made, forgot as soon
   As done.

Rabelais, III, xv.
[Panurge quotes Aesop] : disant chascun homme en ce monde naissant une bezace au coul porter ;... au sachet darriere pendant sont les faultes et malheurs propres : et jamais ne sont veues ne entendues, fors de ceulx qui des cieulx ont le benevole aspect. — (König, 210. König states the source of this passage to be Stobaeus.)

Hamlet.

1) II, ii, 485.
   With eyes like carbuncles...

Rabelais, IV, xli.
Les œilz avoit rouges et flamboyans comme un Pyrope.

2) V, i, 9-13.

   1. *Clown.* It must be " *se offendendo,* " it cannot be else. ...it argues an act, and an act hath three branches ; it is, to act, to do, and to perform...

Rabelais, I, xx.
Ha ! dist Janotus, baudet, baudet, tu ne concluds poinct *in modo et figura.* Voylà de quoy servent les suppositions et *parva logicalia. Pannus pro quo supponit ?* [etc.]

Othello.

1) I, i, 117-18.
   Iago. ...your daughter and the Moor are now making the beast with two backs.

Rabelais, I, iii.
Et faisoient eux deux souvent ensemble la beste à deux doz,.. [W. F. Smith shows that this figure occurred before Rabelais, and was proverbial. — (*R. E. R.*, I, 218.) Sainéan contends that in 16th century French literature it is found only in Rabelais, and hence argues the probability that it was from him that Shakespeare borrowed it. — (*R. E. R.*, IX, 282-85.)]

Macbeth.

1) I, vii, 8-10.
   Macbeth... we but teach Bloody instructions, which, being taught, return To plague the inventor.

Rabelais, IV, lvi.
Et y veids des parolles bien picquantes, des parolles sanglantes, lesquelles le pilot nous disoit quelquefois retourner on lieu duquel estoient proferées, mais c'estoit la guorge couppée ;... — (Smith, *R. E. R.*, I, 219.)

2) II, i, 52-53.
   Macbeth... and wither'd Murder, Alarum'd by his sentinel, the wolf...

Rabelais, IV, xxiii.
...je diz couraige de loup, asceurance de meurtrier. — (Smith, *R. E. R.*, I, 219.)

3) II, iii, 4-5.
   Porter... Here's a farmer, that hang'd himself on the expectation of plenty.

Rabelais, III, iii.
Tesmoings les usuriers de Landerousse, qui n'a gueres se pendirent, voyans les bleds et vins ravaller en pris, et bons temps retourner. — (Smith, *R. E. R.*, I, 220).

4) II, iii, 30-34.
   Macd. What three things does drink especially provoke ?
   Porter. Marry, sir, nose-painting, sleep, and urine. Lechery, sir, it provokes, and unprovokes ; it provokes the desire, but it takes away the performance...

Rabelais, III, xxxi.
...par l'intemperance du vin, advient au corps humain refroidissement de sang, resolution des nerfs, dissipation de semence generative, hebetation des sens, perversion des mouvemens : qui sont toutes impertinances a l'acte de generation. — (Regis, *Garg. und Pant.*, II, 434.)

Timon of Athens.

1) IV, iii, 438-48.
   Timon... I'll example you with thievery :
   The sun's a thief, and with his great attraction

Rabelais, III, iii.
Entre les elemens ne sera symbolisation, alternation, ne transmutation aulcune. Car l'un ne se reputera obligé à l'aultre : il ne luy

Robs the vast sea ; the moon's an
 arrant thief,
And her pale fire she snatches from
 the sun ;
The sea's a thief,... [etc.]

Coriolanus.
1) I, i, 132-45.
 Your most grave belly was deli-
  berate,
 Not rash like his accusers, and thus
  answered :
 " True is it, my incorporate
  friends, " quoth he,
 " That I receive the general food
  at first
 Which you do live upon ; and fit
 it is... "

Tempest.
1) I, i, 30-36.
 Gonzalo. I have great comfort
 from this fellow. Methinks he
 hath no drowning mark upon
 him ; his complexion is perfect
 gallows. Stand fast, good Fate,
 to his hanging ; make the rope of
 his destiny our cable, for our own
 doth little advantage. If he be
 not born to be hang'd, our case
 is miserable.

avoit rien presté. De terre ne sera
faicte eau ; l'eau en aër ne sera
transmuée ; de l'air ne sera faict
feu ; le feu n'eschauffera la terre
[etc.] — (Regis, II, 345).

Rabelais, III, iii.
La teste ne voudra prester la veue de
ses œilz pour guider les pieds et les
mains. Les piedz ne la daigneront
porter ; ...[etc.] ...rien ne prestant,
rien ne empruntant, vous verrez
une conspiration plus pernicieuse
que n'a figurée Æsope en son Apo-
logue. — (König, 207.)

Rabelais.
See above opposite *Two Gentlemen
Verona.*

APPENDIX B

JOHN ELIOT

Borrowings from Rabelais in *Ortho-Epia Gallica. Eliot's Fruits for the French* (London, 1593).

As many of John Eliot's borrowings from Rabelais as I have been able to identify in the second part of his *Ortho-Epia Gallica*, which he entitled *The Parlement of Pratlers*, are indicated in the following pages.

Parl. of Pratlers (Repr. Lindsay)	Rabelais (Transl. Urquhart and Motteux)
a) Epistle to the French Teachers. 1. (pp. 20-21) " ...but after the worthie example of the wise Philosopher *Diogenes*... I haue put my pen to paper : ... " [about 600 words, free adapted].	Prol. III. " When Philip King of Macedon... whilst I should thus set a-going my Diogenical tub. "
b) The drunken mens Banket. 1. (p. 34) " Ho that I am glad ! ...Giue them that they would haue. "	II, III. " Ho, ho, ho, ho, how glad I am ?... send away these poore folks in giving them what they ask... "
1. (p. 37) " ...the odour of wine... delicate is it then oile. "	Prol. I. " The fragrant odour of the wine... then that smell of oile ! "
3. (pp. 37-38) " Tarry a little... Cato neuer tooke pen in hand, but after drinking. To the end that you say not that I liue without example of men laudable and best accounted of.	Prol. III. " Stay a little... Cato never wrote till after he had drunk... to the end you may not say that I live without the Example of Men well praised, and better prised. "
4. (p. 38) Is there any one that will dispute with me of these intricat problems... and Geomancie then, the Philosophie of Hermes Trismegistus. "	II, xx. ...to conferre with him about the insoluble problemes,... Geomancie, Astrologie and Philosophie... "

Parl. of Pratlers	Rabelais

5. (p. 38) " Draw, bring boy, fill wine,... As a land without water. "

Ibid. " Draw, give (page) some wine here... they were very dry. "

6. (p. 39) " Drinke we, drinke we then, as do the camels and dromedaries... So dranke Hercules.

IV, LXV. " ...all Comers and Goers drink before they are a dry. — As the Camels and Dromedaries... so did Hercules. "

7. (p. 39) Truce of thirst,... Who drinks carrouse, and laugheth not a whit. "

Ibid. ante. " A Truce with Thirst, ...Who drinks the Best, yet can be sad. "

8. (p. 39) " Gossip faire and softly,... as the moone doth merrigalds.

II, XIV. " ...Faire and softly, Gossip,... as the Moon doth the catarres and defluxions ;... "

9. (p. 39) This Liuerots head is good for those that have the gout.

I, XXXIX. " The thigh of this leveret is good for those that have the gout. "

10. (p. 39) We shall eate few greene geese this yeare.

Ibid. " We are like to eate no great store of goslings this yeare,... "

11. (p. 39) I had broke my fast well : ...as saint Benets boote.

Ibid. ante. " I have already sup't,... or St. Benedictus boot... "

12. (p. 39) Ha my friend, giue me some pigge. . I die for thirst.

Ibid. " ...friend, reach me some of that rosted pig there. ...I rage for thirst,... "

13. (pp. 39-40) Draw, giue here, turne, broile, poure to me without water : so my friends, firke me this glasse finely. Ha false feuer wilt thou not packe hence ?... *Fœcundi calices quem non fecere disertum.* Lets sing, lets drinke,... If I drinke not, I am dead.

I, v. " ...draw, reach, fill, mixe, give it me without water, so my friend, so whip me off this glasse neatly,... [2 ll.]... Ha thou, false Fever, wilt thou not be gone ?... *Fecundi calices quem non fecere disertum..* [5 ll.] ...let us sing, let us drink,.... I am stark dead without drink,... "

14. (p. 40) For conclusion of mine oration... all honest and learned men. "

I, I. " ...I cannot think but I am come of the race of some rich King... all honest and learned men :... "

c) The Painter.

1. (p. 65) " There is one which is a fine peece of worke,... and woonderfull sumptuous peece.

IV, II. " Panurge bought a large picture... nay a most admirable piece. "

2. (pp. 65-66) This likes me not, ...Polixena written by Euripides. "

Ibid. " Epistemon bought another ...Polyxena's Sacrifice rehearsed by Euripides. "

d) The Mariner.

1. (p. 85) " The Tide swelleth ...It thundreth, it lightneth, it raineth, it haileth... "

IV, XVIII. " Immediately it blowed a Storm,... it Lighten'd, Rain'd, Hail'd... "

Parl. of Pratlers　　　　　　Rabelais

2. (p. 86) " O thrice and foure times happie are those who are on firme land setting of beanes. "

Ibid. " O twice and thrice happy are those that plant Cabbages ! "

3. (p. 86) " Dish, dash, plash, [etc., etc.]... "

Cf. *Ibid.* " Bou, bou, bou, [etc.] ... " and IV, xix, " ...bous, bous, bous, paisch, hu, hu, hu, [etc.]... "

4. (p. 86) " O Saint Michael, Saint Nicholas, now and neuer more. "

IV, xix. " St. Michael of Aure ! St. Nicholas ! Now, now or never. "

5. (p. 86) " I giue eighteen hundred thousand crownes of reuenue to him who will set me a land. "

Ibid. ante. " ...alas, alas, I will give eighteen hundred thousand Crowns to any one that will set me on shoar... "

6. (p. 86) " I see neither heauen nor earth.

IV, xx. " I see neither Heaven nor Earth... "

7. (p. 86) I must make water a litle. "

IV, xviii. " I conskite my self for meer Madness and Fear... "

8. (p. 86) " Truly it hath lightned and thundred lustily... Beleeue that all the fiue hundred thousand hundred millions of Diuels dance the morrice.

IV, xix. " In truth here is a sad Lightning and Thundering ; ...all the Devils dance a Morrice. " [Cf. IV, xxi, " ...in the name of Five hundred thousand Millions of Cart–loads of Devils... "]

9. (p. 86) Thunder Diuels, fart, fist, fissell. A fig for the waue. "

IV, xx. " Grumble, Devils, fart, belch, shite a T — d o' the Wave. "

e) The Inn

1 (p. 90) " Of all fresh fish except the tench, take the wing of a Partridge, or the buttocke of a Nunne. I loue woonderfully the white... they haue no cookes to dresse them. "

I, xxxix. " Of all fishes, but the tench, take the wing of a Partridge, or the thigh of a Nunne... [1 l.]... Our Prior loves exceedingly the white... they have no Cooks to dresse them... "

f) The Slasher

1. (pp. 95-96) " Ho saint Siobe cap de Gascoigne,... They would giue vs drinke then to be rid of vs. " [A very free adaptation of the episode in Rabelais.]

III, xlii. " The Gascon, altogether astonish'd... each upon the pawn of his Sword. "

g) The Bragger

1. (p. 99) The Bragger's genealogy is pieced together from that of Pantagruel, all but one or two names and phrases being exactly transcribed, though in different order.

II, i. The genealogy of Pantagruel.

Parl. of Pratlers

Rabelais

2. (p. 100) " I rage, Diuels I rage, hold me Diuels, hold me.

I, xxxv. " I rage, I rage, devils, ...hold, devils, hold, hold. "

3. (p. 100) Ho Caetzo great Diuel of hell,... I will set you a worke.

Prol. IV. " Take care this be remedied, Son Vulcan ; ...set them at work... "

4. (p. 100) I giue my selfe to an hundred pipes of old Diuels, in case that if you will not fight, if I do not make you eate the two egges of Proserpina.

[Cf. the more characteristic oaths of Friar John, and I, ii, 9th stanza of the poem :
" The bargain was that of that
                   [throatfull she
Should of Proserpina have two egges
                   [free. "

5. (p. 100) Truly Hercules is nothing to you, who being in the cradle, kild the two Serpents : for the said Serpents were verie litle and weake things. "

II, iv. " That which Hercules did was nothing, when in his Cradle he slew two serpents ; for those serpents were but little and weak... "

6. (p. 100) " He would make you pisse vinegre before all the world."

II, xvii. " ...I will make this vainglorious Englishman to skite vineger before all the world. "

7. (p. 100) " Ho ! that I am not a king of France for foure score and ten or a hundred yeares : by God I would make curtald curres of you Gentlemen that ran away from Pauy.

I, xxxix. " Oh that I were but King of France for fourescore or a hundred years ! By G— I should whip like curtail-dogs these runawayes of Pavie. "

8. (p. 100) I hate him more then poyson, who runneth away when tis come to slashing with kniues. "

Ibid. ante. " I hate that man worse than poison that offers to runaway, when he should fight and lay stoutly about him. "

9. (p. 101) " You affright me with swearing so much... These are but heroicall words, and colours of martiall Rhetoricke to adorne my language. "

Ibid. " How now (said Ponocrates) you swear, Friar John ; it is only (said the monk) but to grace and adorn my speech ; they are colours of a Ciceronian Rhetorick. "

10. (p. 101) " My friend, I shock so rudely vpon the enemies,... If our Ladie of Loretto, I cut off his head. " [Freely adapted.]

I, xxvii. " He [Friar John] hurried therefore upon them so rudely,... others cried, Our Lady of Cunaut, of Loretto... "

11. (p. 102) " Masters I am a poore diuell, I beseech you haue pittie on me, I have yet a crowne to pay my *bienvenu*. "

I, xxxiv. " Then cried he out unto them, (My Masters,) I am a poor devil, I desire you to spare me, I have yet one Crown left, come, we must drink it... "

h) The Conclusion of the Parlement of Pratlers.

1. (pp. 107-108) " But did you

Prol. I. " ...or, did you ever see a

Parl. of Pratlers   Rabelais

neuer see a dog meeting with a
mary-bone,... a meate laboured to
the perfection of nature. As
saith Galenus 3 lib. fac. & c.

Dog with a marrow-bone in his
mouth,... a nourishment most perfectly elaboured by nature. "

2. (p. 108) Of all beastes there is
none more sage,... he receiueth of
euerie one so manie blowes and
mowes. "

I, XL. " ...if you conceive how an
Ape in a family is alwayes mocked,...
he hath of all men mocks, frump-
eries and bastonadoes. "

3. (pp. 109-110) " Mistresse your
beautie is so excellent,... humbly
I take my leaue without Adieu. "

II, XXI. " ...yours is so excellent,...
and therefore that we lose no
time... "

4. (p. 111) " He hath eaten his
corne in the grasse. He hath
made then fine greene-sauce. "

III, II. " ...of Corn in the Blade.
You may make good Green-sauce
of a light Concoction... "

5. (p. 113) " See you that man
there ?... he hath two hundred
and fourteene waies to spend
it. " [A very free adaptation of
Rabelais's description of Panurge.]

II, XVI. " Panurge was of a middle
stature,... [etc.] "

APPENDIX C

ULYSSES UPON AJAX (1596)

Sometimes attributed to Sir John Harington.

A sequel to *The Metamorphosis* and *The Anatomy*, called *Ulysses upon Ajax* was published toward the end of 1596. Its authorship is uncertain. It has been attributed to Harington on the grounds of its humanistic contents and pseudo-Rabelaisian style. It lacks Harington's characteristic apophthegms and colloquial manner; and its printer was Thomas Gubbins, whereas the first two works were printed by Richard Field. It is a severe arraignment of *The Metamorphosis* and *The Anatomy*, which seems not to be seriously intended, in four parts [1].

The first is an epistle from " Misodiaboles the Worshipful, to Misacmos the right Worshipful, " in which the latter is censured at length for his " labour without reason. " His wit is good, but his subject gross. Part second continues the argument, which never rises above the level of ostentatious invective, more worthy of Harvey or Nashe than of Harington. The naughty treatise

is an affectation of singularity, a fruit of discontent, a superfluity of wanton wit, a madding with [out] reason, a diligence without judgment, a work fit for Volumnius the jester, not Misacmos the courtier : in form, contrary to all rules of science ; in matter, indecent, filthy, and immodest ; and touching the authorities, they are so weak and so wrested, as no chaste nor Christian ear may in reason endure them.

Part three accuses Misacmos of profaning Scripture, of abusing learned men, and of plagiarism. He is " as deep a philosopher as Metrocles, who could never argue without f—g ; " his name should be inscribed in " Lincoln's Inn Privy, " etc., etc. Part four condemns Misacmos' history of privies, and concludes that the only decent thing

---

1. I am indebted for the material of this appendix to Rehfeld, *Sir John Harington, ein Nachahmer Rabelais'*, 84-93. I do not agree with his conclusion that the work in question *may be* by Harington.

in the book is the description of the engine itself. Even so, he, Miso-diaboles, the critic, knows that a still better could be made with the use of wind instead of water. He brightens up the attack at this point by the introduction of several good latrine jokes, quite at variance in their tone with his chaste precepts.

The best evidence against Harington's authorship is the advice of Misodiaboles that Misacmos should emulate the Athenians, who had learnt from Solon " to cover and colour obscenities and filthiness with apt and decent names. " Harington would not, even in jest, have thus contradicted one of his leading ideas, especially in such a prominent place as the conclusion of the essay. Misodiaboles ends by exhorting Misac-mos to mend his ways and " light the candle of charity before him. "

There is no evidence that the author was familiar with Rabelais [1]. Misodiaboles is almost certainly not Harington, but an imitator of inferior powers, who saw an opportunity to trade on the name of a popular work.

---

1. Rehfeld, *op. cit.*, 85.

APPENDIX D

JOHN OLDHAM (1653-83)

Character of a certain Ugly Old P—, ...First printed in the Year
M. D. C. LXXXIV [1].

No wonder if I am at a Loss to describe him, whom *Nature* was as much puzzled to make. 'Tis here, as in *Painting*, where the most mis-shapen *Figures* are the greatest *Proofs* of *Skill*. To draw a *Thersites*, or *Æsop* well, requires the *Pencil* of *Vandyke* or *Titian*, more than the best *Features* and *Lineaments*. All the Thoughts I can frame of him are as rude and indigested as himself. The very *Idea* and *Conception* of him are enough to Cramp *Grammar*, to disturb *Sense*, and confound Syntax. He's a *Solecism* in the great *Construction*, therefore the best *Description* of him is *Nonsense*, and the fittest *Character* to write it in, that *Pot-hook-hand*, the Devil, at *Oxford* us'd in *Queen's College Library*. He were *Topick* enough for convincing an *Atheist* that the World was made by Chance. The first *Matter*, had more of *Form* and *Order* ; the *Chaos* more of *Symmetry* and *Proportion*. I could call him *Nature's Bye-Blow*, *Miscarriage* and *Abortive*, or say, he is her *Embryo* slink'd before Matu-rity ; but that is stale and flat, and I must flye a higher Pitch to reach his *Deformity*. He is the ugliest *she* ever took Pains to make so, and *Age* to make worse. All the *Monsters* of *Africa* lie kennell'd in his single *Skin*. He's one of the *Grotesques* of the *Universe*, whom the grand *Artist* drew only (as *Painters* do uncouth ugly *Shapes*) to fill up the empty *Spaces* and *Cantons* of this great *Frame*. He's *Man Anagram-matiz'd* : A *Mandrake* has more of *Human Shape* : his *Face* carries *Libel* and *Lampoon* in't. *Nature* at its *Composition* wrote *Burlesque*, and shew'd him how far she could out-do *Art* in *Grimace*. I wonder ' tis not hir'd by the *Play-houses* to draw *Antick Vizards* by. Without doubt

---

1. From *The Works of Mr. John Oldham, Together with his Remains* (London, 1722), II, 323-34. A reference to " Last New-years day (1676) " fixes the approxi-mate date of writing (see p. 225 below). One or two typographical errors have been corrected.

he was made to be laugh'd at, and design'd for the *Scaramuchio* of *Mankind*.   When I see him, I can no more forbear, than at sight of a *Zany* or *Nokes* ; but am like to run the Risque of the *Philosopher* looking on an *Ass* mumbling *Thistles*.   He's more ill-favour'd, than the *Picture* of *Winter* drawn by a Fellow that daubs *Sign-Posts*, more lowring than the last day of *January*.   I have seen a handsomer *Mortal* carv'd in *Monumental Gingerbread*, and woven in *Hangings* at *Mortlack*.   If you have ever view'd that *wooden Gentleman* that peeps out of a Country *Barber's* Window, you may fancy some *Resemblance* of him.   His damn'd squeezing *Close-stool-Face* can be liken'd to nothing better than the *Buttocks* of an old wrinkled *Baboon*, straining upon an *Hillock*.   The very *Sight* of him in a Morning would work with one beyond *Jalap* and *Rhubarb*. A *Doctor* (I'm told) once prescrib'd him to one of his *Parishioners* for a *Purge* :   he wrought the *Effect*, and gave the *Patient* fourteen *Stools*. 'Tis pity he is not drawn at the *City Charges*, and hung up in some publick *Forica*[1] as a *Remedy* against *Costiveness*.

Indeed, by his *Hue* you might think he had been employed to that use :   One would take him for the Picture of *Scoggin* or *Tarleton* on a *Privy-house* Door, which by long standing there has contracted the *Colour* of the neighbouring Excrements.   Reading lately how *Garagantua* came into the *World* at his Mother's *Ear*, it put an unlucky Thought into my Head concerning him : I presently fancied that he was voided, not brought forth, that his *Dam* was deliver'd of him on t'other side, beshit him coming out, and he has ever since retain'd the *Stains*.   His filthy *Countenance* looks like an old *Chimney-piece* in a decay'd Inn, sullied with *Smoak*, and the sprinkling of Alepots. 'Tis dirtier than an ancient *thumb'd Record*, greasier than a Chandler's *Shop-book*.   You'd imagine *Snails* had crawl'd the *Haye* upon it.   The *Case* of it is perfect *Vellum*, and has often been mistaken for it :   A *Scrivener* was like to cheapen it for making *Indentures* and *Deeds* ; besides 'tis as wrinkled as a *walking Buskin* :   It has more *Furrows* than all *Cotswold*[2].   You may resemble it to a *Gammon* of *Bacon* with the *Swerd* off.   I believe the *Devil* travels over it in his Sleep with *Hob-nails* in his *Shoes*.   By the *Maggot-eaten-Sur-Face* you'd swear he had been dug out of his *Grave* again with all his *Worms* about him to Bait *Eel-hooks*.   But enough of it in General, I think it time to descend to *Particulars* ; I wish I could divide his Face, as he does his *Text*, i.e. tear it asunder ; 'Tis fit I begin with the most remarkable part of it.   His *Mouth* (saving your Presence, *Christian Readers*) is like the *Devil's Arse of Peak*, and is just as Large.   By the *Scent*, you'd take it for the *Hole* of a Privy :   He may be winded by a good

---

1. " A Bog-House. "—note by anon. ed.
2. " Hills in *Gloucestershire*, remarkable for their Craggyness. "—note by anon. ed.

Nose at Twelve-score ; I durst have ventur'd at first being in Company
that he dieted on *Assa-foetida*. His very *Discourse* stinks in a *Literal
Sense* ; 'tis *breaking-Wind*, and you'd think he talk'd at the other *End*.
Last *Newyears day* (1676) he tainted a *Loin* of *Veal* with saying Grace :
All the *Guests* were fain to use the *Fanatical-Posture* in their own *Defence*,
and stand with their *Caps* over their *Eyes* like *Malefactors* going to be
turn'd off. That too that renders it the more unsupportable is, that it
can't be stopp'd : The *Breach* is too big ever to be clos'd. Were he a
Milliner, he might measure *Ribbon* by it without the help of his *Yard*
or *Counter*. It reaches so far backwards, those, that have seen him with
his *Peruke* off, say it may be discerned behind. When he gapes, 'twould
stretch the *Duchess* of *Cleaveland* to straddle over : I had almost said,
'tis as wide as from *Dover* to *Calais*. Could he shut it, the *Wrinkles*
round about would represent the Form of the *Sea-mens Compass*, and
should he bluster, 'twere a pretty *Emblem* of those swelling *Mouths*, at
the *Corners* of *Maps* puffing out *Storms*. When he *Smokes*, I am always
thinking of *Mongibello* [1] and its *Eruptions*. His *Head* looks exactly like
a *Device* on a *Kitchin Chimney* ; His *Mouth* the *Vent* and his *Nose* the
Fane. And now I talk of his *Snout*, I dare not mention the *Elephant's*,
for fear of speaking too little : I'd make bold with the old *Wit*, and
compare it to the *Gnomon* of a *Dial* ; but that he has not *Teeth* enough
to stand for the *Twelve Hours*. 'Tis so long, that when he rides a *Journey*, he makes use of it to open *Gates*. He's fain to snite it with both
Hands. It cannot be wip'd under as much as the *Royal Breech*. A *Man*
of ordinary *Bulk* might find Shelter under its *Eves*, were it not for the
Droppings. One protested to me in *Raillery* that when he looks against
the *Sun*, it shadows his whole *Body*, as some Story of the *Sciapodes
Feet* [2]. Another *Hyperbolical Rascal* would make me believe that the
Arches of it are as large as any two of *London-Bridge*, or the great *Rialto*,
at *Venice*. Not long ago I met a one-leg'd *Tarpauling* that had been
begging at his *Door*, but could get nothing : The witty *Whoreson*
(I remember) swore that his *Bow-sprit* was as long as that of the *Royal-
Sovereign*. I confess, stood he in my way, I durst not venture round by
his *Fore-side*, for fear of going half a Mile about. 'Tis perfectly doub-
ling the *Cape*, He has this Privilege for being unmannerly : that it
will not suffer him to put off his *Hat* : And therefore (as 'tis said) at
home he has a *Cord* fasten'd to it, and draws it off with a *Pulley*, and so
receives the *Addresses* of those that visit him. This, I'm very confident
of, he has not heard himself sneeze these *seven Years* : And that leads
me to his *Tools* of Hearing : His *Ears* resemble those of a *Country Jus-*

---

1. " Mount Aetna. " — note by anon. ed.
2. " A Sort of monstrous People in *India*, having but one Leg, with which
they run very swift, and so large a Foot, that lying upon their Backs they can
shade their Body with it. " — note by anon. ed.

tice's Black-Jack, and are of the same *Matter, Hue*, and *Size*. He's as well hung as any *Hound* in the *Country* ; but by their *Bulk* and growing upward, he deserves to be rank'd with a Graver of *Beasts* : His single self [he] might have shewn with *SMEC*[1], and all the *Club Divines*. You may pare enough from the *Sides* of his *Head* to have furnisht a whole *Regiment* of *Round-Heads* : He wears more there, than all the *Pillories* in *England* ever have done. *Mandevile* tells us of a *People* somewhere, that use their *Ears* for *Cushions* : He has reduced the *Legend* to Probability : A *Servant* of his (that could not conceal the *Midas*) told me lately in private, that going to *Bed*, he binds them on his *Crown*, and they serve him instead of *Quilt Night-Caps*. The next observable that falls under my *Consideration* is his Back : Nor need I go far out of my Way to meet it, for it peeps over his *Shoulders* : He was built with a *Buttress* to support the *Weight* of his *Nose*, and help balance it. *Nature* hath hung on him a *Knap-[s]ack*, and made him represent both *Tinker* and *Budget* too. He looks like the visible *Tye* of *Æneas* bolstring up his *Father*, or like a *Beggar-Woman*, endorst with her whole *Litter*, and with *Child* behind. You may take him for *Anti-Christopher* with the *Devil* at his *Back*. I believe the *Atlas* in *Wadham-Garden* at *Oxford*, was carv'd by him. Certainly he was begot in a *Cupping-glass* : his Mother longed for *Pompions*, or went to see some Camel shown while she was conceiving him. One would think a *Mole* has crept into his *Carcass* before 'tis laid in the *Church-Yard*, and Rooted in it or that an *Earthquake* had disorder'd the *Symmetry* of the *Microcosm*, sunk one *Mountain*, and put up another. And now I should descend lower if I durst venture : But I'll not defile my *Pen* : My *Ink* is too cleanly for a farther *Description*. I must beg my *Reader's* Distance : as if I were going to Untruss. Should I mention what is beneath, the very *Jakes* would suffer by the *Comparison*, and 'twere enough to bring a *Bog-House* in Disgrace. Indeed he ought to have been drawn, like the good *People* on the *Parliament-House*, only from the *Shoulders* upwards. To me 'tis a greater *Prodigy* than himself, how his *Soul* has so long endured so nasty a *Lodging*. Were there such a thing as a *Metempsychosis*, how gladly would it exchange its *Carcass* for that of the worst and *vilest Brute* : I'm sufficiently persuaded against the *Whim* of *pre-existence* ; for any thing that had the *Pretence* of *Reason* would never have entered such a *Durance* out of *Choice* : Doubltess it must have been guilty of some unheard of *Sin*, for which *Heaven* dooms it *Penance* in the *Present Body*, and ordains it, its first *Hell* here. And 'tis disputable which may prove the worst, for 'thas suffered half an *Eternity* already. Men can hardly tell which of the *two* will out-live the other. By his *Face* you'd guess him one of the *Patriarchs*, and that he liv'd before the *Flood* : His *Head*

---

1. " The Initial Letters of the Names of *Stephen Marshall* and *Edmund Calamy*. " — note by anon. ed.

looks as if 't had worn out *three* or *four Bodies*, and were Legacied to him by his *Great-Grand-father*. His *Age* is out of *Knowledge*. I believe he was Born before *Registers* were invented. He should have been a *Ghost* in Queen *Mary's* Days. I wonder *Holingshead* does not speak of him. Every *Limb* about him is *Chronicle* : *Par* and *John* of the *Times* were *short-Livers* to him. They say, he can remember when *Pauls* was Founded ; and *London-Bridge* built. I my self have heard him tell all the *Stories* of *York* and *Lancaster* upon his own *Knowledge*. His very *Cane* and *Spectacles* are enough to set up an *Antiquary*. The first was the *Walking-staff* of *Lanfranc* Archbishop of *Canterbury*, which is to be seen by his *Arms* upon the *Head* of it. The other belong'd to the *Chaplain* of *William* the *Conqueror* ; was of *Norman* Make, and travell'd over with him. 'Tis strange the later *Author* of Madam *Fickle* [1] forgot to make his Sir *Arthur Oldlove* swear by them, the *Oath* had been of as good *Antiquity* as St. *Austin's Night-Cap*, or *Mahomet's Threshold*. I have often wonder'd he never set up for a *Conjurer* : His very *Look* would bring him in *Vogue*, draw *Custom*, and undo *Lilly* and *Gadbury*. You'd take him for the *Ghost* of old *Haly* or *Albumazar*, or the Spirit *Frier* in the *Fortune Book* ; his *Head* for the inchanted brazen one of *Frier Bacon*. 'Twould pose a good *Physiognomist* to give *Names* to the *Lines* in his *Face*. I've observ'd all the *Figures* and *Diagrams* in *Agrippa* and *Ptolemy's Centiloquies* there, upon strict View. And t'other Day a *Linguist* of my *Acquaintance* shew'd me all the *Arabick Alphabet* betwixt his *Brow* and his *Chin*. Some have admired how he came to be admitted into *Orders*, since his very *Face* is against the *Canon* : I guess he pleaded the *Qualification* of the *Prophets* of Old, to be *Withered, Toothless* and *Deformed*. He can pretend to be an *Elisha* only by his *Baldness*. The *Devil's Oracles* heretofore were utter'd from such a *Mouth*. 'Twas then the *Candidates* for the *Tripos* were fain to plead *Wrinkles* and *Grey Hairs* ; a *Splay Mouth*, and a *Goggle Eye* were the cheapest *Symony*, and the *Ugly* and *Crippled* were the only *Men* of *Preferment*. And this leads me to consider him a little in the *Pulpit*. And there, 'tis hard to distinguish, whether That, or his *Skin* be the coarser *Wainscot*: He represents a Crackt *Weather-Glass* in a *Frame*. You'd take him by his *Looks* and *Posture* for *Muggleton* doing *Penance,* and paulted with *rotten Eggs*. Had his *Hearers* the Trick of Writing Short-Hand, I should fancy him an *Offender* upon a *Scaffold*, and them Penning his *Confession*. Not a *fluxt Debauchée* in a *Sweating-Tub* makes worse *Faces*. He makes *Doctrine* as Folks do their *Water* in the *Stone* or *Strangury*. *Balaam's* Ass was a better *Divine,* and had a better *Delivery*. The *Thorn* at *Glastenbury* had more *Sense* and *Religion*, and would make more *Converts*. He speaks not, but grunts, like one of the *Gadarene Hogs* after

---

1. " Or, The Witty *False One*, a Comedy written by *Tom Durfey*, 1677. " — note by anon. ed.

the *Devils* enter'd. When I came first to his *Church* and saw him perch'd on high against a *Pillar*, I took him by his gaping for some *Juggler* going to swallow *Bibles* and *Hour-Glasses*. But I was soon convinc'd that other *Feats* were to be play'd, and on a sudden lost all my *Senses* in *Noise*. A Drunken *Huntsman* reeling in, the while he was at *Prayer*, asked if he were giving his *Parishioners* a *Halloo* : He has preached half his *Parish* deaf :   His *Din* is beyond the *Catadupi* of *Nile* [1]:   All his *Patron's Pigeons* are frighted from their *Apartment*, and he's generally believed the *Occasion*.   He may be heard farther than *Sir Samuel Moreland's Flagalet*.   Nay, one damn'd mad *Rogue* swore, should he take a *Text* concerning the *Resurrection*, he might serve for the last *Trumpet*. And yet in one Respect he's fitted for the *Function*.   His *Countenance*, if not *Doctrine*, can scare Men into *Repentance*, like an *Apparition* : Should he walk after he's dead, he would not be more dreadful, than now while he is alive.

A *Maid* meeting him in the Dark in a *Church-Yard*, was frighted into *Fanaticism*.   Another is in Bedlam upo[n] the same Occasion :   I dare not approach him without an *Exorcism*.   *In the Name*, &c. is the fittest *Salutation* :   Some have thought the *Parsonage-House* haunted since he dwelt there.   In *Yorkshire* ('tis reported) they make use of his *Name* instead of *Raw-Head* and *Bloody-bones* to fright *Children*.   He is more terrible than those *Fantoms* Country-Folks tell of by the Fire-side, and pretend to have seen, with *Leathern-wings*, *Cloven-feet*, and *Saucer-Eyes* : If he goes to *Hell* (as 'tis almost an *Article* of my *Creed*, he will) the *Devils* will quake for all their warm *Dwelling*, and crowd up into a *Nook* for fear of him.

---

1. " The *Æthiopians* inhabiting there are naturally Deaf, by the   Noise of the Waters disordering the Organs of Hearing. " — note by anon. ed.

APPENDIX E

TOM BROWN (1663-1704)

I. *A Comical View of the Transactions that will happen in the Cities of* London *and* Westminster. *Together with the* Merry Quack : *Wherein Physick is rectified for both* Beaux *and* Ladies.
Continued Weekly.

[The " Transactions " of the first week are as follows]
From Octob. 16. *to* Octob. 22 [1].

Gentlemen

Whereas the Town has been banter'd near two Months with a sham Account of the Weather, pretended to be taken from Barometers, Thermometers, Microscopes, Telescopes, *and such-like Heathenish Instruments, by which means several of Her Majesties good Subjects have put on their Frieze Coats, expecting it should rain, when it has been fair; and wore their best Clothes, thinking it would be fair when it has rain'd, to the no little Detriment and Prejudice of their aforesaid Clothes and Persons ; and likewise, whereas the Planets that have regulated the Almanacks for about two Thousand Years, have been most wickedly slandered by a late Author, as if they had no influence at all upon the Weather ; the Publisher of this Paper has been persuaded by his Friends, to print these his infallible Predictions, gathered from the Experience of Thirty Years and upwards; and will warrant them to be true, tho' he never travelled abroad, nor pretends to be the Seventh Son of a Seventh Son, nor calls himself the unborn Doctor, nor has the Seed of the Female Fern, The Green and Red Dragon, or any of the like Secrets.*
Wednesday 16.] Cloudy foggy Weather at *Garraway's* and *Jonathan's,* and at most Coffee-Houses at and about Twelve. Crowds of

---

1. Text according to *Works,* 1715, I, 163-65. A few inconsistencies of punctuation and one or two spellings have been corrected, but only ones which seemed accountable to the printer.

People gather at the *Exchange* by One, disperse by Three. Afternoon noisy and bloody at her Majesties Bear-Garden in *Hockley in the Hole*. Night sober broken Captains and others, that have neither Credit nor Money. If rainy, few Night-walkers in *Cheapside* and *Fleetstreet*. This Weeks Transactions censured by the Virtuosoes at *Child's* from Morning till Night.

Thursday 17.] Coffee and Water-gruel to be had at the *Rainbow* and *Nando's* at Four. Hot Furmety at *Fleet-bridge* by Seven. Justice to be had at *Doctor's-Commons*, when People can get it. A Lecture at *Pinnar's-Hall* at Ten. Excellent Pease-potage and Tripe in *Baldwin's-Gardens* at Twelve. At Night much Fornication all over *Covent-Garden*, and five Miles round it. A Constable and two Watchmen killed, or near being so, in *Westminster*; whether by a Lord, or a Lord's Foootman, the Planets don't determine.

Friday 18.] Plenty of Cuckolds trudging from all Parts of the City towards *Horn-Fair* by Eight. Damsels whip'd for their Good-Nature at *Bridewell* about Ten. Several People put in fear of their Lives by their Godfathers at the *Old-Baily* at Eleven. Great destruction of Herrings at One. Much swearing at Three among the Horse-coursers in *Smithfield*; if the Oaths were registered as well as the Horses, good Lord, what a Volume 'twould make ! Several Tails turned up at *Paul's* School, *Merchant-Taylors*, &c. for their Repititions. Night very drunk as the two former.

Saturday 19.] Twenty Butchers Wives in *Leadenhall* and *Newgate*-Markets overtaken with Sherry and Sugar by Eight in the Morning. Shopkeepers walk out at Nine, to count the Trees in *Moorfields*, and avoid Duns. Peoples Houses cleansed in the Afternoon, but their Consciences we dont know when. *Jews* fornicate away the Sabbath in *Drury-Lane* and *Wild-street*. Evening pretty sober.

Sunday 20.] Great jangling of Bells all over the City from Eight to Nine. Psalms murder'd in most Parishes about Ten. Abundance of Doctrines and Uses in the Meetings, and no Application. Vast consumption of Roast Beef and Pudding at One. Afternoon sleepy in most Churches. Store of Handkerchiefs stollen in *Paul's* at Three. Informers busy all Day long. Night not so sober as might be wish'd.

Monday 21.] Whores turned out of the *Temple*, *Grays-Inn*, &c. by Six. Catchpoles up early to seize their Prey against the first Day of the Term. Journeymen Taylors, Shooemakers and Prentices Heads ake with what they had been doing the Day before. Tradesmen begin the Week with Cheating, as soon as they open Shop. If Fair, the Park full of Women at Noon, some virtuous, and some otherwise. Great shaking of the Elbow at *Will's*, &c. about Ten. Two Porters fall out at Putt in a Cellar in the *Strand*, at Twelve precisely.

Tuesday 22.] Wind, whether E. W. N. or S. no matter, but in one Corner or other of the Compass most certain : If high, the Beaux advi-

sed to be merciful to their long Perukes. Muslins and Pepper rise at
the *East-India* House at Twelve. Callicoes fall before Two. Coach'd
Masques calling at the Chocolate-Houses between Eight and Nine. Bas-
tards begot, and Cuckolds made this Week numberless.

Advertisement to the Ladies.

*Women, whether with Child, or no ?   Children whether Male or Female ?
Young Maidens, whether they will have their Sweethearts, or no ?   And
Lovers, whether able and constant ?   The Critical Minute of the Day to
marry in.   What is the best Hour for Procreation.   Husbands, whether
live long or no ?   The second Match whether happy or unhappy ?   What
part of the Town best for a Sempstress to thrive in ?   What the most fortunate Signs for a Shopkeeper, and under what Planet to set up ?   With
other like Questions, fully and satisfactorily Resolved by me* Sylvester Partridge, *Student in Physick and Astrology, near the* Gun *in* Moorfields.

II. " Francis Rablais, to the Physicians of Paris " and " The Answer of
   Mr. Fagon, first Physician to Lewis XIV, to Francis Rablais, " the thirty-
   sixth and thirty-seventh of the *Letters from the Dead to the Living* [1].

Francis Rablais, to the Physicians of Paris.

'Tis in vain for your Flatterers to cry you up for able Doctors, for you
will never arrive at my Knowledge ; and I'm asham'd every Hour to
hear such Asses are admitted into the College.   Do not believe 'tis a
sensible Vanity that induces me to say this, but the perfect Knowledge I
have of my own worth ; and tho' I was design'd for a more lazy Profession, yet that does not in the least diminish my Merit.   You know I
was born at *Chinon*, and that my parents, hoping I should one day make
a precious Saint, put me in my foolish Infancy, into a Convent of *Cor-
deliers* :   But that greasie Habit, in a little time, seem'd to me as heavy
and uneasie as the Armour of a Giant ; so that by Intercession made to
Pope Clement the Seventh, I was permitted to change my gray Frock
for a Black ; so I quitted the Equipage of St. *Francis*, for that of St.
Benedict, and that I was as weary of in a short time as of the other.   As
I had learnt a great deal of Craft, and but little Religion, during my
Noviciate in those good Schools, so I found a way to get loose from that
Cloyster for ever, and took to the study of *Hippocrates*.   Besides that
I had a subtle and clear Genius, my Comrades discover'd in me an
acute natural Raillery, which made me acceptable to the best Com-
panions.   Cardinal *Bellay*, who made me his Physician, took me to *Rome*

---

1. *Works*, 1715, II, 111-16.

with him in that Quality, where the Sanctity of the Tripple-Crown, the ador'd Slipper, and all-opening Key, could not hinder me from jesting in the Presence of his *Holiness*. 'Twas *Paul* the Third, before called *Alexander Fernese*, who then fill'd the Apostolical Chair, and was more remarkable for his Lewdness than Piety. I had the good Fortune to please him with the Inclination he found in me to Lewdness, and he gave me a Bull of Absolution for my Apostacy, free from all Fee and Duties, which I think was a gracious Reward for a foreign Atheistical Buffoon. After I had compil'd a Catalogue of his Vices, to make use of as I should find an Opportunity, the Cardinal my patron return'd to *Paris*, and I with him, where he immediately gratified me with a Canon-ship of St. *Maur*, and the Benefice of *Meudon*. Having all I could desire, I liv'd luxuriously ; and the Love of *Satyr* pleasing me much more than the Service of God, after I had wrote several things without success for the Learned, I composed the history of *Gargantua* and *Pantagruel* for the ignorant, Things which some call a *Cock and a Bull*, and others the Product of a lively Imagination. I know most Men understand them as little as they do *Arabick* ; and as it is not to our present Pur-pose, so do not I intend to explain that Stuff to them, but will now, since 'tis more a *Propos*, give you some Advice concerning the Malady of your blustering Monarch. The Residence I made at the Court of *France*, in the reign of *Francis* the First, make[s] me more bold in judging of the Nature of those Distempers. You conceal the virulency of *Lewis* the *Fourteenth's* Disease because you dare not examine into the bot-tom of the Cause, and are more modest in proposing Remedies, than he has been in contracting the Distemper. Yet every one talks according to his Interest, and the News-Mongers always keep a Blank to set down the manner of his Death. If he does not tremble he must be thorow-pac'd in Iniquity, for he has several Reckonings to make up with Heaven, which are not so easily adjusted ; and as he has often affronted the Majesty of several *Popes*, he will scarce obtain a Pasport to go Scot-free into the other World. We are told here, by some of his good Friends, he begins to putrifie, and [h]as Ulcers a Yard in Length, where Vermin, very Soldier like, intrench themselves. There is no other Remedy for this, according to old *Æsculapius*, but to make him a new Man, by a severe penitential Pilgrimage into some of the Provinces of *Mercury* and *Turpentine*. If he still fears the danger of War, let him go in Disguise ; and if at this Age hecannot be without a *She-Compa-nion*, let him take his old Friend *Maintenon* along with him, she is Poison-proof and may, to save Charges, serve him in three Capacities, *viz*. As a Bed-fellow, Nurse and Guide ; keep him also to a strict Diet ; scrape his Bones, and purge him thorowly, and all may be sound again but his Conscience. You cannot imagine, how merrily we Gentlemen of the Faculty live at *Pluto's* Court : I am Secretary to the same *Paul* the Third who pardon'd me gratis the Violation of my Vows, my Irreverence for the Church, and my want of Respect for him ; *Scaramouche* is his Gentleman Usher, *Harlequin* his page, and *Scarron* his Poet Laureat. Don't suppose I was such a Blockhead as to kiss his sweaty Toe, when I visited him in the *Vatican* ; he had nothing from me but such an hypocritical Hug, as your *Monks* give each other at the ridiculous Ceremony of High-Mass. This old *Goat* still keeps his Amorous Inclinations, and I, who have so often made others Blush, am often asham'd to hear his Ribaldry. He'd certainly make Love to *Proserpine*, but our Sultan wou'd not be pleas'd with his Courtship ; and besides, his Seraglio is as well guarded as the *Grand Seignior's*, otherwise we might have a Litter of fine Puppies betwixt them. Little hump-Shoulder'd *Luxemberg*, late Marshal of *France*, is the Captain of her Guards, and so damnably jealous, that he will not suffer any to come near her; at which *Pluto* is very well pleas'd, and does not mistrust him, thinking it impossible for any Body to be in Love with such a lump of Deformity. But to return to our friend *Paul*, he scorns to copy after the *Devil*, who turn'd *Hermit* when he was old, and I am now making another Collection of his Impieties and Amours, which will be ready to come out with a *Gazetie Nostradamus* has been composing since the Year 1600. That sly Conjurer is so earnest upon the Matter, that he lifts not up his Head, though *Pluto's* black-guard Boys are continually burning Brimstone under his Nose. However, I do not know but this Mountain may bring forth a Mouse ; for to speak freely, I put as little Faith in those Prophets, who like Sots lose their Reason in the Abyss of Futurity, as the honest *Whigs* of *England* do in the Oaths and Treaties of your swaggering Master. As for you, Brother Doctor[s], Cut, Scarifie, Blister, and Clyster, since 'tis your Profession, but take this along with you, that they who do the least Mischief, pass with me for the ablest Men. But I wou'd advise you not to suffer any longer those barbarous Names of *Assassins*, *Poisoners*, *Close-stool-mongers*, *Factors of Death*, &c. the World gives you. I have had high Words with *Moliere* on your Account, and I expect that fine Rhiming Fellow *Boileau* will give him a wipe over the Nose in one of his *Satyrs*. For tho' I have made bold to talk freely with you, yet I do not mean all the World should take the same Liberty.

The Answer of Mr. Fagon, First Physician to Lewis XIV, to
Francis Rablais.

You're a very pretty Gentleman, Friend *Rablais*, to boast of your self so much, and value the rest of your Fraternity so little. Do not you know that I am of the Tribe of *Juda*, and perhaps related to some of the Kings of *Israel* ? Had you heard me preach in a Synagogue, you'd soon be convinc'd whether I am an illiterate Fellow or no. Is it such an Honour to be of your College ? Or wou'd it be any Advantage to be like you ? You have been by your own Confession, a most horrid

Rake-hell ; and I would not for all the *Mammon of Unrighteousness, in my King's Coffer*, transgress one Point of the Law. You ought not to be astonish'd at my Greatness, for I concern my self with more than one Trade, and no man was ever in such Favour, and grew so Rich, by only applying warm Injections to the Back-side. If you enjoy'd a Prebend, and other Benefices, you must I know, have assisted Cardinal *Bellay* in his amours. For my part, I boast of having been a *Broker, Sollicitor*, and under the Rose, *Billet-doux Carrier* and *Door-Keeper*, because all Employments at Court are honourable, especially in that great Concern of *S - - - y*. Do not think you were the first that thought of the Remedy you speak of ; we had several learned Consultations about it, but know not which way to mention it, for *Madam Scarron*, who is very tender of her Reputation, and reigns sovereignly at Court, will say we accuse her of bringing the *Neopolitan* Distemper to *Versailles*, and have us sent to the Gallies, or hang'd for our good Advice. I have often reflected on the scandalous bantering Stuff of those they call Wits, have said, and do say of us ; and wish with all my Heart, the first *Brimstone* they take for the *Itch*, and *Mercury* for the *Pox*, may *Poyson* 'em ; but for us to stir in't, would bring 'em all about our Ears ; and we know the consequence of that from a neighbouring Country, where they have mumbled a poor Physician, and one that can Versifie also, almost as severely as a Troop of hungry *Wolves* would a fat Ass. However, we thank you for your Zeal, but at the same time advise you not to make a Quarrel for so small a Business ; and I, in a particular manner kiss your Hand, and desire you'll give my service to *Nostradamus*. I cannot beat it out of my Head, but that he has put me into his *Centuries*, and that an ingenious Man might discover me there. I own 'tis looking for a Needle in a Bottle of Hay ; but you know I sprung up like a *Mushroum*, and that he foretells nothing but Prodigies.

III. Extract from " Beau Norton to his Brothers at Hippolito's in Covent Garden, " the forty-first of the *Letters from the Dead to the Living* [1].

Taking a solitary walk on the gloomy Banks of *Acheron*, I met a finical Fellow, powder'd from Top to Toe, his Hands in his Pocket, *a-la-Mode de Paris*, humming a new Minuet ; and who should it be but *Gondamour*, that famous *Spaniard*. *Hellen* of *Greece* cry'd Kitchin-Stuff, and *Roxana* had a little basket of *Tripe* and *Trotters* ; *Agamemnon* sold bak'd Ox-Cheek, hot, hot ; *Hannibal* sells Spanish-Nuts, come crack it away ; the so famous *Hector* of *Troy* is a Head-dresser ; the *Decii* keep a Coblers Stall, in the Corner of the *Forum*, and the *Horatii* a Chandler's-

---

1. *Works*, II, 144-46.

Shop ; *Sardanapalus* cries Lilly-white-Vinegar, and *Heliogabalus* Bakers Fritters, in the *Via Appia* of this Metropolis ; *Lucius Emilius Paulus* is a Bayliff's Follower, and the famous Queen *Tomyris* proportions out the Offals for *Cerberus* ; *Tarquin* sweeps his Den, and *Romulus* is a Turnspit in *Pluto's* Kitchin ; *Artaxerxes* is an Under-Scullion, and *Pompey* the Magnificent, a Rag-Man ; *Mark Anthony*, that disputed his Mistress at the Price of the whole Universe, goes now about with Dancing-Dogs, a Monkey and a Rope ; *Cleopatra*, that could swallow a Province at one Draught, when it was to drink her Lover's Health, submits now to the humble Employment of feeding *Proserpine's* Pigs ; that luxurious *Roman*, who was once so dissolv'd in Ease, that a very Rose-Leaf doubled under him, prevented his Rest, is now labouring at the Anvil with a half hundred Hammer ; *Oliver Cromwel* is a Rat-Catcher, and my Lord *Bellew* a Chimney-Sweeper.

There was, besides these, a List of People nearer hand ; but you may easily guess upon what score they are left out of the List. We needed not have gone so far back in the Records of Persons and Things, to have met Instances of Barbarity, Luxury, Avarice, Lust of Dominion, as well as of Sensuality : Malversations of Government in Sovereigns and Subjects ; public Justice avoided, private Feuds fomented, every thing sacrific'd to a *Colbert, Maintenon*, or a *Louvois*.

There is somebody hollows most damnably on the other Side of *Styx*, and lest I lose this Opportunity, I shall only relate some memorable Things to you: Therefore pray pardon me that I cannot dilate upon every Particular. In short, then, *Alexander* the Great is Bully to a Guinea-Dropper ; and Cardinal *Mazarine* keeps a Nine-Holes ; *Mary* of *Medicis* foots Stockings, and *Katharine*, Queen of *Swedeland*, cries *two Bunches a Penny Card-Matches, two Bunches a Penny* ; *Henry* the Fourth of *France* carries a *Rary-Show* ; and *Mahomet, muscles* ; *Seneca* keeps a *Fencing-School*; and *Julius Caesar* a *Two penny Ordinary* ; *Xenophon*, that great Philosopher, cries *Cowcumbers to pickle* ; and *Cato* is the perfectest Sir *Courtly* of the whole *Plutonian* Kingdom ; *Richlieu* cries *topping Bunno* ; and the late Pope, *Any thing to-day* ; *Lewis* the Thirteenth is a *Corn-Cutter* ; *Gustavus Adolphus* cries *Sparagrass* ; with a thousand more Particulars of this Nature. You must allow the Scenes to be mightily alter'd from their former Stations : but alas ! Sir, this Change we suffer, and as Pleasure is the Reward of Virtue, so Disgrace and Infamy is of Cruelty, Pride and Hypocrisie. What can be more surprising, than to see the renowned *Penthesilea*, Queen of the *Amazons*, crying new Almanacks, and *Darius* Ginger-Bread, *Van Trump* cries Ballads, and Admiral *de Ruyter*, long and strong Thread-Laces.

APPENDIX F

EDMUND GAYTON (1608-66)

Extract from *Pleasant Notes upon Don Quixot* (London, 1654) [1].

And I shall put my conceit upon the judgment of the World, which of the two they thinke most probable. Therefore I conjecture that this story of *Quixot*, with many more eminent *Opuscula* of that nature, were all preserv'd in that famous and wonderfull hollow tooth of *Gargantua*, from the irruptions of the *Goths* and *Vandals*, and the *Barbarismes* of the *Ottoman* cruelty : which said tooth, *John Pontaeus*, his *Ter-qua-terque retro-Tritavus* descended into, by the assistance of a Colledge of Physitians (for there was room enough) and Chirurgions also, with all those huge engines, tooth-pick-axes, tooth-mattocks, and all manner of mouth-Pionery, provided for the scouring, cleansing, and purging of that stupendious concavity. In the rubbish of that vast *Hiatus*, were these two Volumes of the *Don* preserv'd safe and unperisht ; which how they came thither, will be the hardest thing to make good : But it is of no such difficulty to salve the scruple. For that exceeding Gyant being troubled with no small paine in his tooth, called the *Hodontalgia*, it caused such a *vacuum* in the place, that so much wind had gathered thither, as it was enough (as out of *Æolus* cavernes) from thence at any time to have caus'd a tempest ; wherefore from all places there were helps and councels call'd, and when stopping of it was concluded upon, they thought not at the instant, with what to doe it, (mens braines being not alwaies ready for every punctilio) but then finding what an intolerable charge it would amount to in Cotton-wooll, Linnen or Canvas, they thought it best, (and best cheape) to doe it with wast paper, which was approved on, and the Gyant willing to save his purse, condescended to it : So all the Pamphlets then extant, all Romances, English, Spanish, French, and throughout the world were bought up, and amongst

---

1. Pp. 33-34.

the rest, this of our *Don*, which being chiefly to be preserv'd, was laid next the root of his tooth, many piles of lesse worthy labours lying betwixt it and the casualties of the continuall defluxions that fell upon the place. So have you him uncorrupt, and by the help of *Rablais* sweet as a nut.

WORKS AND EDITIONS CITED

Addison, Joseph. *The Spectator*, ed. G. Gregory Smith, 4 Vols. (London : Dent, 1924).

Amory, Thomas. *The Life and Opinions of John Buncle Esquire*, ed. E. A. Baker (London : Library of Early Novelists).

Almond for a Parrat, An, anon. (1589 ; Repr. in *The Works of Thomas Nashe*, ed. McKerrow, III, 341 ff.).

Anders, H. R. D. *Shakespeare's Books* (Berlin, 1904).

Anglia (Halle, 1878 ff.).

Arber, Edward. *A Transcript of The Registers of the Company of Stationers of London, 1554-1640*, 5 Vols. (London, 1873 ff.).

Arbuthnot, John. *Life and Works*, G. A. Aitken (Oxford, 1892). The text of the *Works* is complete.

Aretino, Pietro, *Un Pronostico Satirico*, ed. Aless. Luzio (Bergamo, 1900).

Bacon, Francis. *Works*, ed. Spedding, Ellis, and Heath, 14 Vols. (London, 1857-74).

Barnes, Barnabe. *The Devils Charter* (1607 ; ed. R. B. McKerrow, Louvain, 1904).

Bastide, C. *Anglais et Français du XVIIe siècle* (Paris, 1912).

Bensley, Edward. *" A Debt of Sterne's,"* letter to *Times Lit. Sup.* (Nov. Ist, 1928).

Bentley, Richard. *Critical Remarks Upon Gulliver's Travels ; Particularly his Voyage to the Houyhnhms Country*, 3rd ed. (Dublin, 1735).

Bernard, Jean Frédéric. *Etat de L'Homme Dans le Péché Originel* (1714).

Berni, Francesco. *Opere*, 2 Vols. in one (Milan, 1864).

Béroalde de Verville. *Le Moyen de Parvenir, Œuvre contenant la raison de tout ce qui a été, est et sera* (1610 ; Repr. Paris : Librairie Garnier Frères, n. d.).

Beverland, Adrian. *De Peccato Originali, sic nuncupato, Dissertatio* (1679).

Bibliotheca Fanatica : or, the Fanatick Library. Being a Catalogue of such Books as have been lately made, and, by the Authors, presented to the College of Bedlam, anon. (1660) ; Repr. in *Harl. Misc.*, VII, 141-44).

Birck, Paul. *Literarische Anspielungen in den Werken Ben Jonsons* (Strassburg, 1908).

Blanchard, Frederick T. *Fielding the Novelist* (New Haven, 1926).

Bodleian Library. *Catalogus Impressorum Librorum Bibliothecae Bodlejanae in Academia Oxoniensi* (Oxford, 1674).

Borkowsky, Th. " Quellen zu Swift's 'Gulliver', " *Anglia*, XV, 345-90.

Boswell, Jas. *Life of Johnson*, ed. G. Birkbeck Hill, 6 Vols. (London, 1887).

Bouchet, Guillaume. *Les Sérées*, ed. C. E. Roybet, 6 Vols. (Paris, 1873-82).

Boulenger, Jacques. *Rabelais à Travers les Ages* (Paris, 1925).

Bourgeois, A.-F. " Rabelais en Angleterre, " *R. E. R.*, III, 80-83.

Brown, Huntington. " Ben Jonson and Rabelais, " *M. L. N.*, XLIX, 6-13.

Brown, Tom. *Works* (London, 1715).

> *Remains* (London, 1720).
> *Amusements Serious and Comical, and Other Works*, ed. A. L. Hayward (London, 1927).

Browne, Sir Thomas. *Works*, ed. Simon Wilkin, 4 Vols (London, 1835).

Bruscambille. See des Lauriers, N.

Bullen, A. H. *A Collection of Old English Plays*, 4 Vols (London, 1882-85).

Burton, Robert. *The Anatomy of Melancholy*, 3 Vols. (London : Bohn's Library, 1926).

Butler, Samuel. *Characters and Passages from Note-Books*, ed. A. R. Waller (Cambridge, 1908).

> *Hudibras*, ed. T. R. Nash (New York, 1874).
> *Poetical Works*, ed. Robert Bell, 3 Vols. (London, 1855).

Cambridge History of English Literature, 14 Vols. (London and New York, 1907-17).

Castelain, Maurice. *Ben Jonson, L'Homme et L'Œuvre* (Paris, 1907).

Catalogue of Books, of the newest Fashion, To be sold by Auction, at the Whigs Coffee-House, at the Sign of the Jackanapes, in Pratling-Alley, near the Deanery of St. Pauls, A (n. d. ; Repr. in *Harl. Misc.*, XII, 257-62).   On p. 262 Dame Britannia is said to have been a voluntary adultress for five years.   If King William be the paramour, the date of writing would be 1694).

Caxton, William. *Dialogues in French and English* (c. 1483 ; ed. H. Bradley, London : E. E. T. S., Ext. Ser., No. 79, 1900).

Chamberlain, Frederick. *The Sayings of Queen Elizabeth* (London, 1923).

Chesterfield, Philip Dormer Stanhope, Earl of. *Letters*, 4 Vols. (London, 1845).

Churchill, Charles. *Poetical Works*, ed. Hannay and Tooke, 2 Vols. (London and New York, 1892).

Cooke, John. *Greenes Tu Quoque, or, The Cittie Gallant* (London, [1614 ?]. Repr. Dodsley in *A Select Collection*, 1825, VII, 7-98).

Coryat, Thomas. *Crudities* (1611 ; Repr. in 2 Vols., Glasgow, 1905).

Cotgrave, Randle. *A French and English Dictionary* (London, 1632).

Cross, W. L. *The Life and Times of Laurence Sterne*, 2 Vols. (New Haven, 1925).

Dekker, Thomas. *Selected Plays*, ed. Ernest Rhys (London : Mermaid Series).

> *The Rauens Almanacke ; foretelling of a Plague, Famine, and Civill Warre, that shall happen this present year* 1709, Repr. in *The Non-Dramatic Works*, ed. Grosart, 4 Vols. (1885), IV, 167-266.

Dering, Edward. *A Briefe and Necessary Catechisme or instruction Very needfull to be known of al housholders* (n. d. ; the dedicatory epistle is dated April 22nd, 1572).

Des Lauriers, N. *Les Fantaisies de Brvscambille. Contenant plusieurs Discours, Paradoxes, Harangues & Prologues facécieux* (Paris, 1615).

Dictionary of National Biography, The.

Dodsley, Robert. *A Select Collection of Old Plays*, 12 Vols. (London, 1825).

Donne, John. *Poems*, ed. H. J. C. Grierson, 2 Vols. (Oxford, 1912).

Drayton, Michael. *Nymphidia & The Muses Elizium*, ed. John Gray (London, 1896).

Dunbar, William. *Poems*, ed. J. Schipper (Vienna, 1891).

Dunn, Esther C. *Ben Jonson's art : Elizabethan life and Literature as reflected therein* (Nortampton, Mass., 1925).

Dyer, Sir Edward. *Verse and Prose*, ed. Grosart (Miscellanies of The Fuller Worthies' Library, IV, 1876).

Eachard, John. *The Grounds & Occasions of the Contempt of the Clergy and Religion Enquired into* (London, 1670 ; Repr. in *An English Garner*, ed. J. Churton Collins, London, 1903).

Eckhardt, Eduard. *Die Dialekt-und Ausländer-typen des älteren Englischen Dramas*, 2 Vols. (Louvain, 1911).

Eddy, W. A. " Rabelais, a Source For Gulliver's Travels, " *M. L. N.*, XXXVII, 416-18.

Eliot, John. *Ortho-Epia Gallica. Eliots Frvits for the French* (London, 1593).

Encyclopedia Britannica, 13th edition.

Farrer, Lucy E. *La vie et les Œuvres de Claude de Sainliens, alias Claudius Holyband* (Paris, 1908).

Ferriar, John. *Illustrations of Sterne : with Other Essays and Verses*, 2 Vols, 2nd ed. (London, 1812).

Fielding, Henry. *Works*, ed. G. H. Maynadier, 12 Vols. (London, 1903).

Ford, John. *The Dramatic Works of Massinger and Ford*, ed. Hartley Coleridge (London, 1839).

Gargantua. See Girault.

Gaselee, [initials unknown]. Note on *Gargantua* in England in 1546, —*Rev. du XVIe Siècle*, I, 261.

Gayton, Edmund. *Pleasant Notes upon Don Quixot* (London, 1654).

Gentillet, Innocent. See Patericke, Simon.

Girault, François. *The Tale of Gargantua and King Arthur*, ed. Huntington Brown (Cambridge, Mass., 1932). This volume contains *Les croniques admirables du puissant Roy Gargantua*, by François Girault (c. 1534), and, in an appendix, *Les grandes et inestimables cronicques*, anon. (Lyon, 1532).

Glapthorne, Henry. *Plays and Poems*, ed. John Pearson (London, 1874).

Goldsmith, Oliver. *Works*, ed. J. W. M. Gibbs, 5 Vols. (London, 1884-86).

Guez, Giles du. See Palsgrave, John.

Hall, Joseph. *Die Satiren*, ed. Konrad Schulze (Berlin, 1910).

　　Mnvdvs alter et idem. Sive Terra australis antehac semper incognita ; longis itineribus peregrinia cademici nupperime lustrata. Authore Mercvrio Britannico. Accessit propter affinitatem materiae Thomae Campanellae, Civitas solis (1643).

Hallam, Henry. *Introduction to The Literature of Europe in the Fifteenth, Sixteenth, and Seventeenth Centuries*, 3 Vols., 3rd ed. (London, 1847).

Harington, Sir John. *Epigrams*, ed. N. E. McLure (Philadelphia, 1926).

　　The Metamorphosis of Aiax (1596 ; ed. Jack Lindsay, London, 1927).

Harleian Miscellany, The, ed. Sir Walter Scott, 12 Vols. (London, 1808-11).

Harris, Wm. J. *The First Printed Translations into English of the Great Foreign Classics* (London, 1909).

Harvey, Gabriel. *Marginalia*, ed. G. C. Moore Smith (Stratford-upon-Avon, 1913).

　　Works, ed. Grosart, 3 Vols. (1884).

Hayman, Robert. *Quodlibets, Lately Come Over from New Britanolia, Old Newfoundland... With two Epistles of that excellently wittie Doctor, Francis Rablais : Translated out of his French at large* (London, 1628).

Hazlitt, William. *Lectures on English Poets, etc.*, ed. A. R. Waller (London : Dent, 1922).

Head, Richard, and Kirkman, Francis. *The English Rogue : described in the Life of Meriton Latroon, a Witty Extravagant, being a Compleat History of the most Eminent Cheats of both Sexes*, 4 Vols. (London, 1665-80).

Heywood, John. *The Playe Called the Foure PP.* (c. 1530 ; Repr. in J. Q. Adams, *Chief Pre-Shakespearean Dramas*, Boston, 1924).

Holyband, Claudius. See Farrer, Lucy E.

Howell, James. *Epistolae Ho-Elianae*, ed. Joseph Jacobs, 2 Vols. (London, 1892).

Huguet, Edmond. *Etude sur la Syntaxe de Rabelais* (Paris, 1894).

Johnson, Samuel. *Johnson on Shakespeare. Essays and Notes*, ed. Walter Raleigh (London, 1908).

　　　Lives of The English Poets, ed. G. B. Hill, 3 Vols. (London, 1905). See Boswell, James.

Johnstone, Charles. *Chrysal or the Adventures of a Guinea*, ed. E. A. Baker (London : Library of Early Novelists).

Jonson, Ben. *Works*, ed. Gifford and Cunningham, 9 Vols. (London, 1875).

　　　Works, ed. Herford and Simpson, Vols. I and II (Oxford, 1925).
　　　Epicoene, ed. Aurelia Henry (New York, 1906).
　　　Every Man in His Humour, ed. Percy Simpson (Oxford, 1919).
　　　The Staple of News, ed. De Winter (New York, 1905).
　　　Volpone, ed. John D. Rea (New Haven, 1919).

Juillière, Pierre de la. *Les Images dans Rabelais* (Halle, a. S. : Beih. z. Zeitschr. f. Rom. Phil., XXXVII, 1912).

Jusserand, J. J. *The English Novel in the Time of Shakespeare*, Transl. Elizabeth Lee (London, 1890).

　　　Histoire Littéraire du Peuple Anglais, 2 Vols. (Paris, 1894, ff.).

Kirkman, Francis. See Head, Richard.

König, Wilhelm. " Ueber die Entlehnungen Shakespeare's, insbesondere aus Rabelais und einigen italienischen Dramatikern, " *Jahrbuch der Deutschen Shakespeare-Gesellschaft*, IX, 195 ff. (1874).

Köppel, Emil. *Ben Jonson's Wirkung auf zeitgenössische Dramatiker usw.* (Heidelberg, 1906).

Lady Alimony. See Habington, William.

Laneham, Robert. *Letter : Describing a Part of The Entertainment unto Queen Elizabeth at the Castle of Kenilworth in 1575*, ed. F. J. Furnivall (1907).

Lee, Sidney. *The French Renaissance in England* (New York, 1910).

Lefranc, Abel. " Les plus anciennes mentions du *Gargantua* et du *Pantagruel*, " *R. E. R.*, V, 105 ff.

Lingua : or The Combat of The Tongue and The Five Senses for Superiority (1607 ; Repr. Dodsley, *A Select Collection*, 1825, V, 103-214).

Lodge, Thomas, *Works*, ed. E. W. Gosse, 4 Vols. (Glasgow : Hunterian Club, 1883).

Magnus, Laurie. *English Literature in Its Foreign Relations 1300-1800* (London, 1927).

Mayne, Jasper. *The City-Match* (1639 ; Repr. Dodsley, *A Select Collection*, 1825, IX, 231-330).

Mayor, A. Hyatt. *Cervantes, With Especial Reference to Don Quijote, in English Literature Until 1781*, Diss., unpublished (1926 ; a copy is on file in the library of Princeton University).

McKillop, A. D. " Some Early Traces of Rabelais in English Literature, " *M. L. N.*, XXXVI, 469-74.

Melville, Lewis. *The Life and Letters of Laurence Sterne*, 2 Vols. (London, 1910).

Meres, Francis. *Palladis Tamia* (1598 ; Repr. G. Greg. Smith, *Elizabethan Critical Essays*, II).

Meyer, Eduard. *Machiavelli and the Elizabethan Drama* (Weimar, 1897).

Miller, Hugh. *Scenes and Legends of The North of Scotland* (Edinburgh and London, 1835).

M. L. N. Modern Language Notes, I ff. (Baltimore, 1886 ff.).

Motteux, Peter. See Rabelais.

Nashe, Thomas. *Works*, ed. R. B. McKerrow, 5 Vols. (London, 1910).

Nicéron, J. P. *Mémoires pour servir à l'Histoire des Hommes Illustres dans la République des Lettres*, 43 Vols. (Paris, 1729-45). Deals with Rabelais in XXXII, 337-408.

Oldham, John. *Works*, 2 Vols. (London, 1722).

Oxford Dictionary (Oxford, 1884-1928).

Ozell, John. See Rabelais.

Palsgrave, Jean. *L'Eclaircissement de la Langue Française, suivi de la grammaire de Giles du Guez*, ed. François Génin (Paris, 1852).

Pater, Walter. *Works*, 8 Vols. (London, 1901).

Patericke, Simon. *A Discourse Upon The Meanes of Wel Governing And Maintaining In Good Peace, A Kingdome, Or Other Principalitie...*

Against Nicholas Machiavel the Florentine. Translated into English [from the French of Innocent Gentillet] (London, 1608). The Epistle Dedicatorie is dated " Kalends Augusti. Anno 1577. "

Phillips, John. *Speculum Crape-Gownorum : or, an Old Looking-Glass for the Young Academicks, new Foyl'd : with Reflections on some of the late High-Flown Sermons. To which is added, an Essay towards a Sermon of the Newest Fashion. By a Guide to the Inferiour Clergy,* 2nd ed. (London, 1682).

Philological Quarterly, The, I ff. (Iowa City, 1922 ff.).

Plattard, Jean. *L'Œuvre de Rabelais* (Paris, 1910).

    La Vie de François Rabelais (Paris et Bruxelles, 1928).

Pope, Alexander. *Works,* ed. Croker, Elwin, and Courthope, 10 Vols. (London, 1886).

Prior, Matthew. *The Shorter Poems,* ed. Francis Bickley (London : The Abbey Classics, No. XIX).

Putnam, Samuel. See Rabelais.

Rabelais, François.

    Œuvres, ed. Lefranc, 5 Vols. (Paris, 1913 ff.).

    Œuvres, ed. Louis Moland and Henri Clouzot (Paris : Garnier Frères).

    Gargantua and Pantagruel, Transl. Urquhart and Motteux, ed Charles Whibley, 3 Vols. (London : Tudor Translations, 1900).

    Gargantua and Pantagruel, Transl. Urquhart and Motteux, 3 Vols. (London : Chatto and Windus, 1921).

    Works... Now carefully revised, and compared throughout with the late new Edition of M. Le du Chat, by Mr. [John] *Ozell,* 5 Vols. (London, 1737).

    The Five Books and Minor Writings, Transl. W. F. Smith, 2 Vols. (London, 1893).

    All The Extant Works, Transl. Samuel Putnam, 3 Vols. (New York, 1929).

    Gargantua und Pantagruel aus dem Französischen, Transl. Gottlob Regis (Leipzig, 1832-41).

    See also, Girault, Huguet, Juillière, Plattard, Sainéan, Schneegans, and Spitzer.

Randolph, Thomas. *Poetical and Dramatic Works,* ed. W. Carew Hazlitt, 2 Vols. (London, 1875).

Regis, Gottlob. See Rabelais.

Rehfeld, G. *Sir John Harington, ein Nachahmer Rabelais* (Halle, a., S., 1914).

R. E. R. Revue des Etudes Rabelaisiennes, I-X (Paris, 1903-12).
Revue Archéologique, nouvelle série, I-XLIV (Paris, 1860-82).
Revue du seizième siècle, I ff. (Paris, 1913 ff.).
Reyher, Paul. *Les Masques Anglais* (Paris, 1909).
Rymer, Thomas. *A Short View of Tragedy* (1692 ; Repr. Spingarn, *Critical Essays of The Seventeenth Century,* Oxford, 1908-09, III).
Sainéan, Lazare. *L'Influence et la Réputation de Rabelais* (Paris, 1930).
   La Langue de Rabelais, 2 Vols. (Paris, 1922).
   " Les Interprètes de Rabelais en Angleterre et en Allemagne, " *R. E. R.,* VII, 137-258.
Sainliens, Claude de. See Farrer, Lucy E.
Saintsbury, George. *A History of Criticism,* 3 Vols. (London, 1900 ; 4th ed., 1922).
   The Peace of The Augustans (London, 1916).
Salyer, Sandford M. " Renaissance Influences in Hall's *Mundus Alter et Idem,* " *Philol. Quarterly,* VI, 321-34.
Schelling, F. E. *Elizabethan Drama, 1558-1642,* 2 Vols. (Boston and New York, 1908).
Scheengans, Heinrich. *Geschichte der Grotesken Satire* (Strassburg, 1894).
Sells, Arthur L. *Les Sources Françaises de Goldsmith* (Paris, 1924).
Shakespeare, William. *Complete Works* (London and New York : Cambridge edition, 3rd ed., 1910).
Shirley, James. *Dramatic Works and Poems,* ed. W. Gifford and A. Dyce, 6 Vols. (London, 1833).
Sichel, Walter. *Sterne, A Study* (London, 1910).
Sidney, Sir Philip. *An Apologie for Poetrie,* ed. Arber (London : Constable and Co.).
Smith, G. Gregory. *Ben Jonson* (London, 1919).
Smith, W. F. " Rabelais et Shakespeare, " *R. E. R.,* I, 217-221.
   " Samuel Butler, " *Camb. Hist. of Eng. Lit.,* VIII, Ch. II.
   See also Rabelais.
Smollett, Tobias. *Select Works,* 2 Vols. in one, memoir by Sir Walter Scott (New York : Stringer and Townsend).
South, Robert. *Sermons,* 5 Vols. (Oxford, 1842).
Spence, Joseph. *Anecdotes, Observations, and Characters, of Books and Men. Collected from the Conversation of Mr. Pope, and other Eminent Persons of his Time,* ed. S. W. Singer, 2nd ed. (London, 1858).
Spitzer, Leo. *Die Wortbildung als stilistisches Mittel, exemplifiziert an Rabelais* (Halle a. S., 1910 ; *Beih. z. Zeitschr. f. Rom. Phil.,* XXIX).
Stapfer, Paul. *Laurence Sterne — Sa personne et ses ouvrages* (Paris, 1870).

Stationer's Registers. See Arber.

Sterne, Laurence. *The Life and Opinions of Tristram Shandy Gentleman* (1760-67 ; Oxford, 1921). The so-called " Grenville copy " of *Tristram Shandy* is a copy of the edition in 9 Vols., 16° printed by D. Lynch, London, 1760-67 (British Museum, A. 13443-45). The author's name occurs in the preface to Vol. V. The second and third volumes are a reprint, probably surreptitious, of the 2nd edition. The whole contains marginal annotations in one or more unknown hands which indicate many instances of Sterne's indebtedness to Rabelais and several other authors, but they are by no means exhaustive.

    A Sentimental Journey Through France and Italy (1768 ; London : The Abbey Classics).

    Crazy Tales (London, 1762).

    See also Cross, Ferriar, Sichel, Stapfer, Stevenson, John Hall.

Swift, Jonathan. *Prose Works*, ed. Temple Scott, 12 Vols. (London, 1925).

    Poems, ed. W. E. Browning, 2 Vols. (London, 1910).

    Correspondence, ed. F. Elrington Ball, 6 Vols. (London, 1911).

Taylor, John (the " Water-Poet "). *Works*, Repr. Spenser Soc., Fol. of 1630 (1869), and Qu. I-V (1870-78).

Temple, Sir William. *Of Poetry* (1690) and *Essay upon The Ancient and Modern Learning* (1690), Repr. Spingarn, *Critical Essays of The Seventeenth Century* (Oxford, 1908-09), III.

Toldo, Pietro. " Les voyages merveilleux de Cyrano de Bergerac et de Swift et leurs rapports avec l'œuvre de Rabelais, " Pt. I, *R. E. R.*, IV, 295-334 ; Pt. II, *Ibid.*, V, 22-44.

Tucker, T. G. *The Foreign Debt of English Literature* (London, 1907).

Upham, A. H. *The French Influence in English Literature* (New York, 1908).

Urquhart, Sir Thomas. *Works*, ed. G. Maitland (Edinburgh : Maitland Club, No. 30, 1834).

    See also Rabelais.

Voltaire, François Marie Arouet de. *Œuvres complètes*, ed. Condorcet, 13 Vols. (Paris, 1876-78).

    Dictionnaire Philosophique, ed. Georges Bengesco, 2 Vols. (Paris : Librairie des Bibliophiles).

Webster, John. *Complete Works*, ed. F. L. Lucas, 4 Vols., (London, 1927).

Whibley Charles. " Rabelais en Angleterre, " *R. E. R.*, I, 1 ff.

    " Translators, " *Camb. Hist. of Eng. Lit.*, IV, Ch. I.

Literary Studies (London and New-York, 1919).
See also Rabelais.
Wilkins, John. *An Essay Towards a Real Character and a Philosophical Language* (London, 1668).
Willcock, John. *Sir Thomas Urquhart of Cromartie Knight* (Edinburgh and London, 1899).
Wilson, Sir Thomas. *The Art of Rhetorique* (1553 ; Repr. of ed. of 1560, ed. G. H. Mair, Oxford, 1909).
Wonderfvll Strange and Miracvlovs Astrologicall Prognostication, A (1591 ; Repr. McKerrow, *The Works of Thomas Nashe*, III, 377-95).
Young, Edward. *Poetical Works*, ed. J. Mitford, 2 Vols. (Boston, 1854).

INDEX